THE JUDICIAL

BRANCH OF THE FEDERAL GOVERNMENT

PURPOSE, PROCESS, AND PEOPLE

U.S. GOVERNMENT: THE SEPARATION OF POWERS

THE JUDICIAL BRANCH OF THE FEDERAL GOVERNMENT

PURPOSE, PROCESS, AND PEOPLE

EDITED BY BRIAN DUIGNAN, SENIOR EDITOR, RELIGION AND PHILOSOPHY

Britannica®
Educational Publishing
IN ASSOCIATION WITH
ROSEN
EDUCATIONAL SERVICES

Published in 2010 by Britannica Educational Publishing
(a trademark of Encyclopædia Britannica, Inc.)
in association with Rosen Educational Services, LLC
29 East 21st Street, New York, NY 10010.

Distributed exclusively by Rosen Educational Services.
For a listing of additional Britannica Educational Publishing titles, call toll free (800) 237-9932.

First Edition

Britannica Educational Publishing
Michael I. Levy: Executive Editor
Marilyn L. Barton: Senior Coordinator, Production Control
Steven Bosco: Director, Editorial Technologies
Lisa S. Braucher: Senior Producer and Data Editor
Yvette Charboneau: Senior Copy Editor
Kathy Nakamura: Manager, Media Acquisition
Brian Duignan: Senior Editor, Religion and Philosophy

Rosen Educational Services
Hope Lourie Killcoyne: Senior Editor and Project Manager
Nelson Sá: Art Director
Nicole Russo: Designer
Introduction by Richard Worth

Library of Congress Cataloging-in-Publication Data

The judicial branch of the federal government: purpose, process, and people / edited by Brian Duignan.—1st ed.
p. cm.—(U.S. government: the separation of powers)
"In association with Britannica Educational Publishing, Rosen Educational Services."
ISBN 978-1-61530-001-3 (library binding)
1. Courts—United States. 2. Judicial power—United States. 3. Judges—United States.
4. Separation of powers—United States I. Duignan, Brian.
KF8717.J83 2010
347.73—dc22

2009038304

Manufactured in the United States of America

Photo credit: cover © *www.istockphoto.com/dra_schwartz; p. 12* © *www.istockphoto.com; p. 20* © *www.istockphoto.com/Stefan Klein.*

CONTENTS

91

106

WE DEMAND EQUAL RIGHTS NOW!
121

129

140

165

169
WAR

231

261

277

290

315

Introduction

In 1787, a convention of delegates from all but one of the American states met in Philadelphia, where they rewrote the framework of the national government. Before the Constitutional Convention, most political power had been in the hands of the states. As a result, the national government lacked the authority to conduct foreign affairs, conclude treaties with other nations, or raise an army for the nation's defense. While most delegates agreed that a change was necessary to preserve the independence of the United States, they did not want to create an all-powerful central government. While still part of Great Britain, the colonies had been ruled by the British Parliament and King George III, and they did not want to repeat that situation.

Instead, the founders devised a system of government consisting of three branches. The executive branch is embodied in the president. The legislative branch comprises both houses of Congress. The third branch, the judiciary, includes the U.S. Supreme Court and the lower federal district and appeals courts. The founders also wrote into the Constitution an ingenious system of checks and balances that enabled each branch of government to prevent or revoke certain actions by the other two, thereby contributing to a balance of power among the branches.

Each branch of the U.S. federal government holds separate and distinct authority when it comes to governing the nation. Aided by the vice president and members of the cabinet, who are also part of the executive branch, the president enacts and implements laws. Congress is charged with passing the legislation that the president signs into law. Because they are elected officials, the president and federal legislators are subject to the influence of the citizens who voted them into office.

Not so with the judiciary. As sole interpreters of the nation's laws, federal judges and Supreme Court justices are appointed to lifetime terms by the president and confirmed by the Senate. Lifetime appointments are a means of shielding judges and justices from political pressure, leaving them free to decide cases solely on the basis of the law. As each justice or judge is replaced by a new appointment, the complexion of the courts may change, and with it the interpretation of the law.

Judicial review—that is, the right to declare acts unconstitutional—was not part of the Constitution. Yet, it has become central to checks and balances. The right of review for the federal courts was first established in *Marbury* v. *Madison*, in which the Supreme Court, led by Chief Justice John Marshall ruled that the Court had the power to declare an act of Congress unconstitutional. This established the court's doctrine of judicial review, a power held by few other courts in the world. Sixteen years later, the Supreme Court handed down a pair of rulings, *McCulloch* v. *Maryland* and *Gibbons* v. *Ogden*, that more clearly defined the power of the federal government over the states.

The actions of the judicial branch of the U.S. government can have a significant impact on the course of the country's history. Consider the landmark *Dred Scott* ruling. During the mid-19th century, the burning issue in the United States was the institution of slavery. Approximately four million people were held as slaves in the South, and southern political leaders wanted to extend slavery into the western territories. Dred Scott, a slave originally from Missouri, had lived for several years with his owner in Illinois—a free state. After returning to Missouri, where he was still considered a slave, Scott sued to be declared a free man.

Eventually, the case reached the U.S. Supreme Court, where it was decided in 1857. Led by Chief Justice Roger Taney, a majority of the court ruled that, under the Constitution, no slave was considered a citizen with the rights of citizenship. Therefore, Dred Scott was still a slave no matter where he lived, and a slave owner could not be prevented from claiming his slaves—his property—even if they had lived in a free state. The conflict between North and South over slavery increased as a result of the *Dred Scott* decision, leading to the outbreak of the Civil War in 1861.

After the defeat of the South four years later, slavery was formally abolished in the United States by the ratification of the Thirteenth Amendment to the Constitution. Later amendments granted citizenship and equal civil and legal rights to African Americans and slaves (the Fourteenth Amendment) and prohibited the states from denying anyone the right to vote on the basis of "race, color, or previous condition of servitude" (the Fifteenth Amendment).

Despite the latter two amendments, however, many states—especially in the South—soon passed a series of laws, known as Jim Crow laws, that enforced various forms of racial discrimination and segregation. African Americans were prohibited from riding in the same railroad cars as whites, using the same public bathrooms, staying in the same hotels, eating in the same restaurants, or attending the same schools. In an attempt to overturn this injustice in the courts, Homer Plessy, a 30-year-old African American shoemaker who "passed" for white, purchased a train ticket in a whites-only car. He then informed the conductor that he was indeed black and was duly arrested. The case was eventually brought to trial, reaching the U.S. Supreme Court as *Plessy* v. *Ferguson* in 1896. In an 8-1 decision, Justice Henry Brown wrote that the Fourteenth Amendment could "not have been intended to abolish distinctions based upon color, or enforce social, as distinguished from political equality. . . ." As a result, "separate but equal" facilities continued to operate across the United States.

The lone dissenting opinion in the case was written by Justice John Marshall Harlan, who said that "In my opinion, the judgment this day rendered will, in time, prove to be quite as pernicious as the decision made by this tribunal in the *Dred Scott* case." Harlan was right, but it would take the Court almost 60 years before the ruling in *Plessy* v. *Ferguson* was reversed. This occurred in 1954, when the Supreme Court led by Chief Justice Earl Warren handed down a landmark unanimous decision in the case of *Oliver L. Brown et al.* v. *Board of Education of Topeka (Kansas)*. The Court ruled that states such as Kansas, which provided separate elementary schools for white and African-American children, were violating the equal-protection clause of the Fourteenth Amendment. As a result of the decision, Topeka began to end segregation, but many other states refused to comply, and the Federal Government started to enforce desegregation in local schools.

In the 60 years between *Plessy* v. *Ferguson* and *Brown*, the judiciary became involved in other important legal cases. In 1890, Congress had passed the Sherman Antitrust Act (named after Republican Sen. John Sherman of Ohio), designed to stop large companies from achieving a monopolies in various industries. One such company was Standard Oil of New Jersey, which had used a variety of tactics—some of them unethical—to drive out competition and take control of the American oil refining business. Antitrust cases began in the lower federal courts, but many of them were appealed and eventually reached the Supreme

Court. In 1911, the Court delivered a unanimous decision in the case of *Standard Oil of New Jersey Co.* v. *United States*, breaking up the giant trust. In this and other cases, the courts tried to restore fair competition among businesses operating within the same industry.

During this period, the court also heard cases involving basic liberties protected by the Bill of Rights—the first 10 amendments to the U.S. Constitution. Among them was *Gitlow* v. *New York*. In this case, a majority of the court led by Chief Justice William Howard Taft decided in 1925 that the limitations on government power contained in the Bill of Rights apply as much to the states as to the federal government. In 1963, the Warren court overruled a Florida court that had convicted Clarence Earl Gideon of a felony after he had been denied free legal counsel. The Supreme Court ruled that Gideon's rights had been violated under the equal-protection clause of the Fourteenth Amendment. Gideon received a court-appointed attorney and was eventually acquitted of all charges.

One of the Warren court's landmark decisions involved Ernesto Miranda. Miranda had been arrested by police in Phoenix, Ariz. who questioned him for two hours, finally obtaining Miranda's signed confession, wherein he admitted kidnapping, raping, and robbing several women. When the confession was read at his trial, Miranda was found guilty. However, the case was appealed because Miranda had never been told that he had a constitutional right to remain silent during police questioning and to have an attorney present. Miranda appealed the case, which eventually reached the Supreme Court, where the justices ruled that his rights had been violated.

As a result of that decision, people who are arrested by police always receive a fourfold warning from police, one formulation of which is: "You have the right to remain silent; anything you say can and will be used against you in a court of law; you have the right to consult a lawyer present before any questioning and to have him present during questioning; and if you cannot afford legal counsel, one will be provided."

After *Brown* v. *Board of Education*, the Warren court and the court under Chief Justice Earl Warren and later by Chief Justice Warren Burger, continued to hear civil rights cases, and by virtue of their decisions, moved the country further toward desegregation. The U.S. Congress had passed the 1964 Civil Rights Act and the Voting Rights Act of 1965, designed to enforce the liberties granted to all citizens under the Constitution. In 1964, the Warren court handed down a decision in the case of *Heart of Atlanta Motel* v. *United States*, stating that a motel that refused to serve African Americans had violated the Civil Rights Act. In the 1971 case *Swann* v. *Charlotte-Mecklenburg Board of Education*, the Burger court, in a unanimous decision, declared that local courts could step in and order school desegregation plans, many of which included busing, in districts that had not integrated their classrooms.

Another of the judiciary's responsibilities, established back in the Marshall era in the early 19th century, has been to act as a check on the power of Congress and the president. In 1971, the *New York Times* began publishing excerpts from the Pentagon Papers, a detailed account commissioned by the federal government regarding U.S. involvement in the Vietnam War. The information was classified, and the administration of Pres. Richard Nixon asked a district court judge to issue an order preventing the *Times* from continuing to run articles from the report as doing so would cause "irreparable injury to the defense interests of the United States," which was still engaged in the war. The judge refused, saying that the administration had not proven that publication would cause grave and irreparable danger to the American people. When the case was appealed to the Supreme Court, the justices agreed with the decision of the lower courts.

In another landmark decision, the Supreme Court ruled in 1973 that women have a right to obtain an abortion. The majority decision, written by Associate Justice Harry Blackmun, was unique for relying on the Ninth Amendment, which implies the existence of rights not specifically mentioned in the Constitution. The Court found that each person has a right to privacy and that unduly restrictive laws against abortion violate that right. The *Roe* v. *Wade* case continues to create enormous controversy, especially among many Americans who oppose abortion.

Since the 1970s, the judiciary has continued to make many important rulings having enormous impact on American society. In 2000, the Supreme Court, led by Chief Justice William Rehnquist, helped decide the presidential election. The contest between Vice Pres. Al Gore and Gov. George W. Bush hinged on the results in Florida, where a few thousand votes were being contested. The Florida Supreme Court ordered a manual recount of contested votes across the state. After halting the recount to consider an appeal by the Bush campaign, the U.S. Supreme Court ruled in *Bush* v. *Gore* that Florida's method of recounting the votes violated the equal-protection clause of the Fourteenth Amendment and that a fair recount could not be performed in time to meet the deadline for certifying the state's electors (members of the electoral college, the body that formally elects the president). As a result, George W. Bush was declared the winner in Florida and became president of the United States.

In this book, readers will learn how, from its beginnings in the late 18th century to the present day, the federal judiciary has shaped the powers and functions of American government and the character of American society.

Constitutional Background

Chapter I

THE ARTICLES OF CONFEDERATION AND THE CONSTITUTION OF THE UNITED STATES

The U.S. Constitution, which provides the principles of government for the United States, is a landmark document of the Western world. It is the oldest written national constitution in use and was the first to provide constitutional protections for its citizens against government infringement. Adopted in 1789, the Constitution divides governmental authority between a central national government and various separate state governments. It defined the principal organs of government and their jurisdictions as well as the basic rights of citizens, but it was not, however, the first such document created for the task in the United States. Its predecessor, the Articles of Confederation, was a kind of template for the Constitution, providing the new nation with its first, instructive experience in self-government under a written document

The Articles of Confederation, in force from 1781 to 1789, served as a bridge between the early government by the Continental Congress during the Revolutionary period and the federal system of government provided under the U.S. Constitution. Because the experience of overbearing British central authority was vivid in colonial minds, the drafters of the Articles deliberately established a confederation of sovereign states. Their intention is manifest in the name of the new nation, established in Article I: the United States of America. The Articles were written in

PRIMARY SOURCE: THE ARTICLES OF CONFEDERATION (EXCERPTS)

Articles of Confederation and Perpetual Union Between the States of New Hampshire, Massachusetts Bay, Rhode Island and Providence Plantations, Connecticut, New York, New Jersey, Pennsylvania, Delaware, Maryland, Virginia, North Carolina, South Carolina, and Georgia.

Article I. The style of this confederacy shall be "The United States of America."

Article II. Each state retains its sovereignty, freedom, and independence, and every power, jurisdiction, and right which is not by this confederation expressly delegated to the United States in Congress assembled.

Article III. The said states hereby severally enter into a firm league of friendship with each other, for their common defense, the security of their liberties, and their mutual and general welfare, binding themselves to assist each other against all force offered to, or attacks made upon them, or any of them, on account of religion, sovereignty, trade, or any other pretense whatever.

Article IV. The better to secure and perpetuate mutual friendship and intercourse among the people of the different states in this union, the free inhabitants of each of these states, paupers, vagabonds, and fugitives from justice excepted, shall be entitled to all privileges and immunities of free citizens in the several states. ...

Article V. For the more convenient management of the general interests of the United States, delegates shall be annually appointed in such manner as the legislature of each state shall direct, to meet in Congress on the first Monday in November, in every year. ...

No state shall be represented in Congress by less than two nor by more than seven members; and no person shall be capable of being a delegate for more than three years in any term of six years. ...

In determining questions in the United States in Congress assembled, each state shall have one vote. ...

Article VI. No state, without the consent of the United States in Congress assembled, shall send any embassy to, or receive any embassy from, or enter into any conference, agreement, alliance, or treaty with any king, prince, or state. ...

No state shall engage in any war without the consent of the United States in Congress assembled unless such state be actually invaded by enemies. ...

Article VII. When land forces are raised by any state for the common defense, all officers of or under the rank of colonel shall be appointed by the legislature of each state respectively, by whom such forces shall be raised, or in such manner as such state shall direct. ...

Article VIII. All charges of war and all other expenses that shall be incurred for the common defense or general welfare, and allowed by the United States in Congress assembled, shall be defrayed out of a common treasury, which shall be supplied by the several states in proportion to the value of all land within each state. ...

Article IX. The United States in Congress assembled shall have the sole and exclusive right and power of determining on peace and war, except in the cases mentioned in the sixth article. ...

The United States in Congress assembled shall also have the sole and exclusive right and power of regulating the alloy and value of coin struck by their own authority or by that of the respective states ... regulating the trade and managing all affairs with the Indians not members of any of the states ... [and] establishing or regulating post offices from one state to another. ...

The United States in Congress assembled shall have authority to appoint a committee, to sit in the recess of Congress, to be denominated "A Committee of the States," and to consist of one delegate from each state; ... to borrow money or emit bills on the credit of the United States ... to build and equip a navy — to agree upon the number of land forces, and to make requisitions from each state for its quota, in proportion to the number of white inhabitants in such state, which requisition shall be binding. ...

Article X. The Committee of the States, or any nine of them, shall be authorized to execute, in the recess of Congress, such of the powers of Congress as the United States in Congress assembled, by the consent of nine states, shall from time to time think expedient to vest them with. ...

Article XI. Canada acceding to this Confederation, and joining in the measures of the United States, shall be admitted into and entitled to all the advantages of this union; but no other colony shall be admitted into the same unless such admission be agreed to by nine states.

Article XII. All bills of credit emitted, moneys borrowed, and debts contracted by or under the authority of Congress, before the assembling of the United States, in pursuance of the present Confederation, shall be deemed and considered as a charge against the United States, for payment and satisfaction whereof the said United States and the public faith are hereby solemnly pledged.

Article XIII. Every state shall abide by the determinations of the United States in Congress assembled on all questions which by this Confederation are submitted to them. And the Articles of this Confederation shall be inviolably observed by every state, and the union shall be perpetual; nor shall any alteration at any time hereafter be made in any of them; unless such alteration be agreed to in a Congress of the United States and be afterward confirmed by the legislatures of every state.

1776–77 and adopted by the Congress on Nov. 15, 1777. However, the document was not fully ratified by the states until March 1, 1781.

On paper, the Congress had power to regulate foreign affairs, war, and the postal service and to appoint military officers, control Indian affairs, borrow money, determine the value of coin, and issue bills of credit. In reality, however, the Articles gave the Congress no power to enforce its requests to the states for money or troops, and by the end of 1786 governmental effectiveness had broken down.

Nevertheless, some solid accomplishments had been achieved: certain state claims to western lands were settled, and the Northwest Ordinance of 1787 established the fundamental pattern of evolving government in the territories north of the Ohio River. Though on balance a flawed document, severely limiting the power of the central government, the short-lived Articles by their very weaknesses paved the way for the Constitutional Convention of 1787 and the present form of U.S. government.

Constitutional Convention

The Constitution was written during the summer of 1787 in Philadelphia, Pa., by 55 delegates to a Constitutional Convention that was called ostensibly to amend the Articles of Confederation. The Constitution was the product of political compromise after long and often rancorous debates over issues such as states' rights, representation, and slavery. Delegates from small and large states disagreed over whether the number of representatives in the new federal legislature should be the same for each state—as was the case under the Articles of Confederation—or different depending on a state's population. In addition, some delegates from Northern states sought to abolish slavery or, failing that, to make representation dependent on the size of a state's free population. At the same time, some Southern delegates threatened to abandon the convention if their demands to keep slavery and the slave trade legal and to count slaves for representation purposes were not met. Eventually the framers resolved their disputes by adopting a proposal put forward by the Connecticut delegation. The Great Compromise, as it came to be known, created a bicameral legislature with a Senate, in which all states would be equally represented, and a House of Representatives, in which representation

George Washington presiding over the delegates to the 1787 Constitutional Convention in Philadelphia. Hulton Archive/Getty Images

would be apportioned on the basis of a state's free population plus three-fifths of its slave population. (The inclusion of the slave population was known separately as the three-fifths compromise.) A further compromise on slavery prohibited Congress from banning the importation of slaves until 1808 (Article I, Section 9). After all the disagreements were bridged, the new Constitution was submitted for ratification to the 13 states on Sept. 28, 1787.

In 1787–88, in an effort to persuade New York to ratify the Constitution, Alexander Hamilton, John Jay, and James Madison published a series of essays on the Constitution and republican government in New York newspapers. Their work, written under the pseudonym "Publius" and collected and published in book form as *The Federalist*

(1788), became a classic exposition and defense of the Constitution.

In June 1788, after the Constitution had been ratified by nine states (as required by Article VII), Congress set March 4, 1789, as the date for the new government to commence proceedings (the first elections under the Constitution were held late in 1788). Because ratification in many states was contingent on the promised addition of a Bill of Rights, Congress proposed 12 amendments in September 1789; 10 were ratified by the states, and their adoption was certified on Dec. 15, 1791. (One of the original 12 proposed amendments, which prohibited midterm changes in compensation for members of Congress, was ratified in 1992 as the Twenty-seventh Amendment. The last one, concerning the ratio of citizens per member of the House of Representatives, has never been adopted.)

The authors of the Constitution were heavily influenced by the country's experience under the Articles of Confederation, which had attempted to retain as much independence and sovereignty for the states as possible and to assign to the central government only those nationally important functions that the states could not handle individually. But the events of the years 1781 to 1787, including the national government's inability to act during Shays's Rebellion (1786–87) in Massachusetts, showed that the Articles were unworkable because they deprived the national government of many essential powers, including direct taxation and the ability to regulate interstate commerce. It was hoped that the new Constitution would remedy this problem.

The framers of the Constitution were especially concerned with limiting the power of government and securing the liberty of citizens. The doctrine of legislative, executive, and judicial separation of powers, the checks and balances of each branch against the others, and the explicit guarantees of individual liberty were all designed to strike a balance between authority and liberty—the central purpose of American constitutional law.

Provisions

The Constitution concisely organizes the country's basic political institutions. The main text comprises seven articles. Article I vests all legislative powers in the Congress—the House of Representatives and the Senate. The Great Compromise stipulated that representation in the House would be based on population, and each state is entitled to two senators. Members of the House serve terms of two years, senators terms of six. Among the powers delegated to Congress are the right to levy taxes, borrow money, regulate interstate commerce, provide for military forces, declare war, and determine member seating and rules of procedure. The House initiates impeachment proceedings, and the Senate adjudicates them.

Article II vests executive power in the office of the presidency of the United States. The president, selected by an electoral college to serve a four-year term, is given responsibilities common to chief executives, including serving as commander in chief of the armed forces, negotiating treaties (two-thirds of the Senate must concur), and granting pardons. The president's vast appointment powers, which include members of the Federal Judiciary and the cabinet, are subject to the "advice and consent" (majority approval) of the Senate (Article II, Section 2). Originally presidents were eligible for continual reelection, but the Twenty-second Amendment (1951) later prohibited any person from being elected president more than twice. Although the formal powers of the president are constitutionally quite limited and vague in comparison with those of the Congress, a variety of historical and technological factors—such as the centralization of power in the executive branch during war and the advent of television—have increased the informal responsibilities of the office extensively to embrace other aspects of political leadership, including proposing legislation to Congress.

Article III places judicial power in the hands of the courts. The Constitution is interpreted by the courts, and the Supreme Court of the United States is the final court of appeal from the state and lower federal courts. The power of American courts to rule on the constitutionality of laws, known as judicial review, is held by few other courts in the world and is not explicitly granted in the Constitution. The principle of judicial review was first asserted by Supreme Court Chief Justice John Marshall in *Marbury* v. *Madison* (1803), when the court ruled that it had the authority to void national or state laws.

Beyond the body of judicial rulings interpreting it, the Constitution acquires meaning in a broader sense at the hands of all who use it. Congress on innumerable occasions has given new scope to the document through statutes, such as those creating executive departments, the federal courts, territories, and states; controlling succession to the presidency; and setting up the executive budget system. The chief executive also has contributed to constitutional interpretation, as in the development of the executive agreement as an instrument of foreign policy. Practices outside the letter of the Constitution based on custom and usage are often recognized as constitutional elements; they include the system of political parties, presidential nomination procedures, and the conduct of election campaigns. The presidential cabinet is largely a constitutional "convention" based on custom, and the actual operation of the electoral college system is also a convention.

PRIMARY SOURCE: THE CONSTITUTION OF THE UNITED STATES: ARTICLE III, SECTIONS 1 AND 2

Section 1. The judicial power of the United States shall be vested in one Supreme Court, and in such inferior courts as the Congress may from time to time ordain and establish. The judges, both of the Supreme and inferior courts, shall hold their offices during good behavior, and shall, at stated times, receive for their services a compensation which shall not be diminished during their continuance in office.

Section 2. The judicial power shall extend to all cases, in law and equity, arising under this Constitution, the laws of the United States, and treaties made, or which shall be made, under their authority; to all cases affecting ambassadors, other public ministers and consuls; to all cases of Admiralty and maritime jurisdiction; to controversies to which the United States shall be a party; to controversies between two or more states; between a state and citizens of another state; between citizens of different states; between citizens of the same state claiming lands under grants of different states; and between a state, or the citizens thereof, and foreign states, citizens, or subjects.

In all cases affecting ambassadors, other public ministers, and consuls, and those in which a state shall be party, the Supreme Court shall have original jurisdiction. In all the other cases beforementioned, the Supreme Court shall have appellate jurisdiction, both as to law and fact, with such exceptions and under such regulations as the Congress shall make.

The trial of all crimes, except in cases of impeachment, shall be by jury; and such trial shall be held in the state where the said crimes shall have been committed; but when not committed within any state, the trial shall be at such place or places as the Congress may be law have directed.

Article IV deals, in part, with relations between the states and privileges of the citizens of the states. These provisions include the full faith and credit clause, which requires states to recognize the official acts and judicial proceedings of other states; the requirement that each state provide citizens from other states with all the privileges and immunities afforded the citizens of that state; and the guarantee of a republican form of government for each state.

Article V stipulates the procedures for amending the Constitution. Amendments may be proposed by a two-thirds vote of both houses of Congress or by a convention called by Congress on the application of the legislatures of two-thirds of the states. Proposed amendments must be ratified by three-fourths of the state legislatures or by conventions in as many states, depending on the decision of Congress. All subsequent amendments have been proposed by Congress, and all but one—the Twenty-first Amendment, which repealed prohibition—have been ratified by state legislatures.

Article VI, which prohibits religious tests for officeholders, also deals with public debts and the supremacy of the Constitution, citing the document as "the supreme Law of the Land; . . . any Thing in the Constitution or Laws of any State to the Contrary notwithstanding." Article VII stipulated that the Constitution would become operational after being ratified by nine states.

The national government has only those constitutional powers that are delegated to it either expressly or by implication; the states, unless otherwise restricted, possess all the remaining powers (Tenth Amendment). Thus, national powers are enumerated (Article I, Section 8, paragraphs 1–17), and state powers are not. The state powers are often called "residual," or "reserved," powers. The elastic, or necessary and proper, clause (Article I, Section 8, paragraph 18) states that Congress shall have the authority "To make all Laws which shall be necessary and proper for carrying into Execution" the various powers vested in the national government. Thus, it follows that, in addition to the delegated powers, Congress possesses "implied" powers, a proposition established by

IN FOCUS: *MCCULLOCH V. MARYLAND*

On March 6, 1819, in *McCulloch* v. *Maryland*, the U.S. Supreme Court affirmed the constitutional doctrine of Congress's "implied powers." It determined that Congress had not only the powers expressly conferred upon it by the Constitution but also all authority "appropriate" to carry out such powers. In the specific case the court held that Congress had the power to incorporate a national bank, despite the Constitution's silence on both the creation of corporations and the chartering of banks. It was concluded that since a national bank would facilitate the accomplishment of purposes expressly confided to the federal government, such as the collection of taxes and the maintenance of armed forces, Congress had a choice of means to achieve these proper ends. The doctrine of implied powers became a powerful force in the steady growth of federal power.

Competing concepts of federal supremacy and states' rights were brought into sharp relief in questions about commercial regulation. The commerce clause simply authorized Congress "To regulate Commerce with foreign Nations, and among the several States, and with the Indian Tribes." Particularly since a series of decisions in 1937, the court has interpreted Congress's regulatory power broadly under the commerce clause as new methods of interstate transportation and communication have come into use. States may not regulate any aspect of interstate commerce that Congress has preempted.

Chief Justice Marshall in *McCulloch* v. *Maryland* (1819). The issue of national versus state power was not fully resolved by this decision, however.

Civil Liberties and the Bill of Rights

The federal government is obliged by many constitutional provisions to respect the individual citizen's basic rights. Some civil liberties were specified in the original document, notably in the provisions guaranteeing the writ of habeas corpus and trial by jury in criminal cases (Article III, Section 2) and forbidding bills of attainder and ex post facto laws (Article I, Section 9). But the most significant limitations to government's power over the individual were added in 1791 in the Bill of Rights. The Constitution's First Amendment guarantees the rights of conscience, such as freedom of religion, speech, and the press, and the right of peaceful assembly and petition. Other guarantees in the Bill of Rights require fair procedures for persons accused of a crime—such as protection against unreasonable search and seizure, compulsory self-incrimination, double jeopardy, and excessive bail—and guarantees of a speedy and public trial by a local, impartial jury before an impartial judge and representation by counsel. Rights of private property are also guaranteed. Although the Bill of Rights is a broad expression of individual civil liberties, the ambiguous wording of many of its provisions—such as the Second Amendment's right "to keep and bear arms" and the Eighth Amendment's prohibition of "cruel and unusual punishments"—has been a source of constitutional controversy and intense political debate. Further, the rights guaranteed are not absolute, and there has been considerable disagreement about the extent to which they limit governmental authority. The Bill of Rights originally protected citizens only from the national government. For example, although the Constitution prohibited the establishment of an official religion at the national level, the official state-supported religion of Massachusetts was Congregationalism until 1833. Thus, individual citizens had to look to state constitutions for protection of their rights against state governments.

The Fourteenth Amendment

After the American Civil War, three new constitutional amendments were adopted: the Thirteenth, which abolished slavery; the Fourteenth, which granted citizenship to former slaves; and the Fifteenth, which guaranteed former male slaves the right to vote. The Fourteenth Amendment placed an important federal limitation on the states by forbidding them to deny to any person "life, liberty, or property, without due process of law" and guaranteeing every person within a state's jurisdiction "the equal protection of its laws." Later interpretations by the Supreme Court in the 20th century gave these two clauses added significance. In *Gitlow* v. *New York* (1925), the due process clause was interpreted by the Supreme Court to broaden the applicability of the Bill of Rights' protection of speech to the states, holding both levels of government to the same constitutional standard. During subsequent decades, the Supreme Court selectively applied the due process clause to protect other liberties guaranteed in the Bill of Rights, including freedom of religion and the press and guarantees of a fair trial, including the defendant's right to an impartial judge and the assistance of counsel. Most controversial was the Supreme Court's application of this due process clause to the *Roe* v. *Wade* case, which led to the legalization of abortion in 1973.

The Supreme Court applied the equal-protection clause of the Fourteenth Amendment in its landmark decision in *Brown* v. *Board of Education of Topeka* (1954), in which it ruled that racial segregation in public schools was unconstitutional. In the 1960s and '70s the equal-protection clause was used by the Supreme Court to extend protections to other areas, including zoning laws, voting rights, and gender discrimination. The broad interpretation of this clause has also caused considerable controversy.

The Constitution as a Living Document

Twenty-seven amendments have been added to the Constitution since 1789. In addition to those mentioned above, other far-reaching amendments include the Sixteenth (1913), which allowed Congress to impose an income tax; the Seventeenth (1913), which provided for direct election of senators; the Nineteenth (1920), which mandated woman suffrage; and the Twenty-sixth (1971), which granted suffrage to citizens 18 years of age and older.

In more than two centuries of operation, the United States Constitution has proved itself a dynamic document. It has served as a model for other countries, its provisions being widely imitated in national constitutions throughout the world. Although the Constitution's brevity and ambiguity have sometimes led to serious disputes about its meaning, they also have made it adaptable to changing historical circumstances and ensured its relevance in ages far removed from the one in which it was written.

SEPARATION OF POWERS AND CHECKS AND BALANCES

The Constitution created three separate branches of government and a system whereby each branch could check and balance the power of the other two. Separation of powers is the division of the legislative, executive, and judicial functions of government among separate and independent bodies. Such a separation, it has been argued, limits the possibility of arbitrary excesses by government, since the sanction of all three branches is required for the making, executing, and administering of laws. Checks and balances is a principle of government under which separate branches are empowered to prevent actions by other branches and are induced to share power. It is applied primarily in constitutional governments and is of fundamental importance in tripartite governments, such as that of the United States, which divide powers among legislative, executive, and judicial branches.

Separation of Powers

The doctrine may be traced to ancient and medieval theories of mixed government, which argued that the processes of government should involve the different elements in society such as monarchic, aristocratic, and democratic interests. The first modern formulation of the doctrine was that of the French writer Montesquieu in *The Spirit of Laws* (1748), although the English philosopher John Locke had earlier argued that legislative power should be divided between king and Parliament.

Montesquieu's argument that liberty is most effectively safeguarded by the separation of powers was inspired by the English constitution, although his interpretation of English political realities has since been disputed. His work was widely influential, most notably in America, where it profoundly influenced the framing of the Constitution. The U.S. Constitution further precluded the concentration of political power by providing staggered terms of office in the key governmental bodies.

Charles Louis de Secondat, baron de La Brède et de Montesquieu, c. *1750*. Hulton Archive/Getty Images

Modern constitutional systems show a great variety of arrangements of the legislative, executive, and judicial processes, and the doctrine has consequently lost much of its rigidity and dogmatic purity. In the 20th century, and especially since World War II, governmental involvement in numerous aspects of social and economic life has resulted in an enlargement of the scope of executive power. Some who fear the consequences of this for individual liberty have favoured establishing means of appeal against executive and administrative decisions (for example, through an ombudsman), rather than attempting to reassert the doctrine of the separation of powers.

Checks and Balances

The framers of the U.S. Constitution, who were influenced by Montesquieu and the English jurist and common-law scholar William Blackstone, among others, saw checks and balances as essential for the security of liberty under the Constitution: "It is by balancing each of these powers against the other two, that the efforts in human nature toward tyranny can alone be checked and restrained, and any degree of freedom preserved in the constitution" (John Adams). Though not expressly covered in the text of the Constitution, judicial review—the power of the courts to examine the actions of the legislative and the executive and administrative arms of government to ensure that they are constitutional—became an important part of government in the United States. Other checks and balances include the presidential veto of legislation (which Congress may override by a two-thirds vote) and executive and judicial impeachment by Congress. Only Congress can appropriate funds, and each house serves as a check on possible abuses of power or unwise action by the other. Congress, by initiating constitutional amendments, can in practice reverse decisions of the Supreme Court. The president appoints the members of the Supreme Court but only with the consent of the Senate, which also approves certain other executive appointments. The

John Adams, oil painting by Gilbert Stuart, 1826; in the National Collection of Fine Arts, Washington, D.C. Courtesy of the National Collection of Fine Arts, Smithsonian Institution, Washington D.C.

Senate also must approve treaties.

From 1932 the U.S. Congress exercised a so-called legislative veto. Clauses in certain laws qualified the authority of the executive branch to act by making specified acts subject to disapproval by the majority vote of one or both houses. In 1983, in a case concerning the deportation of an alien, the U.S. Supreme Court held that legislative vetoes were unconstitutional (the House of Representatives had overturned the Justice Department's suspension of the alien's deportation). The decision affected clauses in some 200 laws covering a wide range of subjects, including presidential war powers, foreign aid and arms sales, environmental protection, consumer interests, and others. Despite the court's decision, Congress continued to exercise this power, including the legislative veto in at least 11 of the bills it passed in 1984 alone.

Checks and balances that evolved from custom and Constitutional conventions include the congressional committee system and investigative powers, the role of political parties, and presidential influence in initiating legislation.

THE FEDERALIST PAPERS

The proposed Constitution was a well-crafted instrument, but convincing voters that it should be ratified—particularly anti-Federalists and other opponents of the Constitution—was a project unto itself. Because by late 1787 New York had yet to ratify the Constitution, Alexander Hamilton, James Madison, and John Jay wrote a series of essays on the proposed new Constitution in an effort to persuade New York voters to do so. Formally called *The Federalist*, the Federalist Papers was a series of 85 essays published between 1787 and 1788. Seventy-seven of the essays first appeared serially in New York newspapers, were reprinted in most other states, and were published in book form as *The Federalist* on May 28, 1788; the remaining eight papers appeared in New York newspapers between June 14 and August 16.

The authors of the Federalist Papers presented a masterly defense of the new federal system and of the major departments in the proposed central government. They also argued that the existing government under the Articles of Confederation, the country's first constitution, was defective and that the proposed Constitution would remedy its weaknesses without endangering the liberties of the people.

As a general treatise on republican government, the Federalist Papers are distinguished for their comprehensive analysis of the means by which the ideals of justice, the general welfare, and the rights of individuals could be realized. The authors assumed that the primary political motive of man was self-interest and that men—whether acting individually or collectively—were selfish and only imperfectly rational. The establishment of a republican form of government would not of itself provide protection against such characteristics: the representatives of the people might betray their trust; one segment of the population might oppress another; and both the representatives and the public might give way to passion or caprice. The possibility of good government, they argued, lay in man's capacity to devise political institutions that would compensate for deficiencies in both reason and virtue in the ordinary conduct of politics. This theme was predominant in late 18th-century political thought in America and accounts in part for the elaborate system of checks and balances that was devised in the Constitution.

In one of the most notable essays, "Federalist 10," Madison rejected the then common belief that republican government was possible only for small states. He argued that stability, liberty, and justice were more likely to be achieved in a large area with a numerous and heterogeneous population. Although frequently interpreted as an attack on majority rule, the essay is in reality a defense of both social, economic, and cultural pluralism and of a composite majority formed by compromise and conciliation. Decision by such a majority, rather than by a monistic one, would be more likely to accord with the proper ends of government. This distinction between a proper and an improper majority typifies the fundamental philosophy of the Federalist Papers; republican institutions, including the principle of majority rule, were not considered good in themselves but were good because they constituted the best means for the pursuit of justice and the preservation of liberty.

All the papers appeared over the signature "Publius," and the authorship of some of the papers was once a matter of scholarly dispute. However, computer analysis and historical evidence has led nearly all historians to assign authorship in the following manner: Hamilton wrote numbers 1, 6–9, 11–13, 15–17, 21–36, 59–61, and 65–85; Madison, numbers 10, 14, 18–20, 37–58, and 62–63; and Jay, numbers 2–5 and 64.

IN FOCUS: JAMES MADISON: "FEDERALIST 10" (EXCERPTS)

Among the numerous advantages promised by a well-constructed Union, none deserves to be more accurately developed than its tendency to break and control the violence of faction. ... The instability, injustice, and confusion introduced into the public councils have, in truth, been the mortal diseases under which popular governments have everywhere perished. ...

By a faction, I understand a number of citizens, whether amounting to a majority or minority of the whole, who are united and actuated by some common impulse of passion, or of interest, adverse to the rights of other citizens, or to the permanent and aggregate interests of the community. ...

If a faction consists of less than a majority, relief is supplied by the republican principle, which enables the majority to defeat its sinister views by regular vote. ...When a majority is included in a faction, the form of popular government, on the other hand, enables it to sacrifice to its ruling passion or interest both the public good and the rights of other citizens. To secure the public good and private rights against the danger of such a faction, and at the same time to preserve the spirit and the form of popular government, is then the great object to which our inquiries are directed. ...

The two great points of difference between a democracy and a republic are: first, the delegation of the government, in the latter, to a small number of citizens elected by the rest; secondly, the greater number of citizens, and greater sphere of country, over which the latter may be extended.

The effect of the first difference is, on the one hand, to refine and enlarge the public views by passing them through the medium of a chosen body of citizens, whose wisdom may best discern the true interest of their country, and whose patriotism and love of justice will be least likely to sacrifice it to temporary or partial considerations. ...

The other point of difference is the greater number of citizens and extent of territory which may be brought within the compass of republican than of democratic government; and it is this circumstance principally which renders factious combinations less to be dreaded in the former than in the latter. The smaller the society, the fewer probably will be the distinct parties and interests composing it; ... and the smaller the number of individuals composing a majority, and the smaller the compass within which they are placed, the more easily will they concert and execute their plans of oppression. Extend the sphere and you ... make it less probable that a majority of the whole will have a common motive to invade the rights of other citizens. ...

In the extent, and proper structure of the Union, therefore, we behold a republican remedy for the diseases most incident to republican government. And according to the degree of pleasure and pride we feel in being republicans, ought to be our zeal in cherishing the spirit and supporting the character of Federalists.

FEDERAL VERSUS STATE POWER: STATES' RIGHTS AND NULLIFICATION

Many political battles in U.S. history have been based on conflicting interpretations of the extent of the implied powers granted to the federal government by the U.S. Constitution. Historically, proponents of the rights of states, or states' rights, particularly in the South, upheld a narrow interpretation of the implied powers of the federal government and an expansive interpretation of the residual powers of the state governments. An extreme example of this view was the historical doctrine of nullification, according to which states have the power to nullify within their boundaries any act of the federal government with which they disagree.

States' Rights

States' rights are the rights or powers retained by the state, provincial, or regional governments of a federal union under the provisions of a federal constitution. In the United States, Switzerland, and Australia, the powers of the regional governments are those that remain after the powers of the central government have been enumerated in the constitution. In contrast, the powers at both the state or regional level and the national level of government are defined clearly by specific provisions of the constitutions of Canada and Germany.

The concept of states' rights is closely related to that of state rights, which was invoked from the 18th century in Europe to legitimate the powers vested in sovereign national governments. Doctrines asserting states' rights were developed in contexts in which states functioned as distinct units in a federal system of government. In the United States, for example, Americans in the 18th and 19th centuries often referred to the rights of states, implying that each state had inherent rights and sovereignty. Before and following the American Civil War (1861–65), the U.S. states—particularly the Southern states—shared the belief that each of them was sovereign and should have jurisdiction over its most important affairs. Today the term is applied more broadly to a variety of efforts aimed at reducing the powers of national governments, which had grown considerably in both size and scope.

Advocates of states' rights put greater trust and confidence in regional or state governments than in national ones. State governments, according to them, are more responsive to popular control, more sensitive to state issues and problems, and more understanding of the culture and values of the state's population than are national governments. For these reasons, they argue, state governments are better able to address important problems and protect individual rights. In the United States, states' rights proponents also have maintained that strong state governments are more consistent with the vision of republican government put forward by the Founding Fathers. They cite in support of their view the Tenth Amendment to the U.S. Constitution, which reserves for the states the residue of powers "not delegated to the United States by the Constitution, nor prohibited by it to the States."

In the United States, the term *states' rights* has been applied to a variety of political programs. Before the American Civil War, it was the rallying cry of Southern opponents of Northern-inspired tariffs and Northern proposals to abolish or restrict slavery. The notion of states' rights also was used as an argument for the doctrine of nullification and for the claim that the states, by virtue of their sovereignty, had the right to secede from the Union. This constitutional question was resolved only by the victory of the North (federal government) in the Civil War. A century later the doctrine was used to justify opposition to the federal government's efforts to enforce racial desegregation.

Such uses of the doctrine of states' rights in the United States and elsewhere prompted some critics to claim that it serves parochial interests. According to them, states' rights are invoked by majorities in the states to justify laws and practices that discriminate against various ethnic, religious, or other minority groups. They contend that a strong national government is necessary to ensure that states respect the rights guaranteed to all citizens in the national constitution.

States' rights advocates also addressed issues related to environmental protection and education. In the western United States, for example, some citizen groups questioned the power of the federal government to issue pollution standards and regulations on water and land use, arguing that they amounted to an unconstitutional infringement on the right of states to manage their own natural resources. Many states also resisted the imposition of national educational testing standards out of concern that they would undermine the states' historical control over education.

Nullification

Nullification is the doctrine in U.S. history that upheld the right of a state to declare null and void within its boundaries an act of the federal government. Thomas Jefferson and James Madison advocated nullification in the Virginia and Kentucky Resolutions of 1798. The Union was a compact of sovereign states, Jefferson asserted, and the federal government was their agent with certain specified, delegated powers. The states retained the authority to determine when the federal government exceeded its powers, and they could declare acts to be "void and of no force" in their jurisdictions.

John C. Calhoun furthered the nullification doctrine in his *South Carolina Exposition and Protest*, published and distributed by the South Carolina legislature (without Calhoun's name on it) in 1829. Writing in response to Southern bitterness over the Tariff of 1828 ("Tariff of Abominations"), Calhoun took the position that state "interposition" could block enforcement of a federal law. The state would be obliged to obey only if the law were made an amendment to the Constitution by three-fourths of the states. The "concurrent majority"—i.e., the people of a state having veto power over federal actions—would protect minority rights from the possible tyranny of the numerical majority.

When the Tariff of 1832 only slightly modified the Tariff of 1828, the South Carolina legislature decided to put Calhoun's nullification theory to a practical test. The legislature called for a special state convention, and on Nov. 24, 1832, the convention adopted the Ordinance of

John Caldwell Calhoun, depicted in 1825. He championed states' rights and slavery and was a symbol of the Old South. Hulton Archive/ Getty Images

Nullification. The ordinance declared the tariffs of 1828 and 1832 "null, void, and no law, nor binding upon this State, its officers or citizens." It also forbade appeal of any ordinance measure to the federal courts, required all state officeholders (except members of the legislature) to take an oath of support for the ordinance, and threatened secession if the federal government tried to collect tariff duties by force. In its attempts to have other Southern states join in nullification, however, South Carolina met with total failure.

On Dec. 10, 1832, Pres. Andrew Jackson issued his "Proclamation to the People of South Carolina," asserting the supremacy of the federal government and warning that "disunion by armed force is treason." Congress then (March 1, 1833) passed both the Force Bill—authorizing Jackson to use the military if necessary to collect tariff duties—and a compromise tariff that reduced those duties. The South Carolina convention responded on March 15 by rescinding the Ordinance of Nullification but three days later maintained its principles by nullifying the Force Bill.

As a consequence of the nullification crisis, Jackson emerged a hero to nationalists. But Southerners were made more conscious of their minority position and more aware of their vulnerability to a Northern majority as long as they remained in the Union.

FEDERAL SYSTEMS OF GOVERNMENT

The U.S. Constitution embodies a mode of political organization known as federalism. Federal systems of government unite separate states or other polities within an overarching political system in such a way as to allow each to maintain its own fundamental political integrity. Federal systems do this by requiring that basic policies be made and implemented through negotiation in some form, so that all the members can share in making and executing decisions. The political principles that animate federal systems emphasize the primacy of bargaining and negotiated coordination among several power centres; they stress the virtues of dispersed power centres (separation of powers) as a means for safeguarding individual and local liberties.

The various political systems that call themselves federal differ in many ways. Certain characteristics and principles, however, are common to all truly federal systems: a written constitution, noncentralization of power, and areal (or geographic) division of power.

Written Constitution

First, the federal relationship must be established or confirmed through a perpetual covenant of union, usually embodied in a written constitution that outlines the terms by which power is divided or shared; the constitution can be altered only by extraordinary procedures. These constitutions are distinctive in being not simply compacts between rulers and ruled but involving the people, the general government, and the states constituting the federal union. The constituent states, moreover, often retain constitution-making rights of their own.

Noncentralization

Second, the political system itself must reflect the constitution by actually diffusing power among a number of substantially self-sustaining centres. Such a diffusion of power may be termed noncentralization. Noncentralization is a way of ensuring in practice that the authority to participate in exercising political power cannot be taken away from the general or the state governments without common consent.

A Real Division of Power

A third element of any federal system is what has been called in the United States territorial democracy. This has two faces: the use of areal (geographic) divisions to ensure neutrality and equality in the representation of the various groups and interests in the polity and the use of such divisions to secure local autonomy and representation for diverse groups within the same civil society. Territorial neutrality has proved highly useful in societies that are changing, allowing for the representation of new interests in proportion to their strength simply by allowing their supporters to vote in relatively equal territorial units. At the same time, the accommodation of very diverse groups whose differences are fundamental rather than transient by giving them territorial power bases of their own has enhanced the ability of federal systems to function as vehicles of political integration while preserving democratic government. One example of this system may be seen in Canada, which includes a population of French descent, centred in the province of Quebec.

Elements Maintaining Union

Modern federal systems generally provide direct lines of communication between the citizenry and all the governments that serve them. The people may and usually do elect representatives to all the governments, and all of them may and usually do administer programs that directly serve the individual citizen.

The existence of those direct lines of communication is one of the features distinguishing federations from leagues or confederations. It is usually based on a sense of common nationality binding the constituent polities and people together. In some countries this sense of nationality has been inherited, as in Germany, while in the United States, Argentina, and Australia it had to be at least partly invented. Canada and Switzerland have had to evolve this sense in order to hold together strongly divergent nationality groups. In the relatively new federal systems of India, Malaysia, and Nigeria, the future of federalism is endangered by the absence of such a common national sense.

Geographic necessity has played a part in promoting the maintenance of union within federal systems. The Mississippi Valley in the United States, the Alps in Switzerland, the island character of the Australian continent, and the mountains and jungles surrounding Brazil have all been influences promoting unity; so have the pressures for Canadian union arising from that country's situation on the border of the United States and the pressures upon the German states generated by their neighbours to the east and west. In this connection, the necessity for a common defense against common enemies has stimulated federal union in the first place and acted to maintain it.

Elements Maintaining the Federal Principle

Several devices found in federal systems serve to maintain the federal principle itself. Two of these are of particular importance.

The maintenance of federalism requires that the nation and its constituent polities each have substantially complete governing institutions of their own, with the right to modify those institutions unilaterally within limits set by the compact. Both separate legislative and separate administrative institutions are necessary.

The contractual sharing of public responsibilities by all governments in the system appears to be a central characteristic of federalism. Sharing, broadly conceived, includes common involvement in policy making, financing, and administration. Sharing may be formal or informal; in federal systems, it is usually contractual. The contract is used as a legal device to enable governments to engage in joint action while remaining independent entities. Even where there is no formal arrangement, the spirit of federalism tends to infuse a sense of contractual obligation.

Federal systems or systems strongly influenced by federal principles have been among the most stable and long-lasting of polities. But the successful operation of federal systems requires a particular kind of political environment, one that is conducive to popular government and has the requisite traditions of political cooperation and self-restraint. Beyond this, federal systems operate best in societies with sufficient homogeneity of fundamental interests to allow a great deal of latitude to local government and to permit reliance upon voluntary collaboration. The use of force to maintain domestic order is even more inimical to the successful maintenance of federal patterns of government than to other forms of popular government. Federal systems are most successful in societies that have the human resources to fill many public offices competently and the material resources to afford a measure of economic waste as part of the price of liberty.

Chapter 2 THE JUDICIAL BRANCH OF GOVERMENT

THE JUDICIARY IN PERSPECTIVE

The judiciary is the branch of government whose task is the authoritative adjudication of controversies over the application of laws in specific situations. Conflicts brought before the judiciary are embodied in cases involving litigants, who may be individuals, groups, legal entities (e.g., corporations), or governments and their agencies. Conflicts that allege personal or financial harm resulting from violations of law or binding legal agreements between litigants—other than violations legally defined as crimes—produce civil cases. Judicial decisions in civil cases often require the losing or offending party to pay financial compensation to the winner. Crimes produce criminal cases, which are officially defined as conflicts between the state or its citizens and the accused (defendant) rather than as conflicts between the victim of the crime and the defendant. Judicial decisions in criminal cases determine whether the accused is guilty or not guilty. A defendant found guilty is sentenced to punishments, which may involve the payment of a fine, a term of imprisonment, or, in the most serious cases in some legal systems, state-imposed physical mutilation or even death.

Judiciaries also frequently resolve administrative cases, disputes between individuals, groups, or legal entities and government agencies over the application of laws or the implementation of government programs. Most legal systems have incorporated the principle of state sovereignty, whereby governments may not be sued by nonstate litigants without their consent. This principle limits the right of litigants to pursue remedies against government actions. Nevertheless, the right of citizens to be free from the arbitrary, improper, abusive application of laws and government regulations has long been recognized and is the focus of administrative cases.

Legal systems differ in the extent to which their judiciaries handle civil, criminal, and administrative cases. In some, courts hear all three kinds of disputes. In others there are specialized civil, criminal, and administrative courts. Still others have some general and some specialized courts.

In many cases the conflicts that are nominally brought to courts for resolution are uncontested. The majority of civil cases in the United States—such as those involving divorce, child custody, or the interpretation of contracts—are settled out of court and never go to trial. The same is true for criminal cases in the United States, where the practice of extrajudicial plea bargaining is used extensively. The different criminal process that characterizes the United Kingdom and civil-law countries makes plea bargaining of the sort practiced in the United States less likely—or even officially impossible. Nevertheless, there is evidence that analogous practices for generating and accepting guilty pleas are common in the United Kingdom and are not unknown in Germany. In cases of plea bargaining the court's function is administrative, limited to officially ratifying and recording the agreement the parties have reached out of court.

When the judiciary does decide a controversy, a body of regulations governs what parties are allowed before the court, what evidence will be admitted, what trial procedure will be followed, and what types of judgments may be rendered. Judicial proceedings involve the participation of a number of people. Although the judge is the central figure, along with the parties to the controversy and the lawyers who represent them, there are other individuals involved, including witnesses, clerks, bailiffs, administrators, and jurors when the proceeding involves a jury.

The stated function of the courts is the authoritative adjudication of controversies over the application of laws in specific situations. However, it is unavoidable that courts also make law and public policy, because judges must exercise at least some measure of discretion in deciding which litigant claims are legally correct or otherwise most appropriate. Lawmaking and policy making by courts are most evident when powerful national supreme courts (e.g., those in the United States, Germany, and India) exercise their power of judicial review to hold laws or major government actions unconstitutional. They also can occur, however, when judiciaries are behaving as administrators, even when they are merely ratifying agreements reached out of court. Patterns of settlement for suits between employers and employees may be more favourable to employees than formal law would seem to require, because they are influenced by de facto changes in the law that may result from the decisions by juries or trial judges who may regularly be more sympathetic to workers. Formal laws regulating child custody or financial settlements in divorce cases can similarly be altered over time as juries process the claims of the litigants before them in persistent ways.

After a court decision has been made, it may or may not require enforcement. In many cases the parties accept the judgment of the court and conform their behaviour to it. In other cases a court must order a party to cease a particular activity. The enforcement of such orders is carried out by the executive branch and may require funding from the legislative branch.

JUDICIAL LEGITIMACY

Legal scholars are fond of quoting the maxim that courts have neither the "power of the purse nor of the sword," meaning that they, unlike other institutions of government, rarely have the power to raise and spend money and do not command the institutions of coercion (the police and the military). Without force or monetary inducements, courts are weak institutions, because they are denied the most efficacious means of ensuring that their decisions are complied with and enforced.

The lack of formal institutional powers has led some observers to conclude that courts are the least-effective agents of government. However, such arguments ignore what is surely the most significant powers of courts—their institutional legitimacy. An institution is legitimate when it is perceived as having the right or the authority to make decisions and when its decisions are viewed as worthy of respect or obedience. Judicial legitimacy derives from the belief that judges are impartial and that their decisions are grounded in law, not ideology and politics. Often in sharp contrast to other political institutions (such as legislatures), courts are respected—indeed often revered—because their decisions are viewed as being principled rather than motivated by self-interest or partisanship. To the extent that courts are perceived as legitimate by their constituents, their decisions—even their unpopular ones—are respected, acquiesced to, and accepted.

The justices of the U.S. Supreme Court, for example, often make reference to legitimacy as one of the institution's most precious (and perhaps most volatile) resources. Justices have asserted that frequent reversals of existing precedents undermine the legitimacy of the judiciary. Others have argued that some issues are simply too politically sensitive for courts to intervene in (e.g., the president's war-making powers). If courts become embroiled in ordinary political disputes and are seen as just another political actor trying to advance its ideology, interests, and preferences, then the legitimacy of the institution can be gravely damaged. Some have argued that just this kind of damage was done when the U.S. Supreme Court intervened in the 2000 presidential election and, ultimately, determined the winner. In general, judges are mindful of threats to the legitimacy of the courts and are unwilling to put it at risk in order to prevail in any particular political or legal controversy.

Courts are not naturally and universally endowed with legitimacy; rather, a sense of legitimacy is accrued and built over time. Throughout the world, the decisions of courts have often been ignored or violently opposed. In some countries, unpopular rulings have resulted in riots (Bulgaria); court buildings have been attacked and burned (Pakistan); judges have been intimidated and removed from office (Zimbabwe), assassinated (Uganda), or reassigned to courts in the hinterland (Japan); courts have been stripped of their jurisdiction (United States); and, in the most extreme cases, judicial institutions have been suspended (United States) or abolished (Russia).

COURTS IN THE COMMON-LAW TRADITION

Common law, also called Anglo-American law, is the body of customary law, based upon judicial decisions and embodied in reports of decided cases, that has been administered by the common-law courts of England since the Middle Ages. From it has evolved the type of legal system now found also in the United States and in most of the member states of the Commonwealth (formerly the British Commonwealth of Nations). In this sense common law, practiced throughout the United States (except in Louisiana, which utilizes civil law) is also now widespread in continental Europe and elsewhere. In civil-law systems, judges apply principles embodied in statutes, or law codes, rather than relying on precedents established in earlier cases. Used in another sense, the term "civil law" refers to the law that governs the private relations between individuals or businesses, as distinguished from the law that applies to criminal matters.

FUNCTIONS OF COURTS

Keeping the Peace

The primary function of any court system—to help keep domestic peace—is so obvious that it is rarely considered or mentioned. If there were no institution that was accepted by the citizens of a society as an impartial and authoritative judge of whether a person had committed a crime and, if so, what type of punishment should be meted out, vigilantes offended by the person's conduct might well take the law into their own hands and proceed to punish the alleged miscreant according to their uncontrolled discretion. If no agency were empowered to decide private disputes impartially and authoritatively, people would have to settle their disputes by themselves, with power rather than legitimate authority likely being the basis of such decisions. Such a system might easily degenerate into anarchy. Not even a primitive society could survive under such conditions. Thus, in this most basic sense, courts constitute an essential element of society's machinery for keeping peace.

Deciding Disputes

In the course of helping to keep the peace, courts are called upon to decide controversies. If, in a criminal case, the defendant (one charged with a crime) denies committing the acts charged against him, the court must choose between his version of the facts and that presented by the prosecution. If the defendant asserts that his actions did not constitute criminal behaviour, the court (often aided by a jury) must decide whether his view of the law and facts or the prosecution's is correct. In a civil case, if the defendant disputes the plaintiff's account of what happened between them—for example, whether they entered into a certain contract or agreement—or if he disputes the plaintiff's view of the legal significance of whatever occurred—for example, whether the agreement was legally binding—the court again must choose between the contentions of the parties. The issues presented to, and decided by, the court may be either factual, legal, or both.

Courts do not, however, spend all their time resolving disputes between opposing parties. Many cases brought before the courts are not contested (e.g., a "no-fault" divorce or a routine debt-collection case). As no dispute exists over the facts or the law, the court's role in such cases is more administrative than adjudicatory. Moreover, the mere existence of a court may render the frequent exercise of its powers unnecessary. The fact that courts operate by known rules and with reasonably predictable results leads many of those who might otherwise engage in legal action to reach a compromise, because people are typically unwilling to incur the expense of going to court if they believe that there is a good chance that they will lose.

Most people arrested and charged with a crime plead guilty. If they do so with full understanding and without any coercion, the judge generally accepts their admission of guilt. The sole question for the court is to decide whether the defendant should go to jail, pay a fine, pay restitution to the victim, or be subjected to other corrective treatment (the judgment may entail more than one of these punishments). In civil-law countries, some judicial inquiry into the question of guilt or innocence is typically required even after a confession, but the inquiry is generally brief and tends to be perfunctory. The main problem to be resolved is the sentence that should be imposed.

The vast majority of civil cases are also uncontested or, at least, are settled prior to trial. In some instances, serious negotiations begin only after a lawsuit has been filed. Many suits are settled by the parties themselves, without the intervention of the court. Because courts are usually under strong caseload pressures, they encourage such settlements. Consequently, in many Western systems, only a small fraction of civil cases are actually tried. Indeed, in many countries a notable trend since the late 20th century has been the decreased reliance upon trials to settle disputes.

The decline in court usage reflects several legal and social trends, most notably the increased desire of the parties to seek immediate relief and the increased options in the systems available to do just that. In the United States, for example, most divorce cases are uncontested, both parties usually being eager to terminate the marriage and often agreeing on related questions concerning support and the custody of children. All the court does in such cases is review what the parties have agreed upon and give the agreement official approval and the legitimacy of law. In other instances, disputes are settled through various methods of alternative dispute resolution, such as arbitration, in which the parties agree that the decision of the arbitration (or arbitration panel or tribunal) will carry the full, binding force of law. Arbitration is commonly used in commercial and labour disputes.

Many other uncontested matters come before courts, such as the adoption of children, the distribution of assets in trusts and estates, and the establishment of corporations.

Occasionally questions of law or fact arise that have to be decided by the court, but normally all that is required is judicial supervision and approval. Thus, much of what courts do is administrative in nature.

Judicial Lawmaking

All courts apply preexisting rules (statutes) formulated by legislative bodies, though the procedures vary greatly between common-law and civil-law countries. In applying these rules, however, courts must also interpret them, typically transforming the rules from generalities to specifics and sometimes filling gaps to cover situations never addressed by lawmakers when the legislation was first drafted. As courts decide disputes in individual cases, they create an important by-product beyond peaceful settlements—that is, they develop rules for deciding future cases. The judicial decisions embodying these interpretations then become controlling for future cases, sometimes to the extent that they virtually supplant the legislative enactments themselves. In common-law systems, such decisions are called precedents, and they are rules and policies with just as much authority as a law passed by a legislature. Thus, law is made not only by legislatures but also by the courts.

The common-law system of creating precedents is sometimes called stare decisis (literally, "to stand by decided matters"). Judges are generally expected to follow earlier decisions, not only to save themselves the effort of working out fresh solutions for the same problems each time they occur but also, and primarily, because the goal of the law is to render uniform and predictable justice. Fairness demands that if one individual is dealt with in a certain way today, then another individual engaging in substantially identical conduct under substantially identical conditions tomorrow or a month or year hence should be dealt with in the same way. Reduced to its essentials, precedent simply involves treating similar cases similarly. This system of stare decisis is sometimes referred to as judge-made law, as the law (the precedent) is created by the judge, not by a legislature.

In civil-law countries, all judicial decisions are, in theory, based upon legislative enactments, and the doctrine of judicial precedent does not apply. Judges merely "apply" the law created by the legislature. Practice, however, often departs from theory. Although the civil code adopted in these countries is quite comprehensive, attempting to cover nearly every aspect of human conduct and purporting to supply ready-made answers for all problems that can arise, many of the provisions are exceedingly vague (because they are abstract) and are sometimes almost meaningless until applied to concrete situations, when judicial interpretation gives them specific meaning. Furthermore, the legislative codes cannot anticipate all situations that may arise and come before the courts (e.g., the situation in which advances in medical technology enable doctors to keep a legally dead person alive). The gaps in legislation must be and are filled by judicial decisions, as a court is unlikely to refuse to decide a case merely on the grounds that it has not been told in advance the answers to the questions presented to it. Decisions dealing with circumstances unforeseen by the legal codes and giving specific meaning to vague legislative provisions are published in legal volumes in most civil-law countries and are frequently referred to by lawyers and relied upon by judges. They are not considered "binding" in the sense that judges are legally obliged to follow earlier decisions, but they are also not forgotten or disregarded. In actual practice, they have almost as much influence as statutory interpretations in countries that formally adhere to the doctrine of stare decisis.

Judicial lawmaking is more pervasive and more frankly acknowledged in common-law countries than in civil-law ones. In addition to rendering decisions that authoritatively interpret statutes, the courts of common-law countries have created a vast body of law without any statutory foundation whatever. Whenever judges are confronted with a dispute for which there is no clear statutory answer—and this occurs with considerable regularity—they must render decisions in accordance with their own conceptions of justice. Later judges follow these rulings, deciding similar cases in the same manner but distinguishing earlier cases when dissimilar factors are discovered in the cases before them. The later cases also become precedents to be followed in still later cases presenting substantially similar patterns of fact (thus, several precedents may be relevant to a particular case, though they may conflict with each other). The total accumulation of all these judicial decisions is what constitutes "the common law"—the consequence of judges' deciding cases and setting forth their reasons. In common-law countries, legislation is accordingly more limited in scope than it is in civil-law countries. It does not purport to provide for all possibilities, because large areas of conduct are governed solely by judge-made law.

To speak of precedent as "binding" even in common-law systems is somewhat misleading. As already noted, earlier decisions can be and are distinguished when judges conclude that they are based upon situations differing from those before the court in later cases. Even more significant, earlier decisions can be overruled by the courts that rendered them (though not by courts lower in the judicial hierarchy) when the judges conclude that the decisions have proved to be so erroneous or unwise as to be unsuited for current or future application. The Supreme Court of the United States, for example, has overruled many of its own earlier decisions, much to the consternation of those who are unable to accept the inevitability of judicial lawmaking. Many of these reversals have been in the field of constitutional law, in which simple legislative correction of an erroneous judicial interpretation of the Constitution is impossible and in which the only alternative is the exceedingly slow, cumbersome, costly, and difficult process of constitutional amendment. Nevertheless, the power to overrule decisions is not restricted to constitutional interpretations; it also extends to areas of purely statutory and purely judge-made law as well, areas in which legislative action would be equally capable of accomplishing needed changes. Even in the United Kingdom, which does not have a codified constitution and which has traditionally followed a far more rigid doctrine of stare decisis than the United States, the House of Lords, in its role as the highest court, sometimes departs from precedent.

The desirability of judicial lawmaking has long been the subject of lively debate in both civil- and common-law countries. It is universally accepted that courts in democracies should not arrogate to themselves unrestricted legislative power, because the judiciary is rarely subject to the same democratic accountability as legislatures. But when existing statutes and precedents are outmoded or manifestly unfair as applied to specific cases before the courts, should not judges be able to change the law in order to achieve what they conceive to be just results or to avoid what they consider unjust results?

The extent to which the judges should be bound by statutes and case precedents as against their own ethical ideas and concepts of social, political, and economic policy is an important question, as is the matter of which should prevail when justice and law appear to judges to conflict with each other. These are questions upon which reasonable persons disagree vigorously, even when they are in basic agreement on the proposition that some degree of judicial lawmaking is inevitable. The proper tempo and scope of judicial change are what is mainly at issue. How quickly should judges act to remedy injustice, and when should they consider an existing rule to be so established that its alteration calls for constitutional amendment or legislative enactment rather than judicial decision? As many dissenting opinions attest, judges themselves disagree on the answers to these questions, even when they are sitting on the same bench hearing the same case.

Nor should it be assumed that so-called literal or strict interpretation of documents, such as constitutions, precludes judicial policy making. The inherent ambiguity of constitutional interpretation can be seen clearly by considering the First Amendment to the Constitution of the United States, which states that "Congress shall make no law . . . abridging the freedom of speech." This prescription, upon first glance, seems entirely clear. Nevertheless, few people—not least the framers of the Constitution—have interpreted it as meaning that Congress cannot pass any law that abridges any form of speech. Nearly everyone accepts that treasonous or seditious speech, for example, can be proscribed. Most would also accept at least some legal restrictions on libelous speech, and many would accept restrictions on so-called hate speech. Indeed, once one begins to consider the wide variety of actions that might qualify as speech (including "nonverbal," or symbolic, speech), it is easy to conclude that the U.S. Constitution itself has little literal meaning beyond what is given to it by the interpretations of judges.

Constitutional Decisions

In some countries, courts not only interpret legislation but also determine its validity (constitutionality), and in so doing they sometimes nullify statutes passed by legislatures. A court empowered with such authority may declare that a piece of legislation is null and void because it is incompatible with constitutional principles (e.g., some restrictions on the right to have an abortion in the United States have been found by the U.S. Supreme Court to be incompatible with the right to personal privacy—itself a contested constitutional principle that was developed by the court beginning only in the 1960s). This happens only in countries that have written constitutions and that have developed a doctrine of "judicial supremacy" (in contrast to "parliamentary supremacy," which is generally found in countries following the model of the United Kingdom). When scholars speak of "limited government," they mean specifically that the policy options available to governments are constrained by constitutional principles that are enforced by an independent judiciary. The prime example is the United States, and the classic statement of the doctrine is the Supreme Court's decision in

Etching by H.B. Hall after the Henry Inman painting of Chief Justice John Marshall, c. *1810*. Kean Collection/ Hulton Archive/Getty Images

Marbury v. *Madison* (1803), in which Chief Justice John Marshall said:

> *The powers of the legislature are defined and limited; and [so] that those limits may not be mistaken, or forgotten, the Constitution is written. To what purpose are powers limited, and to what purpose is that limitation committed to writing, if these limits may, at any time, be passed by those intended to be restrained? The distinction between a government with limited and unlimited powers, is abolished, if those limits do not confine the persons on whom they are imposed, and if acts prohibited and acts allowed, are of equal obligation. It is a proposition too plain to be contested, that the Constitution controls any legislative act repugnant to it . . . . It is emphatically the province and duty of the judicial department to say what the law is. Those who apply the rule to particular cases, must of necessity expound and interpret that rule. If two laws conflict with each other, the courts must decide on the operation of each.*

Armed with this powerful precedent from this very early date in the development of the U.S. legal system, the U.S. Supreme Court has held many statutes—federal as well as state—unconstitutional and has also invalidated executive actions that it believed violated the Constitution.

Perhaps even more surprising is the fact that all lower courts in the United States also possess and exercise the same powers as the Supreme Court. Whenever a question arises in any U.S. court at any level as to the constitutionality of a statute or executive action, that court is obligated to determine its validity in the course of deciding the case before it. Indeed, the case may have been brought for the sole and express purpose of testing the constitutionality of the statute (e.g., a law requiring racial segregation or restricting freedom of speech), or it may be an ordinary civil or criminal case in which a constitutional question incidental to the main purpose of the proceeding is raised (e.g., the legality of a search and seizure by the authorities). Every judge in the United States is legally empowered to engage in constitutional interpretation. When a lower court decides a constitutional question, however, its decision is subject to appellate review, sometimes at more than one level. When a state statute is challenged as violating the state constitution, the final authority is the supreme court of that state; when a federal or state statute or a state constitutional provision is challenged as violating the Constitution of the United States, the ultimate arbiter is the U.S. Supreme Court.

In a few U.S. states and in many countries, questions as to the constitutional validity of a statute may be referred in abstract form to a high court by the chief executive or the legislature for an advisory opinion. In most systems, however, this is unusual and, in any event, supplementary to the normal procedure of raising and deciding constitutional questions. The normal pattern is for a constitutional question to be raised at the trial-court level in the context of a genuine controversy and decided finally on appellate review of the trial-court decision.

The U.S. pattern of constitutional adjudication is not followed in all countries that have written constitutions. In some countries (e.g., Germany), there is a special court at the highest level of government that handles only constitutional questions and to which all such questions are referred as soon as they arise and before any concrete controversy occurs. A constitutional question may be referred to the special court in abstract form for a declaratory opinion by a procedure similar to that prevailing in the minority of U.S. states that allow advisory opinions. In France, members of the parliament may demand (and increasingly have demanded) that the constitutionality of legislation be certified by the Constitutional Council prior to its becoming law.

In other countries, written constitutions may be in effect but not accompanied by any conception that their authoritative interpretation is a judicial function. Legislative and executive bodies, rather than courts, act as the guardians and interpreters of the constitution, being guided by their provisions but not bound by them in any realistic sense. Modernization in the developing world, the spread of democracy in Latin America in the 1980s and '90s, and the collapse of communism in the states of the former Soviet Union and eastern Europe in 1989–91 have meant that there are now fewer instances of wholly impotent courts. Still, in some countries, the courts remain captive to political elites or open to manipulation by the government, or the courts' authority to exercise the judicial review to which they are constitutionally entitled remains tenuous. In 1993, for example, the Russian constitutional court was dissolved by Pres. Boris Yeltsin and replaced with a system of appointments that ensured greater presidential control.

Finally, some countries, such as the United Kingdom, have no formal written constitution. In such countries, parliamentary supremacy clearly prevails, though European law (i.e., the law of the European Union [EU]) now supersedes parliamentary supremacy in all EU countries, including the United Kingdom. The courts have no power to invalidate statutes, though they can and do interpret them, which is a very important judicial power.

Procedural Rule Making

Distinct from the type of lawmaking just described is a more conscious and explicit type of judicial legislation that is somewhat less controversial. It is directed toward the rules of procedure by which the courts operate; in the

United States and elsewhere, the rules of procedure are generally subsumed under the concept known as due process (known outside the United States as fair procedure). This is a technical area in which expert knowledge of the type possessed by judges and lawyers is needed, in which constant attention to detail is required, and in which major problems of social, economic, or political policy are seldom explicitly encountered. Some legislative bodies, able or willing to devote only sporadic attention to the day-to-day problems of the management of litigation, have delegated the power to regulate procedure to the courts themselves. This is not ad hoc judicial lawmaking as a by-product of deciding cases but openly acknowledged promulgation of general rules for the future, in legislative form, by courts rather than legislatures.

An outstanding example of judicial rule making is found in the United States, where Congress has delegated to the Supreme Court broad power to formulate rules of civil, criminal, and appellate procedure for the federal courts. The Supreme Court also exercises the power to amend the rules from time to time as experience indicates that changes are desirable. Although Congress reserves the power to veto the rules promulgated by the Supreme Court, it has felt no need to do so. These rules of procedure often reflect highly significant biases toward one interest or another; examples include rules regarding the ways in which individual citizens can be aggregated into a "class" so that they can pursue their grievances collectively in the federal court system.

Other legislative bodies, including those of some U.S. states and most of the countries of continental Europe, have been unwilling to place so much trust in the courts and have retained for themselves the power to regulate procedure. The results have been varied. Courts sometimes become so immersed in day-to-day decision making that they fail to pay adequate attention to the proper functioning of the judicial machinery and perpetuate rules that are unduly rigid, unrealistic, and unsuited to the needs of litigants, which was the case in England and the American colonies during the 18th and first part of the 19th century. When such a situation exists, reform through legislative action is necessary. Apart from the occasional necessity of major sweeping changes, however, experience in common-law countries indicates that procedural rule making is better vested in the courts than in legislative bodies.

Review of Administrative Decisions

Administrative agencies of various kinds (e.g., the Food and Drug Administration in the United States) exist alongside the courts in nearly every country. Some do substantially the same kind of work as is done by courts and in substantially the same manner; others, however, have quite different functions (e.g., the issuing of licenses and the payment of social-welfare benefits).

The relationship between such agencies and regular courts differs markedly between common-law and civil-law countries. In common-law countries the actions of administrative agencies are subject to review in the ordinary courts. If the agency decides controversies in substantially the same manner as a court but in a different and more limited area, judicial control takes much the same form of appellate review as is provided for the decisions of lower courts. The objective of reviewing the record of the proceedings is to determine whether the administrative agency acted within the scope of its jurisdiction, whether there was any evidence to support its conclusion, whether procedures were fair, and whether the governing law was correctly interpreted and applied. Administrative decisions are seldom upset by the courts, because most judges believe that administrative agencies have expertise in their area of specialization. However, the agencies can be and occasionally are overruled, which reflects the large degree of judicial control over other agencies of government that characterizes common-law systems. If the administrative agency does not engage in formal adjudication, it produces no record of its proceedings for judicial review. Nevertheless, the agency's decisions can be challenged in court by way of trial rather than appeal. The same problems are presented for judicial determination: did the agency act within its jurisdiction, did it correctly follow the law, and was there any rational or factual basis for its action? The United Kingdom has experienced a dramatic increase in the frequency of this type of litigation.

In many civil-law countries, the ordinary courts have no control over administrative agencies. Their decisions are reviewed by a special tribunal that is engaged exclusively in that work and that has nothing to do with cases of the type that come into the courts. Its function is solely appellate and is limited to the specialized areas entrusted to the administrative agencies. The prototype of this type of tribunal is France's Conseil d'État, which decides and advises on issues put to it by the president, cabinet, or parliament. Such tribunals also have been established in other countries, including Belgium, Egypt, Greece, Spain, and Turkey.

Enforcement of Judicial Decisions

The method of enforcing a judicial decision depends upon its nature. If it does nothing more than declare legal rights, as is true of a simple divorce decree (merely severing marital ties, not awarding alimony or the custody of children) or a declaratory judgment (e.g., interpreting a contract or a statute), no enforcement is needed. If a judgment orders a party to do or to refrain from doing a certain act, as happens when an injunction is issued, the court itself takes the first step in enforcing the judgment by holding in contempt anyone who refuses to obey its order and sentencing him to pay a fine or to go to jail. Thereafter, enforcement is in the hands of the executive branch of government, acting through its law-enforcement and correctional authorities.

In routine criminal cases and in civil cases that result in the award of monetary damages, courts have little to do with the enforcement of their judgments. Instead, this is the function of the executive branch of government, acting through sheriffs, marshals, jailers, and similar officials. The courts themselves have no machinery for enforcement.

Some judgments issued by courts are extremely controversial and encounter intense public opposition (e.g., the decision of the Supreme Court of the United States ordering racial desegregation of the public schools in 1954). When voluntary compliance with such a judgment is refused, forcible methods of enforcement are necessary, sometimes extending to the deployment of armed forces under the control of the executive branch. The withdrawal of executive support seldom occurs, even when decisions are directed against the executive branch itself; when such executive support is withheld, however, the courts are rendered impotent. Judges, being aware of their limited power, seldom render decisions that they know will have so little support that they will not be enforced.

TYPES OF COURTS

There are many different types of courts and many ways to classify and describe them. Basic distinctions must be made between criminal and civil courts, between courts of general jurisdiction and those of limited jurisdiction, and between appellate and trial courts.

Criminal Courts

Criminal courts deal with persons accused of committing a crime, deciding whether they are guilty and, if so, determining the consequences they shall suffer. The prosecution of alleged offenders is generally pursued in the name of the public (e.g., *The People v. ...*), because crimes are considered offenses not just against individual victims but also against society at large. The public is represented by an official such as a district attorney (often called a prosecutor), procurator, or police officer. Although courts are also agencies of the state, they are neutral in criminal proceedings, favouring neither the prosecution nor the defense. The impartiality of the court is strongly reinforced where juries are used to decide the guilt or innocence of the defendant.

The role of the criminal court in civil-law systems is quite different from its role in common-law ones. Civil-law countries assign a more active role to the judge and a more passive role to counsel. Instead of being passive recipients of evidence produced by the prosecution and the defense, judges in civil-law systems often direct the presentation of evidence and even order that certain evidence be produced. Thus, procedure in civil-law systems is considered inquisitorial. Judges in this system have an independent responsibility to discover the facts. In the common-law courts, adversary procedures tend to prevail; the lawyers for both sides bear primary responsibility for producing evidence and do most of the questioning of witnesses. Advocates of the adversarial system hold that a just outcome is most likely to result when all possible relevant information—good (tending to exonerate) and bad (tending to incriminate)—is placed before an impartial adjudicator (the judge or the jury). Self-interest motivates both the defense and the prosecution to provide all possible evidence relevant to its side of the case. Where the jury system is used, the jury is supposed to constitute an unbiased sample of ordinary people predisposed to favouring neither the defense nor the prosecution, and the judge serves as a "legal referee" who ensures that proper legal procedures are followed (e.g., barring the introduction of illegally obtained evidence, such as coerced confessions, or other information deemed inadmissible). The adversarial system, and its associated conception of justice, is a pillar of the common-law tradition, as evidenced in the U.S., British, and Canadian systems of criminal justice.

If a defendant is found guilty, he is sentenced, again according to law and within limits predetermined by legislation. The objective of most punishment is not so much to impose retribution upon the offender as to deter others from committing similar acts; another frequent objective is to rehabilitate the offender. Hence, the most common sentences are fines, short terms of imprisonment, and probation (which allows the offender freedom under state supervision). In extremely serious cases, the goal may be to prevent the offender from committing further crimes, which may call for a long term of imprisonment (e.g., life in prison without the possibility of parole) or even capital punishment. During the last third of the 20th century, however, the death penalty began to disappear from many criminal codes throughout the world; nonetheless, it remains in effect and is imposed widely in several countries, including the United States, Iran, and China.

Civil Courts

Civil courts (not to be confused with the civil-law legal system) deal with "private" controversies, particularly disputes that arise between individuals or between private businesses or institutions (e.g., a disagreement over the terms of a contract or over who shall bear responsibility for an automobile accident). The public is not ordinarily a party to the litigation (as it is in criminal proceedings), for its interest is limited to providing just and acceptable rules for making decisions and a forum where the dispute can be impartially and peacefully resolved. These factors are important because the use of the civil courts is voluntary.

The government may be involved in civil litigation if it stands in the same relation to a private party as another individual might stand. If a government postal truck hits a pedestrian, for example, the government might be sued civilly by the injured person; or if the government contracted to purchase supplies that turned out to be defective, it might sue the dealer for damages in a civil court. In such proceedings, however, the government acts as a private party.

The objective of a civil action is not explicitly punishment or correction of the defendant or the setting of an example to others but rather restoration of the parties so far as possible to the positions they would have occupied had no legal wrong been committed. The most common civil remedy is a judgment for monetary damages, but there are others, such as an injunction ordering the defendant to do—or to refrain from doing—a certain act or a judgment restoring property to its rightful owner. For example, a celebrity might obtain an injunction against an alleged "stalker" requiring that the person not come within a certain distance of the celebrity at any time.

Civil claims do not ordinarily arise out of criminal acts. A person who breaks his contract with another or who causes him a physical injury through negligence may have committed no crime (i.e., no offense against the public has been committed) but only a civil wrong for which he may not be prosecuted criminally by the public. There are, however, areas of overlap, for a single incident may give rise to both civil liability and criminal prosecution. In some countries (e.g., France), both types of responsibility can be determined in a single proceeding under a concept known as adhesion, by which the injured party is allowed to assert his civil claim in the criminal prosecution, agreeing to abide by its outcome. This removes the necessity of two separate trials. In common-law countries, there is no such procedure (even though civil and criminal jurisdiction may be merged in a single court). Two separate actions must be brought independent of each other. For example, in the United States in the mid-1990s, former football star O.J. Simpson was tried in a California criminal court on a charge of having murdered his ex-wife and her friend; although he was acquitted in that litigation (in which a guilty verdict required proof "beyond a reasonable doubt"), in a subsequent civil suit (in which a guilty verdict required proof by a "preponderance of the evidence"), he was found liable and was ordered to pay restitution to the families of the victims. In the United States, such collateral civil lawsuits have become attractive to victims of alleged crimes, particularly because the standard of proof in civil courts is dramatically lower than it is in criminal courts.

O.J. Simpson (centre) *stands with his attorneys F. Lee Bailey* (left) *and Johnnie Cochran at his criminal trial, listening as he is found not guilty of the murders of Nicole Brown Simpson and Ron Goldman, Oct. 3, 1995.* Myung Chun/AFP/Getty Images

Courts of General Jurisdiction

Although there are some courts that handle only criminal cases and others that deal with only civil cases, a more common pattern is for a single court to be vested with both civil and criminal jurisdiction. Examples of such courts include the High Court of Justice for England and Wales and many of the trial courts found in U.S. states. Canada is an instructive example, because the federal government has the exclusive authority to legislate criminal laws, while the provinces have the authority to legislate civil laws. Virtually all cases, criminal and civil, originate in the provincial courts. Often these tribunals are called courts of general jurisdiction, which signifies that they can handle almost any type of controversy, though in fact they may not have jurisdiction over certain types of cases assigned to specialized tribunals (e.g., immigration cases). Often such courts are also described as superior courts, because they are empowered to handle serious criminal cases and important civil cases involving large amounts of money. In addition, most high appellate courts (e.g., the U.S. Supreme Court and the courts of last resort in the U.S. states) are courts of general jurisdiction, hearing both civil and criminal appeals.

Even if a court possesses general or very broad jurisdiction, it may nevertheless be organized into specialized branches, one handling criminal cases, another handling civil cases, another handling juvenile cases, and so forth. The advantage of such an arrangement is that judges can be transferred from one type of work to another, and cases do not fail to be heard for having been instituted in the wrong branch, since they can be transferred administratively with relative ease.

Courts of Limited Jurisdiction

There are many kinds of specialized tribunals, varying from country to country. Some deal only with the administration of the estates of deceased persons (probate courts), some only with disputes between merchants (commercial courts), and some only with disputes between employers and employees (labour courts). Many of the constitutional courts of the democracies that emerged in the 1990s in central and eastern Europe also have limited jurisdiction, confined to disputes grounded in the constitution. Although all these courts are courts of limited jurisdiction, they may exercise substantial power.

Juvenile courts, empowered to deal with misconduct by children and sometimes also with the neglect or maltreatment of children, are a particularly notable court of limited jurisdiction. The procedures of juvenile courts are much more informal than those of adult criminal courts, and the facilities available to them for the pretrial detention of children and for their incarceration, if necessary, after trial are different. Because children are assumed not to be fully capable of rational thought, they are deemed less culpable for their actions, and the emphasis in juvenile courts is therefore usually on saving children, not punishing them. American attitudes are bifurcated on the subject of juvenile law; on the one hand, when minors are victims or can potentially be victimized, law and society typically agree that the purpose of the law is to protect the innocent. This is evident in laws designed to protect minors from exposure to obscene material and from sexual predators and in divorce and custody law. When, however, minors commit a violent act, public and political sentiments often change, and the minor is no longer seen as innocent and deserving of the protection of the law. While some may seek to rehabilitate the youth and desire lenient punishment, others consider a youth of any age who commits a crime as mature enough to be sentenced accordingly.

Traffic courts also deserve mention because they are so common and affect so many people. They process motor vehicle offenses such as speeding and improper parking. Their procedure is summary and their volume of cases heavy. Contested trials are quite infrequent.

Finally, in most jurisdictions there are institutions called, unfortunately and for want of a better term, inferior courts. These are often staffed by part-time judges who are not necessarily trained in the law. They handle minor civil cases involving small sums of money, such as bill collections, and minor criminal cases carrying light penalties. In addition to finally disposing of minor criminal cases, such courts may handle the early phases of more serious criminal cases—including fixing bail, advising defendants of their rights, appointing counsel, and conducting preliminary hearings to determine whether the evidence is sufficient to justify holding defendants for trial in higher superior courts.

Appellate Courts

The tribunals described thus far are trial courts or courts of first instance. They see the parties to the dispute, hear the witnesses, receive the evidence, find the facts, apply the law, and determine the outcome.

Appellate courts are positioned above the trial courts to review their work and to correct any errors that may have occurred. Appellate courts are usually collegiate bodies, consisting of several judges instead of the single judge who typically presides over a trial court. The jurisdiction of the appellate courts is often general; specialized appellate tribunals handling, for example, only criminal appeals or only civil appeals are rare though not unknown (e.g., the U.S. state of Texas has separate supreme courts for civil and criminal cases). The Conseil d'État of France and the Federal Constitutional Court of Germany, mentioned above, are also specialized judicial tribunals.

National judicial systems are organized hierarchically. At the lowest level, there are numerous trial courts scattered throughout the country; above them are a smaller number of first-level appellate courts, usually organized on a regional basis; and at the apex is a single court of last resort.

Appellate review is rarely automatic. It usually must be sought by a party aggrieved by the judgment in the court below. For that reason, and because an appeal may be both expensive and useless, there are far fewer appeals than trials and, if successive appeals are available, as is often the case, far fewer second appeals than first appeals.

Because the principle of due process generally creates a right to at least one review by a higher court, intermediate appeals courts are typically obliged to hear the cases appealed to them. High courts, like many state supreme courts and the U.S. Supreme Court, are not obliged to hear any particular case, and, in fact, they issue decisions in only a tiny fraction of the cases appealed to them.

There are three basic types of appellate review. The first consists of the retrial of the case, with the appellate court hearing the evidence for the second time, making fresh findings of fact, and in general proceeding in much the same manner as the court that originally rendered the judgment under appeal. This trial de novo is used in common-law countries for the first stage of review, but only when the trial in the first instance was conducted by an inferior court—one typically staffed by a part-time judge empowered to try only minor cases and keeping no formal record of its proceedings.

The second type of review is based in part on a dossier, which is a record compiled in the court below of the evidence received and the findings made. The reviewing court has the power to hear the same witnesses again or to supplement their testimony by taking additional evidence, but it need not and frequently does not do so, being content to rely on the record already made in reaching its own findings of fact and conclusions of law. This type of proceeding prevails generally in civil-law countries for the first stage of appellate review, even when the original trial was conducted in a superior court staffed by professional judges and empowered to try important or serious cases.

The third type of review is based solely on a written record of proceedings in the court or courts below. The reviewing court does not itself receive evidence directly but concentrates its effort on discovering from the record whether any errors were committed of such a serious nature as to require reversal or modification of the judgment under review or a new trial in the court below. The emphasis is on questions of law (both procedural and substantive) rather than on questions of fact, and the court typically requests briefs by the litigants delineating their views on the legal issues (including the relevant precedents) at stake in the case. This type of review prevails both in civil-law and common-law countries at the highest appellate level. It is also used in common-law countries at lower levels when the appeal involves a judgment of a superior court. The purpose of this type of review is not merely to ensure that correct results are reached in individual cases but also to clarify and expound the law in the manner described earlier (i.e., the creation of precedents). Lower courts have little to do with the development of the law, because they ordinarily do not write or publish opinions. The highest appellate courts do, and it is their opinions that become the guidelines for future cases.

JUDGES

In common-law countries, such as the United States, the path to judicial office typically begins with a significant amount of time in the private practice of law or, less commonly, in law teaching or governmental legal service before becoming a judge. Judges are appointed or elected to office; there is no competitive examination. In England the appointive system prevails for all levels of judges, including even lay magistrates. Appointments are primarily under the control of the lord chancellor, who, although a cabinet officer, is also the highest judge of the United Kingdom. Judges are kept surprisingly free from party politics. In the United States, the appointive method is used in federal courts and some state courts, but ideological and partisan considerations—particularly at the federal level—play a very significant role in appointments to the bench. In the United States, all appointments to the federal bench, and many appointments to the state judiciary, are made by the chief executive (president or governor), though these appointments are generally subject to legislative approval. In many states, however, judges are popularly elected, sometimes on nonpartisan ballots, sometimes on partisan ballots with all the trappings of traditional political contests.

A third method of judicial selection, devised in an attempt to de-emphasize partisan considerations (and to give more power to the organized bar) while maintaining some measure of popular control over the selection of judges, has grown in popularity. Called the Missouri Plan, it involves the creation of a nominating commission that screens judicial candidates and submits to the appointing authority a limited number of names of persons considered qualified. The appointing authority must select from the list submitted. The person chosen as judge then assumes office for a limited time and, after the conclusion of this probationary period, stands for "election" for a much longer term. The judge does not run against any other candidate; rather, he is judged only against his own record. The ballot, called a retention ballot, often simply reads "Shall Judge X be retained?" In practice, few judges are removed from office through retention ballots. These different selection systems strike different balances between the principles of democratic accountability and judicial independence.

In common-law countries, a person does not necessarily enter the judiciary at a low level; he may be appointed or elected to the country's highest court or to one of its intermediate courts without any prior judicial experience. Indeed, even courtroom experience is not a prerequisite for a judgeship in the United States. There is also no regular pattern of promotion, and judges are not assured of a long tenure with ultimate retirement on a pension. In some courts, life tenure is provided, sometimes subject to mandatory retirement at a fixed age. In others, tenure is limited to a stated term of years. At the conclusion of his term, if not mandatorily retired earlier, the judge must be reelected or reappointed if he is to continue.

While in office, common-law judges enjoy greater power and prestige and more independence than their civil-law counterparts. A common-law judge, who occupies a position to which most members of the legal profession aspire, is not subject to outside supervision and inspection by any council of judges or by a minister of justice; nor is he liable to be transferred by such an official from court to court or from place to place. The only administrative control over common-law judges is exercised by judicial colleagues, whose powers of management are generally slight, being limited to matters such as requiring periodic reports of pending cases and arranging for temporary (and usually consensual) transfers of judges between courts when factors such as illness or congested calendars require them. Only judges who misbehave very badly (e.g., by abusing their office) are in danger of disciplinary sanctions, and then usually only by way of criminal prosecution for the alleged misdeeds or by legislative impeachment and trial, resulting in removal from office—a very cumbersome, slow, ill-defined, inflexible, ineffective, and seldom-used procedure. Some parts of the United States have developed more expeditious methods of judicial discipline, in which senior judges are vested with the power to impose sanctions on erring colleagues ranging from reprimand to removal from office. They are also vested with the power to retire judges who have become physically or mentally unfit to discharge their duties.

The ultimate act of discipline is impeachment. In the United States, federal judges may be removed from office based upon an impeachment by the House of Representatives and a conviction by the Senate. Very few judges have been either impeached or convicted (one associate justice of the Supreme Court, Samuel Chase, was impeached but was not convicted). In other parts of the world, including Latin America, impeachment has been institutionalized. In Argentina, for example, a magistrate council investigates judicial misconduct and may remove judges from office.

Except at the very highest appellate level, common-law judges are no less subject than their civil-law counterparts to appellate reversals of their judgments. But appellate review cannot fairly be regarded as discipline. It is designed to protect the rights of litigants; to clarify, expound, and develop the law; and to help and guide lower-court judges, not to reprimand them.

Chapter 3 Judicial Review

VARIETIES OF JUDICIAL REVIEW

As had been discussed previously, judicial review is the power of the courts of a country to examine the actions of the legislative, executive, and administrative arms of the government and to determine whether such actions are consistent with the constitution. Actions judged inconsistent are declared unconstitutional and, therefore, null and void. The institution of judicial review in this sense depends upon the existence of a written constitution.

The conventional usage of the term judicial review could be more accurately described as "constitutional review," because there also exists a long practice of judicial review of the actions of administrative agencies that require neither that courts have the power to declare those actions unconstitutional nor that the country have a written constitution. Such "administrative review" assesses the allegedly questionable actions of administrators against standards of reasonableness and abuse of discretion. When courts judge challenged administration actions to be unreasonable or to involve abuses of discretion, those actions are declared null and void, as are actions that are judged inconsistent with constitutional requirements when courts exercise judicial review in the conventional or constitutional sense.

Whether or not a court has the power to declare the acts of government agencies unconstitutional, it can achieve the same effect by exercising "indirect" judicial review. In such cases the court pronounces that a challenged rule or action could not have been intended by the legislature because it is inconsistent with some other laws or established legal principles.

Constitutional judicial review is usually considered to have begun with the assertion by John Marshall, chief justice of the United States (1801–35), in *Marbury* v. *Madison* (1803), that the Supreme Court of the United States had the power to invalidate legislation enacted by Congress. There was, however, no express warrant for Marshall's assertion of the power of judicial review in the actual text of the Constitution of the United States; its success rested ultimately on the Supreme Court's own ruling, plus the absence of effective political challenge to it.

Constitutional judicial review exists in several forms. In countries that follow U.S. practice (e.g., Kenya and New Zealand), judicial review can be exercised only in concrete cases or controversies and only after the fact—i.e., only laws that are in effect or actions that have already occurred can be found to be unconstitutional, and then only when they involve a specific dispute between litigants. In France judicial review must take place in the abstract (i.e., in the absence of an actual case or controversy) and before promulgation (i.e., before a challenged law has taken effect). In other countries (e.g., Austria, Germany, South Korea, and Spain) courts can exercise judicial review only after a law has taken effect, though they can do so either in the abstract or in concrete cases. Systems of constitutional judicial review also differ in the extent to which they allow courts to exercise it. For example, in the United States all courts have the power to entertain claims of unconstitutionality, but in some countries (e.g., France, Germany, New Zealand, and South Africa) only specialized constitutional courts can hear such claims.

A number of the constitutions drafted in Europe and Asia after World War II incorporated judicial review in various forms. For example, in France, where the Cour de Cassation (the highest court of criminal and civil appeal) has no power of judicial review, a constitutional council (Conseil Constitutionnel) of mixed judicial-legislative character was established; Germany, Italy, and South Korea created special constitutional courts; and India, Japan, and Pakistan set up supreme courts to exercise judicial review in the manner generally used in the United States and in the British Commonwealth.

After World War II many countries felt strong pressure to adopt judicial review, a result of the influence of U.S. constitutional ideas—particularly the idea that a system of constitutional checks and balances is an essential element of democratic government. Some observers concluded that the concentration of government power in the executive, substantially unchecked by other agencies of government, contributed to the rise of totalitarian regimes in Germany and Japan in the era between World War I and World War II. Although judicial review had been relatively uncommon before World War II, by the early 21st century more than 100 countries had specifically incorporated judicial review into their constitutions. (This number does not include the United States, whose constitution still includes no mention of the practice.)

JUDICIAL REVIEW IN THE UNITED STATES

The practice of judicial review in the United States has been a model for other countries. As noted earlier, despite its overwhelming importance, judicial review is not explicitly mentioned in the U.S. Constitution and is itself a product of judicial construction in *Marbury* v. *Madison* (1803).

In the U.S. system of judicial review, constitutional questions can be raised only in connection with actual "cases and controversies." Advisory opinions to the government are common in other countries but are not rendered by U.S. federal courts. Although the cases and controversies requirement has been relaxed by the Supreme Court—at least to the extent of allowing class-action suits or allowing organizations to sue on behalf of their members who have not personally brought suit—it is still the case that courts will not decide a constitutional

IN FOCUS: *MARBURY* V. *MADISON*

On Feb. 24, 1803, in *Marbury* v. *Madison*, the U.S. Supreme Court ruled for the first time that an act of Congress was unconstitutional, thus establishing the doctrine of judicial review.

The Supreme Court's growing conflict with Pres. Thomas Jefferson and the Republican Congress came to a head after Secretary of State James Madison, on Jefferson's orders, withheld from William Marbury the commission of his appointment (March 2, 1801), by former Pres. John Adams, as justice of the peace in the District of Columbia. Marbury—one of the so-called midnight appointments made in the final hours of Adams's term under the Judiciary Act of 1801—requested the Supreme Court to issue a writ of mandamus compelling Madison to deliver his commission. In denying his request, the Court held that it lacked jurisdiction because Section 13 of the Judiciary Act passed by Congress in 1789, which authorized the Court to issue such a writ, was unconstitutional and thus invalid. Chief Justice Marshall declared that in any such conflict between the Constitution and a law passed by Congress, the Constitution must always take precedence. The apparent "victory" for Jefferson was in fact a landmark in asserting the power of the Supreme Court's life-tenured justices, which Jefferson hated and feared.

question unless it is rooted in a controversy in which the parties have a direct, personal interest. This requirement can sometimes frustrate efforts to obtain pronouncements on disputed issues.

Although the U.S. courts are the guardians of the Constitution, they are not bound to consider all the provisions of the Constitution justiciable. Under the doctrine of political questions, the Supreme Court has refused at times to apply standards prescribed by or deducible from the Constitution to issues that it believed could be better decided by the political branches of government. Since *Luther* v. *Borden* (1849), for example, it is a matter of settled practice that the court will not use Article IV, Section 4—which provides that the states must have a republican form of government—to invalidate state laws; it is for Congress and the president to decide whether a particular state government is republican in form. Many military and foreign policy questions, such as the constitutionality of a particular war, likewise have been considered political and therefore nonjusticiable.

On the other hand, the political-question doctrine has not prevented the Supreme Court from asserting its jurisdiction in cases that are politically sensitive. Thus, in *United States* v. *Nixon* (1974), the court ruled that Pres. Richard Nixon was required to turn over to federal authorities the tape recordings that confirmed his complicity in the Watergate scandal. The doctrine also did not prevent the court from intervening in the presidential election of 2000, when it halted the recount of ballots in the disputed state of Florida and effectively confirmed George W. Bush's victory, despite forceful arguments that, under the Constitution and relevant federal statutes, the matter was clearly one for Florida and Congress to decide.

Pres. Richard M. Nixon boards presidential helicopter Army One after resigning office following the Watergate scandal, Aug. 9, 1974. Bill Pierce/Time & Life Pictures/Getty Images

Judicial review is designed to be more impartial than review by other institutions of government. This does not mean, however, that it is immune to policy considerations or to changes in the needs and political attitudes of the people. As a matter of fact, the Supreme Court's reading of the Constitution has itself evolved in the course of more than two centuries, in accordance with the large transformations that have occurred in American society.

Given the structure of the U.S. Constitution, the Supreme Court historically has resolved constitutional disputes in four main areas: the relations between the states and the national government, the separation of powers within the national government, the right of government to regulate the economy, and individual rights and freedoms. In each of these areas the court's conception of the Constitution has undergone substantial changes.

From 1789 through the Civil War era, the Supreme Court was a crucial participant in nation building, its decisions reinforcing the newly born structures of the federal system. The court's rulings established judicial supremacy in constitutional interpretation, gave force to the national supremacy clause of Article VI of the Constitution—which declared the Constitution the supreme law of the United States—and laid the foundation for the power of the federal government to intervene in the national economy by broadly interpreting its constitutional power to regulate interstate commerce. In contrast, during the decades of industrialization and economic growth that followed the Civil War, the court was very skeptical of attempts at economic regulation by the federal government. Indeed, until the Great Depression spawned the New Deal legislation of Pres. Franklin D. Roosevelt, the court often ruled that many areas of economic activity were matters exclusively for state legislation or not subject to government regulation at all. After 1937, however, the court lifted the obstacles it had previously erected to federal intervention in the economic and social transactions of the country. Within a few years the Supreme Court established that Congress can make laws with respect to practically all commercial matters of national concern.

A foundation of this expansion of the government's power to intervene in the economy and society was laid in the doctrine of federal spending power first enunciated in *United States* v. *Butler* (1936). The outcome of this case was overtly hostile to the expansion of government power, since the Supreme Court ruled unconstitutional a tax provision of the Agricultural Adjustment Act of 1933 that was designed to encourage limitation of production. However, the lasting contribution of the decision emerged from the Supreme Court's conclusion that the Constitution gives Congress a general and broad power to tax and spend in support of the general welfare. As a further example, the new interpretation of the commerce clause laid down in *Wickard* v. *Filburn* (1942) upheld the federal government's right to enforce quotas on the production of agricultural products in virtually all circumstances, even when, as in this case, a farmer exceeding his quota—by an admittedly sizable amount of wheat—proclaimed his intention to consume all his excess production, thereby preventing it from entering interstate commerce at all.

In the area of separation of federal powers, the court gradually came to support a substantial transfer of powers to the executive and to administrative agencies. Because Article I, Section 1 of the Constitution confers all legislative powers upon Congress, the court at first ruled that such powers cannot be delegated by Congress to the executive. This doctrine was much diluted in the 20th century, when it became clear that delegated legislation was necessary to administer a mixed economy. The court's generally favourable attitude toward enhancing the powers of the executive branch has manifested itself in other areas as well, notably in the field of foreign affairs. Nevertheless, the court has set important limits on the powers of the president. It has ruled, for example, that the president does not have an "inherent" power to seize steel mills in time of war (*Youngstown Sheet & Tube Co.* v. *Sawyer*, 1952) and that the prerogative of the president to keep confidential records secret must yield to the need of the judiciary to enforce criminal justice if the secret is not strictly related to military or diplomatic matters (*United States* v. *Nixon*, 1974).

Until the New Deal, the court used the provisions of the Constitution concerning individual rights and freedoms primarily to protect property and economic liberties against state and federal efforts to interfere with the market. Thus, it often used the due process clause of the Fifth and Fourteenth amendments (no person shall be deprived of "life, liberty, or property, without due process of law") to invalidate social legislation, such as laws establishing minimum or maximum working hours. In contrast, the court's agenda was subsequently dominated by litigation directly raising questions involving civil and political rights and freedoms, as well as individual equality before the law. Due process claims focus primarily on procedural rights in criminal and administrative areas. In the mid-20th century, during a period of expansion of individual rights, the court declared unconstitutional racial segregation in the schools (*Brown* v. *Board of Education of Topeka*, 1954) and malapportionment in electoral districts (*Baker* v. *Carr*, 1962; *Wesberry* v. *Sanders*, 1964) and strengthened the rights of criminal defendants and the accused (*Mapp* v. *Ohio*, 1961; *Miranda* v. *Arizona*, 1966). The court also recognized a constitutional right to privacy (*Griswold* v. *State of Connecticut*, 1965), which became the foundation for the right of a woman to obtain an abortion (*Roe* v. *Wade*, 1973; *Planned Parenthood of Southeastern Pennsylvania* v. *Casey*, 1992). Beginning in the 1970s, the court was less willing to support litigant claims that would further expand individual rights and freedoms, though for the most part it did not significantly restrict them.

Through more than two centuries of judicial review, the U.S. Supreme Court typically has supported the values of the prevailing political ideology against challenges from the states or other branches of the federal government. Indeed, it has often been said that the court conducts judicial review by following election returns and public opinion polls. Although there is considerable insight in this observation, it is not true that the court simply tailors its decisions to comport with the political views of the electoral majority. At times, as in the early 20th century, the court's view of economic legislation was out of step with the views of the electorate, the other federal branches, and some states. In the 1950s and early '60s the court also made decisions contrary to public opinion and government policy regarding political and racial equality and other civil, political, and procedural rights.

APPLICATIONS OF JUDICIAL REVIEW

The consequences of judicial review in the United States have been enormous. From the late 1930s through the 1960s, a liberal Supreme Court used its powers of judicial review to broaden democratic participation in government and to expand the rights of citizens, especially those of minorities and the accused. Beginning in the 1970s, a more-conservative Supreme Court resisted the expansion of rights in many areas and limited the effects of previously established rights in others. Nevertheless, it did not, by and large, overturn the panoply of rights created by its predecessor.

In Europe and elsewhere judicial review has been used to advance the same democratic values that inspired the decisions of the U.S. Supreme Court from the late 1930s. European constitutional courts, in particular, have modified the legal systems of their countries here and there by interpreting the rights enumerated in their respective constitutions in ways that bear comparison with the American experience of judicial review. Nevertheless, European courts have tended to be more cautious than the U.S. Supreme Court in expanding the freedoms of the individual at the expense of other competing values.

A few examples may illustrate the differences between American and European applications of judicial review. In the area of freedom of expression, the American doctrine holds that no seditious or subversive speech can be punished unless it poses a "clear and present danger" of inciting immediate unlawful action. Accordingly, the U.S. Supreme Court has been extremely reluctant to approve prior restraint of speech or expression. The freedom to express unorthodox opinions is also clearly recognized by European constitutions and is upheld by the constitutional courts when they are confronted with laws that curtail it. But European doctrine has not accepted the American standard of clear and present danger or prior restraint. Thus, the Italian constitutional court requires, for the punishment of speech advocating the use of violence, that the speech create, in the circumstances, a "danger," but it does not specify that the danger must be "immediate." The Federal Constitutional Court of Germany, judging on the basis of constitutional provisions that forbid speech and associations directed at impairing the liberal-democratic foundations of the state, has dissolved neo-Nazi and other parties without even considering the element of actual "danger." On the same basis it has upheld laws excluding from public employment persons holding subversive beliefs. In the United States the law of libel concerning public figures actively protects free speech inasmuch as, under the doctrine of *New York Times* v. *Sullivan* (1964), plaintiffs who are public figures cannot win unless they prove that the libeler acted with "actual malice" (that he knowingly asserted a false statement). In Europe a finding of liability for the defamation of a public figure does not constitutionally require such proof.

The U.S. Supreme Court has found (*Roe* v. *Wade*, 1973; *Planned Parenthood of Southeastern Pennsylvania* v. *Casey*,

Justice Harry A. Blackmun, 1976. Library of Congress Prints and Photographs Division

1992) that a woman's constitutional right to privacy entitles her to obtain an abortion freely, prior to the point at which the fetus attains viability. European constitutional courts have not gone this far in recognizing a freedom to obtain an abortion. The Italian court held in 1975 that voluntary abortions cannot be punished if performed for the purpose of preserving the life and health—either physical or emotional—of the woman. The Austrian court (1974) and the French Constitutional Council (1975), without addressing the problem of a woman's constitutional right to interrupt pregnancy, have validated statutes that provide in liberal terms for the possibility of voluntary abortions. In a unique ruling in 1975, the Federal Constitutional Court of West Germany held that the West German constitution, by declaring the life of persons inviolable, implicitly protects the life of fetuses and that an adequate protection is afforded by the state only if voluntary abortion is made a crime by law. The law of East Germany was much more permissive, and, a few years after the reunification of the two German states (1990), the Constitutional Court, while reaffirming the principle that the fetus must be protected, held that such protection must be achieved not through punishment but through counseling and other measures aimed at influencing a woman to decide freely to carry her pregnancy to term.

The separation of church and state, as provided for by the First Amendment to the U.S. Constitution, has led the U.S. Supreme Court to rule in a series of cases that officially sanctioned Bible reading, prayer, and religious instruction in public schools are unconstitutional. Separation of church and state, although contemplated in principle also by European constitutions, is sometimes tempered by constitutional provisions making accords between church and state possible in matters of common interest. No European court has ruled that accords giving students the opportunity to attend religious courses in public schools violate the principle of religious freedom or the principle of the equality of all citizens before the law.

In other areas of the law, European constitutional courts have proved to be as ready as, and sometimes even more ready than, the U.S. court to afford protection to the rights of the individual. In the United States, *Mapp* v. *Ohio* (1961) established that illegally obtained evidence cannot be produced at a trial to substantiate criminal charges against the defendant. (In *Herring* v. *United States*, 2009, however, the Supreme Court declared that evidence obtained from an unlawful arrest that results from an innocent error in record keeping by police can be used against the defendant.) This "exclusionary rule" also is in force, at least partially, in much of Europe. The Italian constitutional court, for example, has stated that such a rule is required on constitutional grounds. In *Miranda* v. *Arizona* (1966), the U.S. Supreme Court held that a confession made by the accused under arrest cannot be used as evidence unless he has been previously advised of his rights, among which is the right to remain silent and the right to consult with a lawyer. The Italian constitutional court declared unconstitutional (1970) a law that excluded the suspect's attorney at the interrogation by the investigatory authorities and at other proceedings intended to secure evidence against the accused.

Although courts in the United States can be asked to review the lawfulness of administrative actions, the Supreme Court is still reluctant to establish as a matter of constitutional due process that citizens are always entitled to sue in court in order to have administrative decisions set aside if contrary to ordinary substantive or procedural rules. The Italian and German constitutions explicitly state the principle and admit no exception, and the courts of both countries carefully see to it that the principle is respected and that citizens are not deprived of their day in court, even if the other party is the administrative agency.

While applying the principle of equality in cases of sex discrimination and discrimination against children born out of wedlock, European courts often have gone beyond the doctrines of the U.S. Supreme Court in the same areas. According to the German rule, for example, husband and wife must have the same rights within the family; in particular, parental power over the children belongs equally to both. The Italian court has in many respects reshaped family law to ensure the equal rights of the wife and of children born out of wedlock and has defended the right of women to treatment equal to that of men in labour relations. Effective legislative protection against discrimination aimed at non-European immigrant workers and their families is still deficient in EU countries, and, by and large, constitutional courts have said little in this area. But they have shown remarkable sensitivity when the problem affects local ethnic or linguistic minorities. The U.S. Supreme Court found that programs of affirmative action meant to help minorities who were previously discriminated against did not necessarily constitute "reverse discrimination" in violation of the equal-protection clause of the Constitution. A similar ruling in the 1970s by the Italian court validated laws that reserved a proportion of public jobs and publicly financed housing for the German-speaking population of Alto Adige, who had inhabited the region for centuries.

It is true that European courts thus far have not openly defied the political powers of the state in the way the U.S. Supreme Court has sometimes done. Even when the European courts have somehow challenged such powers by annulling laws that were supposedly of special interest to them, the conflict has not really been acute. But the greater prudence of European courts is not difficult to explain. It is the result of many factors, prominent among which are the facts that their legitimation as independent and active agencies within the political system is recent and that the tradition of judicial review does not yet have the firm roots it possesses in the United States.

Courts of the United States

Chapter 4

THE SUPREME COURT OF THE UNITED STATES

The Supreme Court of the United States is the final court of appeal and final expositor of the Constitution of the United States. Within the framework of litigation, the Supreme Court marks the boundaries of authority between state and nation, state and state, and government and citizen.

Scope and Jurisdiction

The Supreme Court was created by the Constitutional Convention of 1787 as the head of a federal court system, though it was not formally established until Congress passed the Judiciary Act in 1789. Although the Constitution outlined the powers, structure, and functions of the legislative and executive branches of government in some detail, it did not do the same for the judicial branch, leaving much of that responsibility to Congress and stipulating only that judicial power be "vested in one supreme Court, and in such inferior Courts as the Congress may from time to time ordain and establish." As the country's

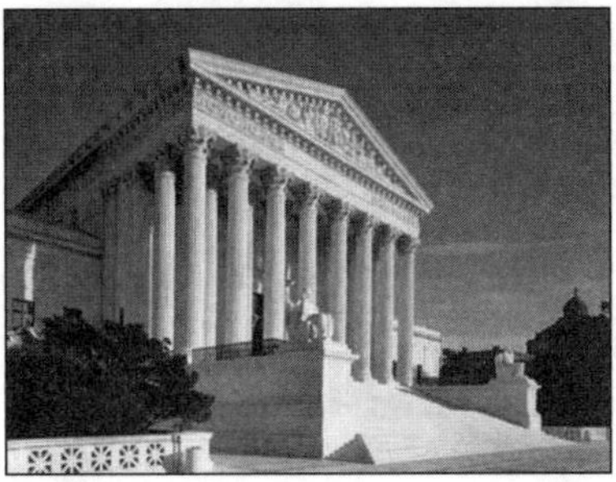

Western facade of the U.S. Supreme Court building. Franz Jantzen/Supreme Court of the United States

The courtroom of the Supreme Court of the United States. Franz Jantzen/Supreme Court of the United States

court of last resort, the Supreme Court is an appellate body, vested with the authority to act in cases arising under the Constitution, laws, or treaties of the United States; in controversies to which the United States is a party; in disputes between states or between citizens of different states; and in cases of admiralty and maritime jurisdiction. In suits affecting ambassadors, other public ministers, and consuls and in cases in which

Pres. George W. Bush posing with members of the U.S. Supreme Court during Chief Justice John Roberts's investiture ceremony, Oct. 3, 2005. Eric Draper/The White House

states are a party, the Supreme Court has original jurisdiction—i.e., it serves as a trial court. Relatively few cases reach the court through its original jurisdiction, however; instead, the vast majority of the court's business and nearly all of its most influential decisions derive from its appellate jurisdiction.

Size, Membership, and Organization

The organization of the federal judicial system, including the size of the Supreme Court, is established by Congress. From 1789 to 1807 the court comprised six justices. In 1807 a 7th justice was added, followed by an 8th and a 9th in 1837 and a 10th in 1863. Since 1869 the number of justices has been set at nine. The size of the court has sometimes been subject to political manipulation; for example, in the 1860s Congress reduced the number of justices to eight to ensure that Pres. Andrew Johnson, whom the House of Representatives had impeached and the Senate only narrowly acquitted, could not appoint a new justice to the court; and in the 1930s Pres. Franklin D. Roosevelt asked

James Earle Fraser's Contemplation of Justice, *on the north side of the main entrance of the U.S. Supreme Court.* Lois Long/ Supreme Court of the United States

The Old Supreme Court Chamber, where the court sat from 1810 to 1860. Franz Jantzen/ Supreme Court of the United States

The Old Senate Chamber, where the Supreme Court of the United States sat from 1860 to 1935, c. *1900.* Franz Jantzen/ Supreme Court of the United States

Congress to consider legislation (which it subsequently rejected) that would have allowed the president to appoint an additional justice for each member of the court aged 70 years or older who refused to retire.

According to the Constitution, appointments to the Supreme Court and to the lower federal courts are made by the president with the advice and consent of the Senate, though presidents have rarely consulted the Senate before making a nomination. The Senate Judiciary Committee ordinarily conducts hearings on nominations to the Supreme Court, and a simple majority of the full Senate is required for confirmation. When the position of chief justice is vacant, the president may appoint a chief justice from outside the court or elevate an associate justice to the position. In either case a simple majority of the Senate must approve the appointment. Members of the Supreme Court are appointed for life terms, though they may be expelled if they are impeached by the House

Check Out Receipt

Danville Public Library (DANP-ZCH)

Tuesday, May 28 2013 3:44PM

Item: 31205002966982
Title: Queenmaker : a novel of King David's Queen
Call no.: F Edg c.2
Due: 06/11/2013

Thank You!

of Representatives and convicted in the Senate. Only one justice has been impeached, Samuel Chase, who was acquitted in 1805. In 1969 Abe Fortas resigned under threat of impeachment for alleged financial improprieties unrelated to his duties on the court.

The federal judicial system originally comprised only trial courts of original jurisdiction and the Supreme Court. As the country grew in size, and in the absence of intermediate appellate courts, the volume of cases awaiting review increased, and fidelity to Supreme Court precedents varied significantly among the lower courts. To remedy this problem, Congress passed the Circuit Court of Appeals Act (1891), which established nine intermediate courts with final authority over appeals from federal district courts, except when the case in question was of exceptional public importance. The Judiciary Act of 1925 (popularly known as the Judges' Bill), which was sponsored by the court itself, carried the reforms farther, greatly limiting obligatory jurisdiction (which required the Supreme Court to review a case) and expanding the classes of cases that the court could accept at its own discretion through the issue of a writ of certiorari. Further changes were enacted in 1988, when Congress passed legislation that required the Supreme Court to hear appeals of cases involving legislative reapportionment and federal civil rights and antitrust laws. Currently, there are 12 geographic judicial circuits and a court of appeals for the federal circuit, located in Washington, D.C. Roughly 98 percent of federal cases end with a decision by one of the lower appellate courts.

Procedures and Power

The term of the Supreme Court begins by statute (set in 1917) on the first Monday in October and typically ends in late June (though from 1873 to 1917 the court began its term on the second Monday in October). Each year the court receives thousands of certiorari requests. The number of these requests has increased dramatically since World War II—a reflection of the country's population growth, a

Bronze entrance doors to the Supreme Court of the United States. Franz Jantzen/ Supreme Court of the United States

progressively more litigious legal culture, and a surge in the demands placed by citizens on government.

All certiorari requests are circulated among the justices. The chief justice leads the court in developing a "discuss list" of potential cases, though the associate justices may request that additional cases be placed on the list. By the so-called Rule of Four, apparently developed in the late 19th century, the decision to grant certiorari requires the assent of at least four justices. Once the decision to hear a case has been made, lower-court records and briefs are delivered to the court and oral arguments are scheduled. Interested third parties also may submit their opinions to the court by filing an amicus curiae (Latin: "friend of the court") brief. With rare exceptions the petitioners and respondents are each allotted 30 minutes of time to present their arguments to the court. The justices hear neither witnesses nor evidence. Each side in the case attempts to persuade the justices that the Constitution should be interpreted in a manner that supports its point of view.

The decision-making process involves two major judgments. First, in a vote that is usually kept secret, the justices decide the merits of the case; then they issue the official written decision of the court. The first judgment determines who will write the official decision. By tradition, if the chief justice is in the majority, he selects which justice (including himself) will author the court's verdict. If he is in the minority, the longest-serving member of the majority makes the decision-writing appointment. Since the era of John Marshall, chief justice from 1801 to 1835, it has been common practice for the court to issue formal opinions to justify its decisions, though the Constitution does not require it to do so. Drafts of all opinions circulate among the justices, and all justices may concur with or dissent from any decision, in full or in part. The final decision effectively represents the supreme law of the land and is expected to be used as controlling constitutional doctrine by lower courts.

The Supreme Court's power of judicial review enables it to declare acts of Congress or the state legislatures unconstitutional. Executive, administrative, and judicial actions also are subject to review by the court. Because judicial review is not explicitly mentioned in the Constitution, some critics have charged that the framers did not intend for the court to exercise such power. Nevertheless, since the late 19th century the vast majority of legal scholars have accepted judicial review as a proper power of the court.

Historical Trends

Any assessment of the unifying forces in American society must ascribe a significant role to the Supreme Court. In its institutional infancy, the court necessarily addressed structural and functional questions involving inter alia federalism, express and implied powers, checks and balances, and the separation of powers. During the mid- to late 19th century, the court employed the Constitution's commerce clause (Article I Section 8) to nullify state laws of taxation or regulation that discriminated against or unduly burdened interstate commerce. The clause subsequently was used to uphold the power of Congress to regulate vast sectors of the economy.

Whereas the commerce clause has been the chief doctrinal source of power over the economy, the due-process clause of the Fifth Amendment and the equal-protection clause of the Fourteenth Amendment have been the principal sources of protection of persons and corporations against arbitrary or repressive acts of government. These clauses were used at first to protect property rights, but in the 1920s they began to be applied

IN FOCUS: THE CHIEF JUSTICE

The chief justice of the United States is the presiding judge in the Supreme Court of the United States and the highest judicial officer of the nation. The chief justice is appointed by the president with the advice and consent of the Senate and has life tenure. His primary functions are to preside over the Supreme Court in its public sessions when the court is hearing arguments and during its private conferences when it is discussing and deciding cases. He serves as chairman in the court and has authority to assign the writing of opinions in cases where he is a member of the majority; otherwise his powers are the same as those of any other Supreme Court justice. The chief justice customarily administers the oath of office to the president and vice president at the time of their inauguration. The chief justice is also the presiding officer of the Judicial Conference of the United States, an assembly of judges representing all the federal courts that reviews and investigates problems relating to the administration of justice in those courts.

When the office is occupied by a person of extraordinary intellectual capacity and dynamic personality, as was the case with John Marshall, the chief justice may exert a great

Portraits of U.S. Chief Justices John Jay, John Rutledge, Oliver Ellsworth, John Marshall, Roger B. Taney, Salmon P. Chase, Morrison R. Waite, and Melville W. Fuller. Library of Congress, Washington, D.C. (neg. no. LC-USZ62-17681)

influence on the court's work. When the occupant of the centre chair is a lesser figure, as has often been the case, he is likely to be overshadowed by other members of the court.

The title of chief justice is also usually accorded the presiding judicial officer within any multijudge court, as well as to the highest judicial officer within a state of the United States. Since 1860, the title of lord chief justice of England has been given to the officer presiding over the Queen's Bench division of the High Court of Justice.

John Marshall. Library of Congress, Washington, D.C.

to civil liberties, particularly in the extension of Bill of Rights guarantees to state actions. By the middle of the century, the equal-protection clause, which had been designed to protect the rights of emancipated slaves, was being used to strike down laws that were racially discriminatory, and all rights guaranteed by the First Amendment had been incorporated (and thusly made applicable to the states) through the due-process clause of the Fourteenth Amendment. By the end of the 20th century, the court found itself addressing issues that had previously been considered off-limits according to the political-question doctrine, which it had invoked to avoid entering into questions that it thought were best decided by legislatures (e.g., prison administration, the operation of districting systems, and even, arguably, the 2000 presidential election). While broadening the concept of justiciable disputes, the court also sought to limit congressional power to control the affairs of the states. In a variety of cases concerning issues such as state immunity from lawsuits, commerce, and criminal procedure, a states' rights approach was adopted by the court's conservative majority.

The opinions of the Supreme Court, including the dissenting opinions of individual justices, often have been considered epitomes of legal reasoning. Through these opinions, the court serves to clarify, refine, and test the philosophical ideals written into the Constitution and to translate them into working principles for a federal union under law. Beyond its specific contributions, this symbolic and pragmatic function may be regarded as the most significant role of the court.

APPELLATE COURTS

The appellate courts of the United States, formally called the United States Courts of Appeals, consist of 13 intermediate appellate courts within the federal judicial system, including 12 courts whose jurisdictions are geographically apportioned and the United States Court of Appeals for the Federal Circuit, whose jurisdiction is subject-oriented and nationwide.

Each regional Court of Appeals is empowered to review all final decisions and certain interlocutory decisions of district courts within its jurisdiction, except those few decisions that are appealable directly to the Supreme Court of the United States. A Court of Appeals may also review and enforce the orders of some federal regulatory agencies, such as the Federal Trade Commission, the

Securities and Exchange Commission, and the National Labor Relations Board. The Courts of Appeals typically sit in panels of three judges, and cases are decided by majority vote. The courts conduct their reviews on the basis of the record of the trial proceedings and typically do not hear witnesses independently or otherwise receive evidence. Their reviews are mostly limited to points of law, not fact. All decisions of the courts of appeals are subject to discretionary review or appeal in the Supreme Court.

The United States has 94 judicial districts, above which there are 12 regional Courts of Appeals: District of Columbia Circuit, for Washington, D.C.; 1st Circuit, for Maine, New Hampshire, Massachusetts, Rhode Island, and Puerto Rico; 2nd Circuit, for Vermont, Connecticut, and New York; 3rd Circuit, for New Jersey, Pennsylvania, Delaware, and the Virgin Islands; 4th Circuit, for Maryland, West Virginia, Virginia, North Carolina, and South Carolina; 5th Circuit, for Mississippi, Louisiana, and Texas; 6th Circuit, for Ohio, Michigan, Kentucky, and Tennessee; 7th Circuit, for Indiana, Illinois, and Wisconsin; 8th Circuit, for Minnesota, Iowa, Missouri, Arkansas, Nebraska, North Dakota, and South Dakota; 9th Circuit, for California, Oregon, Washington, Arizona, Nevada, Idaho, Montana, Alaska, Hawaii, and certain Pacific islands; 10th Circuit, for Colorado, Wyoming, Utah, New Mexico, Oklahoma, and Kansas; and 11th Circuit, for Georgia, Florida, and Alabama.

The Court of Appeals for the Federal Circuit, created by an act of Congress in 1982, hears appeals from U.S. district and territorial courts primarily in patent and trademark cases, though it also hears appeals in cases in which the United States or its agencies is a defendant, as in alleged breaches of contract or in tax disputes. The Court of Appeals for the Federal Circuit is located in Washington, D.C.

DISTRICT COURTS

The district courts of the United States, formally called the United States District Courts, consist of the basic trial-level courts of the federal judicial system. The courts, which exercise both criminal and civil jurisdiction, are based in the 94 judicial districts throughout the United States. Each state has at least one judicial district, as do the District of Columbia and Puerto Rico, and a populous state may have as many as four districts. The number of judges varies widely from district to district.

As of 2009, Congress had authorized some 650 district court judgeships. As required by Article III of the Constitution of the United States, the judges of district courts are nominated by the president and confirmed by the Senate and hold their offices "during good Behaviour." Magistrate judges, who are appointed by federal district judges on a full-time basis for eight-year terms or on a part-time basis for four-year terms, play an increasingly important role in assisting district judges. Indeed, with the consent of the parties to the case, they may conduct trials and enter decisions themselves.

Decisions of the district courts are normally subject to appeal, typically to the United States Court of Appeals for the region in which the district court is located.

Chapter 5 Civil Rights and the Federal Court

SLAVERY

Political Background: Sectional Conflict of the 1840s and '50s

Northerners in the United States generally disliked slavery, but they made few efforts to change the South's "peculiar institution" until the first decades of the 19th century, when the country's acquisition of huge territories in the West (initially through the Louisiana Purchase) raised the question of which of the new territories would permit slavery and which would prohibit it. Sectional differences between the North and the South, centring on the issue of slavery, began to appear in many American institutions in the 1830s. During the 1840s the major national religious denominations, such as the Methodists and the Presbyterians, split over the slavery question. The Whig Party, which had once allied the conservative businessmen of the North and West with the planters of the South, divided and virtually disappeared after the election of 1852. When a bill introduced by Sen. Stephen A. Douglas of Illinois opened up to slavery the huge territories of Kansas and Nebraska—land that had long been reserved for free states—Northerners began to organize into an antislavery political party, called in some states the Anti-Nebraska Democratic Party, in others the People's Party, but in most places, the Republican Party.

Events of 1855 and 1856 further exacerbated relations between the sections and strengthened this new party.

Kansas, once organized by Congress, became the field of battle between the free and the slave states in a contest in which concern over slavery was mixed with land speculation and office seeking. A virtual civil war broke out, with rival free- and slave-state legislatures both claiming legitimacy. Disputes between individual settlers sometimes erupted into violence. A proslavery mob sacked the town of Lawrence, an antislavery stronghold, on May 21, 1856. On May 24–25 John Brown, a free-state partisan, led a small party in a raid upon some proslavery settlers on Pottawatomie Creek, murdered five men in cold blood, and left their gashed and mutilated bodies as a warning to the slaveholders. Not even the U.S. Capitol was safe from the violence. On May 22 Preston S. Brooks, a South Carolina congressman, brutally attacked Sen. Charles Sumner of Massachusetts at his desk in the Senate chamber because he had presumably insulted the Carolinian's "honour" in a speech he had given in support of Kansas abolitionists. The 1856 presidential election made it clear that voting was becoming polarized along sectional lines. Though James Buchanan, the Democratic nominee, was elected, John C. Frémont, the Republican candidate, received a majority of the votes in the free states.

The *Dred Scott* Decision

The following year the Supreme Court of the United States tried to solve the sectional conflicts that had baffled both the Congress and the president. On March 6, 1857, in its *Dred Scott* decision (formally called *Dred Scott* v. *John F.A. Sandford*), the court made slavery legal in all the territories, thereby adding fuel to the sectional controversy and pushing the nation along the road to civil war.

Dred Scott was a slave who was owned by Dr. John Emerson of Missouri. In 1834 Emerson undertook a series

Dred Scott. Library of Congress, Washington, D.C. (digital file no. 3a08411u)

of moves as part of his service in the U.S. military. He took Scott from Missouri (a slave state) to Illinois (a free state) and finally into the Wisconsin Territory (a free territory under the provisions of the Missouri Compromise). During this period, Scott met and married Harriet Robinson, who became part of the Emerson household. In the early 1840s the Emersons (Dr. Emerson had married in 1838) and the Scotts returned to Missouri, and Dr. Emerson died in 1843.

Dred Scott reportedly attempted to purchase his freedom from Emerson's widow, who refused the sale. In 1846, with the help of antislavery lawyers, Harriet and Dred Scott filed individual lawsuits for their freedom in the Missouri state courts on the grounds that their residence in a free state and a free territory had freed them from the bonds of slavery. It was later agreed that only Dred Scott's case would move forward; the decision in that case would apply to Harriet Scott's case as well. Although the case was long thought to have been unusual, historians have demonstrated that several hundred suits for freedom were filed by or on behalf of slaves in the decades before the Civil War.

Dred Scott v. *Irene Emerson* took years to reach a definitive decision. The case was initially filed in the Saint Louis

Circuit Court. In 1850 a lower court declared Scott free, but the verdict was overturned in 1852 by the Missouri Supreme Court. Mrs. Emerson soon left Missouri and gave control of her late husband's estate to her brother, John F.A. Sanford, a resident of New York; his last name was incorrectly spelled Sandford on court documents. Because Sanford was not subject to suit in Missouri, Scott's lawyers filed a suit against him in the U.S. federal courts. The case eventually reached the U.S. Supreme Court, which announced its decision on March 6, 1857, just two days after the inauguration of Pres. James Buchanan.

Though each justice wrote a separate opinion, Chief Justice Roger B. Taney's opinion is most often cited on account of its far-reaching implications for the sectional crisis. As one of the seven justices denying Scott his freedom (two dissented), Taney declared that an African

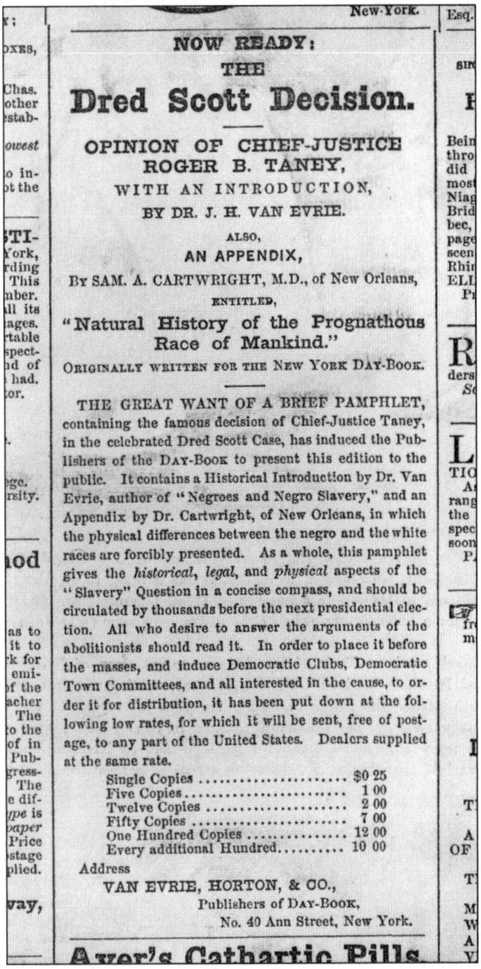

NOW READY:

THE

Dred Scott Decision.

OPINION OF CHIEF-JUSTICE ROGER B. TANEY,

WITH AN INTRODUCTION,

BY DR. J. H. VAN EVRIE.

ALSO,

AN APPENDIX,

BY SAM. A. CARTWRIGHT, M.D., of New Orleans,

ENTITLED,

"Natural History of the Prognathous Race of Mankind."

ORIGINALLY WRITTEN FOR THE NEW YORK DAY-BOOK.

THE GREAT WANT OF A BRIEF PAMPHLET, containing the famous decision of Chief-Justice Taney, in the celebrated Dred Scott Case, has induced the Publishers of the DAY-BOOK to present this edition to the public. It contains a Historical Introduction by Dr. Van Evrie, author of "Negroes and Negro Slavery," and an Appendix by Dr. Cartwright, of New Orleans, in which the physical differences between the negro and the white races are forcibly presented. As a whole, this pamphlet gives the *historical*, *legal*, and *physical* aspects of the "Slavery" Question in a concise compass, and should be circulated by thousands before the next presidential election. All who desire to answer the arguments of the abolitionists should read it. In order to place it before the masses, and induce Democratic Clubs, Democratic Town Committees, and all interested in the cause, to order it for distribution, it has been put down at the following low rates, for which it will be sent, free of postage, to any part of the United States. Dealers supplied at the same rate.

Single Copies	$0 25
Five Copies	1 00
Twelve Copies	2 00
Fifty Copies	7 00
One Hundred Copies	12 00
Every additional Hundred	10 00

Address

VAN EVRIE, HORTON, & CO.,

Publishers of DAY-BOOK,

No. 40 Ann Street, New York.

Newspaper notice for a pamphlet on the U.S. Supreme Court's Dred Scott decision. Library of Congress, ng. No. LC-USZ 62-132561

American could not be entitled to rights as a U.S. citizen, such as the right to sue in federal courts. In fact, Taney wrote, African Americans had "no rights which any white man was bound to respect." The decision might have ended there, with the dismissal of Scott's appeal. But Taney and the other justices in the majority went on to declare that the Missouri Compromise of 1820 (which had forbidden slavery in that part of the Louisiana Purchase north of the latitude 36°30', except for Missouri) was unconstitutional because Congress had no power to prohibit slavery in the territories. Slaves were property, and masters were guaranteed their property rights under the Fifth Amendment. Neither Congress nor a territorial legislature could deprive a citizen of his property without due process of law. As for Scott's temporary residence in a free state, Illinois, the majority said that Scott had still been subject then to Missouri law.

The decision—only the second time in the country's history that the Supreme Court declared an act of Congress unconstitutional—was a clear victory for the slaveholding South. Southerners had argued that both Congress and the territorial legislature were powerless to exclude slavery from a territory. Only a state could exclude slavery, they maintained. This seemed a mortal blow to the newly created Republican Party, formed to halt the extension of slavery into the western territories. It also forced Stephen A. Douglas, advocate of popular sovereignty, to come up with a method (the "Freeport Doctrine") whereby settlers could actually ban slavery from their midst. Pres. Buchanan, the South, and the majority of the Supreme Court hoped that the *Dred Scott* decision would mark the end of antislavery agitation. Instead, the decision increased antislavery sentiment in the North, strengthened the Republican Party, and fed the sectional antagonism that burst into war in 1861.

PRIMARY SOURCE: *DRED SCOTT V. SANDFORD* (EXCERPTS)

Mr. Chief Justice Taney delivered the opinion of the Court. ...

The question is simply this: Can a Negro, whose ancestors were imported into this country and sold as slaves, become a member of the political community formed and brought into existence by the Constitution of the United States, and as such become entitled to all the rights and privileges and immunities, guaranteed by that instrument to the citizen? ...

In the opinion of the Court, the legislation and histories of the times, and the language used in the Declaration of Independence, show that neither the class of persons who had been imported as slaves nor their descendants, whether they had become free or not, were then acknowledged as a part of the people nor intended to be included in the general words used in that memorable instrument. ...

We proceed ... to inquire whether the facts relied on by the plaintiff entitled him to his freedom. ...

The act of Congress upon which the plaintiff relies declares that slavery and involuntary servitude, except as a punishment for crime, shall be forever prohibited in all that part of the territory ceded by France, under the name of Louisiana, which lies north of 36°30' north latitude and not included within the limits of Missouri. And the difficulty which meets us at the threshold of this part of the inquiry is whether Congress was authorized to pass this law under any of the powers granted to it by the Constitution. ...

The counsel for the plaintiff has laid much stress upon that article in the Constitution which confers on Congress the power "to dispose of and make all needful rules and regulations respecting the territory or other property belonging to the United States"; but, in the judgment of the Court, that provision has no bearing on the present controversy, and the power there given, whatever it may be, is confined, and was intended to be confined, to the territory which at that time belonged to, or was claimed by, the United States and was within their boundaries as settled by the treaty with Great Britain, and can have no influence upon a territory afterward acquired from a foreign government. ...

Now, as we have already said in an earlier part of this opinion, upon a different point, the right of property in a slave is distinctly and expressly affirmed in the Constitution. The right to traffic in it, like an ordinary article of merchandise and property, was guaranteed to the citizens of the United States, in every state that might desire it, for twenty years. And the government in express terms is pledged to protect it in all future time if the slave escapes from his owner. ...

Upon these considerations it is the opinion of the Court that the act of Congress which prohibited a citizen from holding and owning property of this kind in the territory of the United States north of the line therein mentioned is not warranted by the Constitution and is therefore void; and that neither Dred Scott himself, nor any of his family, were made free by being carried into this territory; even if they had been carried there by the owner with the intention of becoming a permanent resident.

The Scotts were later bought by the Blow family, who had sold Dred to Dr. Emerson, and they were freed in 1857. Dred died of tuberculosis the following year. Little is known of Harriet's life after that time.

SEGREGATION AND DISCRIMINATION

Racial Segregation

Racial segregation is the practice of restricting people to certain circumscribed areas of residence or to separate institutions (e.g., schools, churches) and facilities (parks, playgrounds, restaurants, restrooms) on the basis of race or alleged race. Racial segregation provides a means of maintaining the economic advantages and superior social status of the politically dominant group. In the West it has been employed primarily by white populations to maintain their ascendancy over other groups by means of legal and social colour bars. Historically, however, various conquerors—among them Asian Mongols, African Bantu, and

Civil rights supporters carrying placards at the March on Washington, D.C., Aug. 28, 1963. Library of Congress, Washington, D.C.; Warren K. Leffler (digital file: cph ppmsca 03128)

American Aztecs—have practiced discrimination involving the segregation of subject races.

Segregation along racial lines has appeared in all parts of the world where there are multiracial communities, except where racial amalgamation has occurred on a large scale, as in Hawaii and Brazil. In such countries there has been occasional social discrimination but not legal segregation. In the Southern states of the United States, on the other hand, legal segregation in public facilities was current from the late 19th century into the 1950s. The civil rights movement was initiated by African Americans in the South in the 1950s and '60s to break the prevailing pattern of racial segregation. This movement spurred the passage of the Civil Rights Act of 1964, which contained strong provisions against discrimination and segregation in voting, education, and the use of public facilities.

Elsewhere, racial segregation was practiced with the greatest rigour in South Africa, where, under the apartheid system, it was an official government policy from 1950 until the early 1990s.

Jim Crow Laws

The Jim Crow system in the United States was built upon laws that enforced racial segregation in the South between the formal end of Reconstruction—the period (1865–77) after the American Civil War during which governments in the former Confederate states were reestablished and the states readmitted to the Union—and the beginning of a strong civil rights movement in the 1950s. Jim Crow was the name of a minstrel routine (actually *Jump Jim Crow*) performed beginning in 1828 by its author, Thomas Dartmouth ("Daddy") Rice, and by many imitators, including actor Joseph Jefferson. The term came to be a derogatory epithet for African Americans and a designation for their segregated life.

From the late 1870s, Southern state legislatures, no longer controlled by carpetbaggers and freedmen, passed laws requiring the separation of whites from "persons of colour" in public transportation and schools. Generally, anyone of ascertainable or strongly suspected African ancestry in any degree was for this purpose a "person of colour"; the pre-Civil War distinction favouring those whose ancestry was known to be mixed—particularly the half-French "free persons of colour" in Louisiana—was abandoned. The segregation principle was extended to parks, cemeteries, theatres, and restaurants in an effort to prevent any contact between blacks and whites as equals. It was codified on local and state levels and most famously with the "separate but equal" decision of the U.S. Supreme Court in *Plessy* v. *Ferguson* (1896).

"Separate But Equal": *Plessy v. Ferguson*

Homer Plessy was a shoemaker in Louisiana around the turn of the 19th century. Of mixed ancestry, Plessy looked white. However, according to the racial guidelines of the day, Plessy was considered black. The Comité des Citoyens ("Citizens' Committee"), a group opposed to racial segregation in the South, therefore chose Plessy as the perfect candidate to defy the segregation laws, which stipulated that there be separate train cars for blacks and whites. Taking a seat in the whites-only car, Plessy informed the conductor that he was black. Arrested according to plan, Plessy and his lawyers hoped to have the "separate but equal" law proven unconstitutional. The court took a different view.

Plessy v. *Ferguson* was handed down by the U.S. Supreme Court on May 18, 1896. In an 8–1 majority the court firmly advanced the controversial "separate but equal" doctrine for assessing the constitutionality of racial segregation laws. Decided nearly 30 years after the passage of the Fourteenth Amendment to the Constitution of the United States, which had granted full and equal citizenship rights to African Americans, the *Plessy* case was the first major inquiry into the meaning of the amendment's equal-protection clause. In upholding a Louisiana law that required the segregation of passengers on railroad cars, the court reasoned that equal protection is not violated as long as reasonably equal accommodations are provided to each racial group. Despite a series of civil rights advances in subsequent years, the ruling served as a controlling judicial precedent until its reversal in the case of *Brown* v. *Board of Education of Topeka* (1954). In the years following,

PRIMARY SOURCE: *PLESSY V. FERGUSON* (EXCERPTS)

Mr. Justice Brown:

This case turns upon the constitutionality of an act of the General Assembly of the state of Louisiana, passed in 1890, providing for separate railway carriages for the white and colored races. ...

The constitutionality of this act is attacked upon the ground that it conflicts both with the Thirteenth Amendment of the Constitution, abolishing slavery, and the Fourteenth Amendment, which prohibits certain restrictive legislation on the part of the states.

That it does not conflict with the Thirteenth Amendment, which abolished slavery and involuntary servitude except as a punishment for crime, is too clear for argument. ... A statute which implies merely a legal distinction between the white and colored races — a distinction which is founded in the color of the two races, and which must always exist so long as white men are distinguished from the other race by color — has no tendency to destroy the legal equality of the two races or reestablish a state of involuntary servitude. Indeed, we do not understand that the Thirteenth Amendment is strenuously relied upon by the plaintiff in error in this connection.

By the Fourteenth Amendment, all persons born or naturalized in the United States and subject to the jurisdiction thereof are made citizens of the United States and of the state wherein they reside; and the states are forbidden from making or enforcing any law which shall abridge the privileges or immunities of citizens of the United States, or shall deprive any person of life, liberty, or property without due process of law, or deny to any person within their jurisdiction the equal protection of the laws. ...

The object of the [latter] amendment was undoubtedly to enforce the absolute equality of the two races before the law, but in the nature of things it could not have been intended to abolish distinctions based upon color, or to enforce social as distinguished from political equality, or a commingling of the two races upon terms unsatisfactory to either. Laws permitting, and even requiring, their separation in places where they are liable to be brought into contact do not necessarily imply the inferiority of either race to the other, and have been generally, if not universally, recognized as within the competency of the state legislatures in the exercise of their police power. The most common instance of this is connected with the establishment of separate schools for white and colored children, which has been held to be a valid exercise of the legislative power even by courts of states where the political rights of the colored race have been longest and most earnestly enforced. ...

We consider the underlying fallacy of the plaintiff's argument to consist in the assumption that the enforced separation of the two races stamps the colored race with a badge of inferiority. If this be so, it is not by reason of anything found in the act, but solely because the colored race chooses to put that construction upon it. The argument necessarily assumes that if, as has been more than once the case, and is not unlikely to be so again, the colored race should become the dominant power in the state legislature and should enact a law in precisely similar terms, it would thereby relegate the white race to an inferior position. We imagine that the white race, at least, would not acquiesce in this assumption.

The argument also assumes that social prejudices may be overcome by legislation and that equal rights cannot be secured to the Negro except by an enforced commingling of the two races. We cannot accept this proposition. If the two races are to meet upon terms of social equality, it must be the result of natural affinities, a mutual appreciation of each other's merits, and a voluntary consent of individuals.

subsequent decisions struck down similar kinds of Jim Crow legislation.

Equal Protection Comes of Age

The Civil Rights Movement

The civil rights movement in the United States that blossomed in the late 1950s applied nonviolent protest action to break the pattern of racially segregated public facilities in the South and eventually to achieve passage of the comprehensive Civil Rights Act (1964).

Denied constitutional guarantees (1787) because of their mainly slave status at the founding of the republic, African

Americans were first promised fundamental citizenship rights in the Thirteenth through Fifteenth constitutional amendments (1865–70). The Civil Rights Act of 1875 required equal accommodations for blacks with whites in public facilities (other than schools), but this legislation was effectively voided by the Supreme Court in 1883. By 1900, 18 states of the North and West had legislated public policies against racial discrimination, but in the South new Jim Crow laws eroded the franchise and reinforced segregation practices, while the U.S. Supreme Court's decision in *Plessy* v. *Ferguson* (1896) legitimized the segregation of blacks from whites.

During World War II, progress was made in outlawing discrimination in defense industries (1941) and after the war in desegregating the armed forces (1948). During the late 1940s and early 1950s, lawyers for the National Association for the Advancement of Colored People (NAACP) pressed a series of important cases before the Supreme Court in which they argued that segregation meant inherently unequal (and inadequate) educational and other public facilities for African Americans. These cases culminated in the Court's landmark decision in *Brown* v. *Board of Education of Topeka* (May 17, 1954). This historic decision was to stimulate a mass movement on the part of African Americans and white sympathizers to try to end the segregationist practices and racial inequalities that were firmly entrenched across the nation and particularly in the South. The movement was strongly resisted by many whites in the South and elsewhere.

After an African American woman, Rosa Parks, was arrested for refusing to move to the black section of a bus in Montgomery, Ala. (Dec. 1, 1955), African Americans staged a one-day local boycott of the bus system to protest her arrest. Fusing these protest elements with the historic force of African American churches, a local Baptist minister, Martin Luther King, Jr., succeeded in transforming a spontaneous racial protest into a massive resistance movement, led from 1957 by his Southern Christian Leadership Conference (SCLC). After a protracted boycott of the Montgomery bus company forced it to desegregate its facilities, picketing and boycotting spread rapidly to other communities. During the period from 1955 to 1960, some progress was made toward integrating schools and other public facilities in the upper South and the border states, but the Deep South remained adamant in its opposition to most desegregation measures.

In 1960 the sit-in movement (largely under the auspices of the newly formed Student Nonviolent Coordinating Committee; SNCC) was launched at Greensboro, N. C., when African American college students insisted on service at a local segregated lunch counter. Patterning its techniques on the nonviolent methods of Indian leader

Participants in the March on Washington, D.C., in August 1963. Library of Congress, Washington, D.C. (digital file no. 04297u); photograph, Warren K. Leffler

Mohandas Gandhi, the movement spread across the nation, forcing the desegregation of department stores, supermarkets, libraries, and movie theatres. In May 1961 the Congress of Racial Equality (CORE) sent Freedom Riders of both races through the South and elsewhere to test and break down segregated accommodations in interstate transportation. By September it was estimated that more than 70,000 students had participated in the movement, with approximately 3,600 arrested; more than 100 cities in 20 states had been affected. The movement reached its climax in August 1963 with the massive March on Washington, D.C., to protest racial discrimination and demonstrate support for major civil rights legislation that was pending in Congress.

The federal government under presidents Dwight D. Eisenhower (1953–61) and John F. Kennedy had been reluctant to vigorously enforce the *Brown* decision when this entailed directly confronting the resistance of Southern whites. In 1961–63 Pres. Kennedy won a following in the African American community by encouraging the movement's leaders, but Kennedy's administration lacked the political capacity to persuade Congress to pass new legislation guaranteeing integration and equal rights. After Kennedy's assassination (November 1963), Congress, under the prodding of Pres. Lyndon B. Johnson, in 1964 passed the Civil Rights Act. This was the most far-reaching civil rights bill in the nation's history (indeed, in world history), forbidding discrimination in public accommodations and threatening to withhold federal funds from communities that persisted in maintaining segregated schools. It was followed in 1965 by the passage of the Voting Rights Act, the enforcement of which eradicated the tactics previously used in the South to disenfranchise African American voters. This act led to drastic increases

Soldiers standing guard in Washington, D.C., during the riots that occurred after the assassination of Martin Luther King, Jr., April 1968. Library of Congress, Washington, D.C. (digital file no. 04301u)

in the numbers of African American registered voters in the South, with a comparable increase in the numbers of African Americans holding elective offices there.

Up until 1966 the civil rights movement had united widely disparate elements in the black community along with their white supporters and sympathizers, but in that year signs of radicalism began to appear in the movement as younger African Americans became impatient with the rate of change and dissatisfied with purely nonviolent methods of protest. This new militancy split the ranks of the movement's leaders and also alienated some white sympathizers, a process that was accelerated by a wave of rioting in the African American ghettos of several major cities in 1965–67. After the assassination of King (April

1968) and further rioting in the cities, the movement as a cohesive effort disintegrated, with a broad spectrum of leadership advocating different approaches and varying degrees of militancy.

In the decades that followed, many civil rights leaders sought to achieve greater direct political power through elective office, and they sought to achieve more substantive economic and educational gains through affirmative-action programs that compensated for past discrimination in job hiring and college admissions. Although the civil rights movement was less militant, it was still persevering.

Equal Protection

Equal protection is the constitutional guarantee in the United States that no person or group will be denied the protection under the law that is enjoyed by similar persons or groups. In other words, persons similarly situated must be similarly treated. Equal protection is extended when the rules of law are applied equally in all like cases and when persons are exempt from obligations greater than those imposed upon others in like circumstances. The Fourteenth Amendment to the U.S. Constitution, one of three amendments adopted in the immediate aftermath of the American Civil War (1861–65), prohibits states from denying to any person "the equal protection of the laws."

Equal Protection's Limited Enforcement

For much of the post–Civil War period, the Supreme Court held that the postwar amendments had but one purpose: to guarantee "the freedom of the slave race . . . and the protection of the newly-made freeman and citizen from the oppressions of those who had formerly exercised unlimited domination over him." Thus, the equal-

PRIMARY SOURCE: THE CONSTITUTION OF THE UNITED STATES: AMENDMENT XIV

[1868] **Section 1**—All persons born or naturalized in the United States, and subject to the jurisdiction thereof, are citizens of the United States and of the State wherein they reside. No State shall make or enforce any law which shall abridge the privileges or immunities of citizens of the United States; nor shall any State deprive any person of life, liberty, or property, without due process of law; nor deny to any person within its jurisdiction the equal protection of the laws.

Section 2—Representatives shall be apportioned among the several States according to their respective numbers, counting the whole number of persons in each State, excluding Indians not taxed. But when the right to vote at any election for the choice of electors for Pres. and Vice Pres. of the United States, Representatives in Congress, the Executive and Judicial officers of a State, or the members of the Legislature thereof, is denied to any of the male inhabitants of such State, being twenty-one years of age,{14} and citizens of the United States, or in any way abridged, except for participation in rebellion, or other crime, the basis of representation therein shall be reduced in the proportion which the number of such male citizens shall bear to the whole number of male citizens twenty-one years of age in such State.

Section 3—No person shall be a Senator or Representative in Congress, or elector of Pres. and Vice President, or hold any office, civil or military, under the United States, or under any State, who, having previously taken an oath, as a member of Congress, or as an officer of the United States, or as a member of any State legislature, or as an executive or judicial officer of any State, to support the Constitution of the United States, shall have engaged in insurrection or rebellion against the same, or given aid or comfort to the enemies thereof. But Congress may by a vote of two-thirds of each House, remove such disability.

Section 4—The validity of the public debt of the United States, authorized by law, including debts incurred for payment of pensions and bounties for services in suppressing insurrection or rebellion, shall not be questioned. But neither the United States nor any State shall assume or pay any debt or obligation incurred in aid of insurrection or rebellion against the United States, or any claim for the loss or emancipation of any slave; but all such debts, obligations and claims shall be held illegal and void.

Section 5—The Congress shall have power to enforce, by appropriate legislation, the provisions of this article.

protection clause of the Fourteenth Amendment was applied minimally—except in some cases of racial discrimination, such as the invalidation of literacy tests and grandfather clauses for voting. In other decisions—such as *Plessy* (1896) and the decisions creating the doctrine of state action, which limited the enforcement of national civil rights legislation—the court diminished the envisioned protections. Indeed, for nearly 80 years after the adoption of the Fourteenth Amendment, the intent of the equal-protection clause was effectively circumvented. As late as 1927, Justice Oliver Wendell Holmes, Jr., referred to equal protection as "the usual last resort of constitutional arguments." Not until the landmark *Brown* v. *Board of Education* (1954) decision did the court reverse its decision in *Plessy*.

Under Chief Justice Earl Warren in the 1960s, the concept of equal protection was dramatically transformed and applied to cases involving welfare benefits, exclusionary zoning, municipal services, and school financing. Equal protection became a prolific source of constitutional litigation. During the tenure of Chief Justices Warren E. Burger and William H. Rehnquist, the court added considerably to the list of situations that might be adjudicated under the doctrine of equal protection, including sexual discrimination, the status and rights of aliens, voting, abortion, and access to the courts. In *Bush* v. *Gore* (2000), which stemmed from the controversial presidential election of that year, the Supreme Court's ruling that a selective recount of ballots in the state of

Florida violated the equal-protection clause helped to preserve George W. Bush's narrow win in that state and in the electoral college.

Brown v. Board of Education of Topeka

The concept of separate but equal was finally overturned over half a century after *Plessy*. In 1954, Linda Brown, a third grader living in Topeka, Kan., was the instrument of change. Though she lived a few blocks from the local white elementary school, the seven-year-old had to walk a mile to attend the black elementary school. In concert with the local NAACP, the Brown family filed suit.

On May 17, 1954, in *Brown* v. *Board of Education of Topeka*, the U.S. Supreme Court ruled unanimously that racial segregation in public schools violated the Fourteenth Amendment to the Constitution, which declares that no state may deny equal protection of the laws to any person within its jurisdiction. The decision declared that separate educational facilities were inherently unequal. Based on a series of Supreme Court cases argued between 1938–50, *Brown* v. *Board of Education of Topeka* completed the reversal of the 1896 *Plessy* decision. Strictly speaking, the 1954 decision was limited to the public schools, but it implied that segregation was not permissible in other public facilities.

A mother explaining to her daughter the significance of the Supreme Court's 1954 ruling in Brown v. Board of Education of Topeka; *photographed on the steps of the U.S. Supreme Court in Washington, D.C., Nov. 19, 1954.* New York World-Telegram & Sun Collection/Library of Congress, Washington, D.C. (digital file no. cph 3c27042)

PRIMARY SOURCE: *BROWN ET AL. V. BOARD OF EDUCATION OF TOPEKA ET AL.* (EXCERPTS)

These cases come to us from the states of Kansas, South Carolina, Virginia, and Delaware. They are premised on different facts and different local conditions, but a common legal question justifies their consideration together in this consolidated opinion.

In each of the cases, minors of the Negro race, through their legal representatives, seek the aid of the courts in obtaining admission to the public schools of their community on a nonsegregated basis. In each instance, they had been denied admission to schools attended by white children under laws requiring or permitting segregation according to race. This segregation was alleged to deprive the plaintiffs of the equal protection of the laws under the Fourteenth Amendment. In each of the cases other than the Delaware case, a three-judge federal District Court denied relief to the plaintiffs on the so-called "separate but equal" doctrine announced by this Court in *Plessy* v. *Ferguson*, 163 U.S. 537. ...

The plaintiffs contend that segregated public schools are not "equal" and cannot be made "equal," and that hence they are deprived of the equal protection of the laws. Because of the obvious importance of the question presented, the Court took jurisdiction. Argument was heard in the 1952 Term, and reargument was heard this Term on certain questions propounded by the Court. ...

We come then to the question presented: Does segregation of children in public schools solely on the basis of race, even though the physical facilities and other "tangible" factors may be equal, deprive the children of the minority group of equal educational opportunities? We believe that it does.

In *Sweatt* v. *Painter, supra*, in finding that a segregated law school for Negroes could not provide them equal educational opportunities, this Court relied in large part on "those qualities which are incapable of objective measurement but which make for greatness in a law school." ... Such considerations apply with added force to children in grade and high schools. To separate them from others of similar age and qualifications solely because of their race generates a feeling of inferiority as to their status in the community that may affect their hearts and minds in a way unlikely ever to be undone. The effect of this separation on their educational opportunities was well stated by a finding in the Kansas case by a court which nevertheless felt compelled to rule against the Negro plaintiffs:

Segregation of white and colored children in public schools has a detrimental effect upon the colored children. The impact is greater when it has the sanction of the law; for the policy of separating the races is usually interpreted as denoting the inferiority of the Negro group. A sense of inferiority affects the motivation of a child to learn. Segregation with the sanction of law, therefore, has a tendency to [retard] the educational and mental development of Negro children and to deprive them of some of the benefits they would receive in a racial[ly] integrated school system.

We conclude that in the field of public education the doctrine of "separate but equal" has no place. Separate educational facilities are inherently unequal. Therefore, we hold that the plaintiffs and others similarly situated for whom the actions have been brought are, by reason of the segregation complained of, deprived of the equal protection of the laws guaranteed by the Fourteenth Amendment. This disposition makes unnecessary any discussion whether such segregation also violates the due process clause of the Fourteenth Amendment.

Baker v. Carr

The issue of apportioning legislative representation in accordance with equal protection was the focus of the landmark case *Baker* v. *Carr*. Decided on March 26, 1962, the U.S. Supreme Court ruled that the Tennessee legislature must reapportion itself on the basis of population. Traditionally, particularly in the South, the populations of rural areas had been overrepresented in legislatures in proportion to those of urban and suburban areas. Prior to the *Baker* case, the Supreme Court had refused to intervene in apportionment cases; in 1946 in *Colegrove* v. *Green* the court said apportionment was a "political thicket" into which the judiciary should not intrude. In the *Baker* case, however, the court held that each vote should carry equal weight regardless of the voter's place of residence. Thus the legislature of Tennessee had violated the constitutionally guaranteed right of equal protection. Chief Justice Earl

Warren described this decision as the most important case decided after his appointment to the court in 1953.

Citing the *Baker* case as a precedent, the court held in *Reynolds* v. *Sims* (1964) that both houses of bicameral legislatures had to be apportioned according to population. It remanded numerous other apportionment cases to lower courts for reconsideration in light of the *Baker* and *Reynolds* decisions. As a result, virtually every state legislature was reapportioned, ultimately causing the political power in most state legislatures to shift from rural to urban areas.

PRIMARY SOURCE: *BAKER* V. *CARR* (EXCERPTS)

This civil action was brought under 42 U.S.C. Sections 1983 and 1988 to redress the alleged deprivation of federal constitutional rights. The complaint, alleging that by means of a 1901 statute of Tennessee apportioning the members of the General Assembly among the state's ninety-five counties, "these plaintiffs and others similarly situated are denied the equal protection of the laws accorded them by the Fourteenth Amendment to the Constitution of the United States by virtue of the debasement of their votes," was dismissed by a three-judge court convened under 28 U.S.C. Section 2281 in the Middle District of Tennessee. ... We hold that the dismissal was in error, and remand the cause to the District Court for trial and further proceedings consistent with this opinion. ...

Tennessee's standard for allocating legislative representation among her counties is the total number of qualified voters resident in the respective counties, subject only to minor qualifications. ...

Between 1901 and 1961, Tennessee has experienced substantial growth and redistribution of her population. The relative standings of the counties in terms of qualified voters have changed significantly. It is primarily the continued application of the 1901 Apportionment Act to this shifted and enlarged voting population which gives rise to the present controversy. ...

In light of the District Court's treatment of the case, we hold today only (a) that the court possessed jurisdiction of the subject matter;

(b) that a justiciable cause of action is stated upon which appellants would be entitled to appropriate relief; and (c) because appellees raise the issue before this Court, that the appellants have standing to challenge the Tennessee apportionment statutes. Beyond noting that we have no cause at this stage to doubt the District Court will be able to fashion relief if violations of constitutional rights are found, it is improper now to consider what remedy would be most appropriate if appellants prevail at the trial.

The District Court was uncertain whether our cases withholding federal judicial relief rested upon a lack of federal jurisdiction or upon the inappropriateness of the subject matter for judicial consideration—what we have designated "nonjusticiability." ...

Our conclusion ... that this cause presents no nonjusticiable "political question" settles the only possible doubt that it is a case or controversy. Under the present heading of "Jurisdiction of the Subject Matter" we hold only that the matter set forth in the complaint does arise under the Constitution and is within 28 U.S.C. Section 1343. ...

We conclude that the complaint's allegations of a denial of equal protection present a justiciable constitutional cause of action upon which appellants are entitled to a trial and a decision. The right asserted is within the reach of judicial protection under the Fourteenth Amendment.

The judgment of the District Court is reversed and the cause is remanded for further proceedings consistent with this opinion.

Civil Rights Legislation of the 1960s

The Civil Rights Act

The Civil Rights Act, enacted on July 2, 1964, intended to end discrimination based on race, colour, religion, or national origin; it is often considered the most important U.S. law on civil rights since the end of Reconstruction. Title I of the act guarantees equal voting rights by removing registration requirements and procedures biased against minorities and the underprivileged. Title II prohibits segregation or discrimination in places of public accommodation involved in interstate commerce. Title VII bans discrimination by trade unions, schools, or employers involved in interstate commerce or doing business with the federal government. The latter section also applies to discrimination on the basis of sex and established a government agency, the Equal Employment Opportunity Commission (EEOC), to enforce these provisions. The act also calls for the desegregation of public schools (Title IV), broadens the duties of the Civil Rights Commission (Title V), and assures nondiscrimination in the distribution of funds under federally assisted programs (Title VI).

The Civil Rights Act was a highly controversial issue in the United States as soon as it was proposed by Pres. John F. Kennedy in 1963. Although Kennedy was unable to secure passage of the bill in Congress, a stronger version was eventually passed with the urging of his successor, Pres. Lyndon B. Johnson, who signed the bill into law following one of the longest debates in Senate history. White

IN FOCUS: THE EQUAL EMPLOYMENT OPPORTUNITY COMMISSION

The Equal Employment Opportunity Commission, also known as the EEOC, is a government agency established on July 2, 1965, by Title VII of the Civil Rights Act of 1964 to "ensure equality of opportunity by vigorously enforcing federal legislation prohibiting discrimination in employment"—particularly discrimination on the basis of religion, race, sex, colour, national origin, age, or disability.

The EEOC investigates claims of discrimination on the federal level and attempts mediation. If mediation is impossible, the EEOC will bring a suit against the offending company. The agency also works with some 90 fair employment practice agencies on the state and local level. In 1991 the EEOC further expanded to include several educational and technical assistance programs to further equal employment practices. The EEOC and its 50 field offices manage more than 80,000 claims of employment discrimination annually.

groups opposed to integration with blacks responded to the act with a significant backlash that took the form of protests, increased support for pro-segregation candidates for public office, and some racial violence. The act gave federal law enforcement agencies the power to prevent racial discrimination in employment, voting, and the use of public facilities. The constitutionality of the Civil Rights Act was immediately challenged in the test case *Heart of Atlanta Motel* v. *United States* (1964).

Heart of Atlanta Motel v. United States

On Dec. 14, 1964, in *Heart of Atlanta Motel* v. *United States*, the U.S. Supreme Court ruled that in passing Title II of the Civil Rights Act (1964), which prohibited segregation or discrimination in places of public accommodation involved in interstate commerce, the U.S. Congress did not exceed the regulatory authority granted to it by the commerce clause of Article I of the U.S. Constitution. The court thereby declared that Title II was constitutional.

After Pres. Lyndon B. Johnson signed the Civil Rights Act on July 2, 1964, the owner of the Heart of Atlanta Motel in Georgia, who had previously refused to accept African American customers, filed suit in federal district court, alleging that the prohibition of racial discrimination contained in Title II of the Civil Rights Act represented an invalid exercise of Congress's constitutional power to regulate interstate commerce. The owner also claimed that the title violated the Fifth Amendment's guarantees of due process and just compensation for the taking of private property because it deprived him of the right to choose his customers and that it violated the Thirteenth Amendment's prohibition of involuntary servitude because it compelled him to rent rooms to African Americans. The district court upheld the constitutionality of Title II and issued a permanent injunction requiring the motel to cease discriminating against African American customers. The case was appealed to the Supreme Court, where oral arguments were heard on Oct. 5, 1964. In a unanimous (9–0) ruling issued on December 14, the court affirmed the district court's finding. In his opinion for the court, Justice Tom C. Clark argued that the motel's transactions clearly affected interstate commerce and thus fell within the purview of congressional regulation, and he rejected the petitioner's arguments that the title violated the Fifth and Thirteenth amendments as misguided in point of both history and law.

The Voting Rights Act

The Voting Rights Act was enacted on Aug. 6, 1965, and aimed to overcome legal barriers at the state and local levels that prevented African Americans from exercising their right to vote under the U.S. Constitution's Fifteenth

Pres. George W. Bush signing the Voting Rights Act Reauthorization and Amendments Act, July 2006. Paul Morse/White House photo

Amendment (1870). The act significantly widened the franchise and is considered among the most far-reaching pieces of civil rights legislation in U.S. history.

Shortly following the end of the Civil War in 1865, the Fifteenth Amendment was ratified, guaranteeing that the right to vote would not be denied "on account of race, color, or previous condition of servitude." Soon afterward the U.S. Congress enacted legislation that made it a federal crime to interfere with an individual's right to vote and that otherwise protected the rights promised to former slaves under both the Fourteenth (1868) and Fifteenth amendments. In some states of the former Confederacy, African Americans became a majority or near majority of the eligible voting population, and African American candidates ran and were elected to office at all levels of government.

Nevertheless, there was strong opposition to the extension of the franchise to African Americans. Following the end of Reconstruction, the Supreme Court of the United States limited voting protections under federal legislation, and intimidation and fraud were employed by white leaders to reduce voter registration and turnout among African Americans. As whites came to dominate state legislatures once again, legislation was used to strictly circumscribe the right of African Americans to vote. Poll taxes, literacy tests, grandfather clauses, whites-only primaries, and other measures disproportionately disqualified African Americans from voting. The result was that by the early 20th century nearly all African Americans were disfranchised. In the first half of the 20th century, several such measures were declared unconstitutional by the U.S. Supreme Court. In 1915, for example, grandfather clauses were invalidated, and in 1944 whites-only primaries were struck down. Nevertheless, by the early 1960s voter registration rates among African Americans were negligible in much of the Deep South and well below those of whites elsewhere.

In the 1950s and early 1960s the U.S. Congress enacted laws to protect the right of African Americans to vote, but such legislation was only partially successful. In 1964 the Civil Rights Act was passed and the Twenty-fourth Amendment, abolishing poll taxes for voting for federal offices, was ratified, and the following year Pres. Lyndon B. Johnson called for the implementation of comprehensive federal legislation to protect voting rights. The resulting act, the Voting Rights Act, suspended literacy tests, provided for federal oversight of voter registration in areas that had previously used tests to determine voter eligibility (these areas were covered under Section 5 of the legislation), and directed the attorney general of the United States to challenge the use of poll taxes for state and local elections. An expansion of the law in the 1970s also protected voting rights for non-English-speaking U.S. citizens. Section 5 was extended for 5 years in 1970, 7 years in 1975, and 25 years in both 1982 and 2006.

The Voting Rights Act resulted in a marked decrease in the voter registration disparity between whites and blacks. In the mid-1960s, for example, the overall proportion of white to black registration in the South ranged from about 2 to 1 to 3 to 1 (and about 10 to 1 in Mississippi); by the late 1980s racial variations in voter registration had largely disappeared. As the number of African American voters increased, so did the number of African American elected officials. In the mid-1960s there were about 70 African American elected officials in the South, but by the turn of the 21st century there were some 5,000, and the number of African American members of the U.S. Congress had increased from 6 to about 40.

Busing

Busing and Racial Integration

Starting in the 1960s the busing of school children for purposes of integration was a highly emotional issue that found vehement opposition among both black and white citizens. The Richard Nixon administration remained decidedly cool to busing for racial balance, but in April 1971 the Supreme Court ruled, in *Swann* v. *Charlotte-Mecklenburg Board of Education*, that desegregation must be achieved even if the methods be "administratively awkward, inconvenient, or even bizarre" and allowed that busing was an acceptable means.

The Nixon administration pressed for a moratorium on busing, and Congress, in July 1972, passed a bill to accomplish this end. There was even talk of a constitutional amendment to outlaw busing. However, the Supreme Court, in four separate rulings during 1972, decided that a moratorium on busing did not apply to court orders written to correct unlawful segregation. Out of all the legal and judicial uncertainty over the issue, there grew a public mood of hostility and defiance toward busing and in favor of local control of the public schools in both the North and South. The Resolution Against Busing to Achieve Integration, adopted by the Georgia Jaycees on Feb. 22, 1970, is representative of this widespread sentiment.

Swann v. Charlotte-Mecklenburg Board of Education

In *Swann* v. *Charlotte-Mecklenburg Board of Education*, handed down on April 20, 1971, the U.S. Supreme Court unanimously upheld busing programs that aimed to

PRIMARY SOURCE: "RESOLUTION AGAINST BUSING TO ACHIEVE INTEGRATION" (EXCERPTS)

Whereas, the Federal Judiciary has recently set forth the concept that a mathematical racial balance of faculty and students must be maintained in the public school systems; and

Whereas, this concept will force school systems to classify and locate people according to their race in order to achieve a mythical racial balance; and

Whereas, it is strongly felt that the busing of children to areas in which they do not live for the purpose of obtaining a mathematical racial balance is a denial of individual dignity, worth and equality, and is a denial of the constitutional rights of these children to the freedom of choice of attending a school in close proximity to their homes; and

Whereas, we believe that the implementation of a mathematical racial balance of teachers and pupils will be utterly chaotic and will prevent the continued growth of quality education; and

Whereas, school children and teachers, by federal courts' orders, are being regimented and moved about like pawns on a chessboard to achieve an unlawful objective in direct contradiction to the position taken by the United States Congress and the Pres. of the United States.

Now, therefore, The Georgia Jaycees does unanimously oppose the busing and transferring of school children and teachers for the purpose of accomplishing a mathematical racial balance of faculty and students in the public school systems and deplore the absolute disregard of the Federal Judiciary in creating a chaotic condition by requiring mass transfers of teachers to the detriment of a quality education being obtained by innocent children.

Be it further resolved that the Georgia Jaycees favors an unitary school system accomplished by the children having a freedom of choice of attending schools in close proximity to their homes without regard to achieving mathematical balances based on race, creed or color. ...

speed up the racial integration of public schools in the United States.

Although 17 years earlier, in *Brown* v. *Board of Education of Topeka*, the Court had struck down racial segregation in public schools because of racially segregated housing patterns and resistance by local leaders, many schools remained as segregated in the late 1960s as they were at the time of the *Brown* decision.

In Charlotte, N.C., for example, in the mid-1960s less than 5 percent of African American children attended integrated schools. Indeed, busing was used by white officials to maintain segregation. The NAACP, on behalf of Vera and Darius Swann, the parents of a six-year-old child, sued the Charlotte-Mecklenburg school district to allow their son to attend Seversville Elementary School, the school closest to their home and then one of Charlotte's few integrated schools. James McMillan, the federal district judge in the case, ruled in favour of the Swanns and oversaw the implementation of a busing strategy that integrated the district's schools. McMillan's decision was appealed to the U.S. Supreme Court, which upheld it. The busing strategy was adopted elsewhere in the United States and played an instrumental role in integrating U.S. public schools.

In later decades, court-ordered busing plans were criticized not only by whites but also by African Americans, who often charged that busing harmed African American students by requiring them to endure long commutes to and from school. Busing continued in most major cities until the late 1990s.

Affirmative Action

History of Affirmative Action

Affirmative action programs were implemented in the United States beginning in the 1960s to improve employment or educational opportunities for members of minority groups and for women. It began as a government remedy to the effects of long-standing discrimination against such groups and has consisted of policies, programs, and procedures that give preferences to minorities and women in job hiring, admission to institutions of higher education, the awarding of government contracts, and other social benefits. The typical criteria for affirmative action are race, disability, gender, ethnic origin, and age.

Affirmative action was initiated by the administration of President Johnson in order to improve opportunities for African Americans while civil rights legislation was dismantling the legal basis for discrimination. The federal government began to institute affirmative action policies under the landmark Civil Rights Act of 1964 and an executive order in 1965. Businesses receiving federal funds were prohibited from using aptitude tests and other criteria that tended to discriminate against African Americans. Affirmative action programs were monitored by the Office of Federal Contract Compliance and the EEOC. Subsequently, affirmative action was broadened to cover women and Native Americans, Hispanics, and other minorities and was extended to colleges and universities and state and federal agencies.

By the late 1970s the use of racial quotas and minority set-asides led to court challenges of affirmative action as a form of "reverse discrimination." The first major challenge was *Regents of the University of California* v. *Bakke* (1978), in which the U.S. Supreme Court ruled (5–4) that quotas may not be used to reserve places for minority applicants if white applicants are denied a chance to compete for those places. Although the court outlawed quota programs, it allowed colleges to use race as a factor in making college admissions decisions. Two years later a fragmented court upheld a 1977 federal law requiring that 10 percent of funds for public works be allotted to qualified minority contractors.

The Supreme Court began to impose significant restrictions on race-based affirmative action in 1989. In several decisions that year, the court gave greater weight to claims of reverse discrimination, outlawed the use of minority set-asides in cases where prior racial discrimination could not be proved, and placed limits on the use of racial preferences by states that were stricter than those it applied to the federal government. In *Adarand Constructors* v. *Pena* (1995), the court ruled that federal affirmative action programs were unconstitutional unless they fulfilled a "compelling governmental interest."

Opposition to affirmative action in California culminated in the passage in 1996 of the California Civil Rights Initiative (Proposition 209), which prohibited all government agencies and institutions from giving preferential treatment to individuals based on their race or sex. The Supreme Court effectively upheld the constitutionality of Proposition 209 in November 1997 by refusing to hear a challenge to its enforcement. Legislation similar to Proposition 209 was subsequently proposed in other states and was passed in Washington in 1998. The Supreme Court also upheld a lower-court ruling that struck down as unconstitutional the University of Texas's affirmative action program, arguing in *Hopwood* v. *University of Texas Law School* (1996) that there was no compelling state interest to warrant using race as a factor in admissions decisions. Afterward there were further legislative and electoral challenges to affirmative action in many parts of the country. In the 2003 *Bollinger* decisions, two landmark rulings involving admissions to the University of Michigan and its law school, the U.S. Supreme Court reaffirmed the constitutionality of affirmative action, though it ruled that race could not be the preeminent factor in such decisions as it struck down the university's undergraduate admissions policy that awarded points to students on the basis of race.

Regents of the University of California v. Bakke

On June 28, 1978, in *Regents of the University of California* v. *Bakke*, also known as the *Bakke* decision, the U.S. Supreme Court declared affirmative action constitutional but invalidated the use of racial quotas. The medical school at the University of California, Davis, as part of the university's affirmative action program, had reserved 16 percent of its admission places for minority applicants. Allan Bakke, a white California man who had twice unsuccessfully applied for admission to the medical school, filed suit against the university. Citing evidence that his grades and test scores surpassed those of many minority students who had been accepted for admission, Bakke charged that he had suffered unfair "reverse discrimination" on the basis of race, which he argued was contrary to the Civil Rights Act of 1964 and the equal-protection clause of the U.S. Constitution's Fourteenth Amendment. The Supreme Court, in a highly fractured ruling (six separate opinions were issued), agreed that the university's use of strict racial quotas was unconstitutional and ordered that the medical school admit Bakke, but it also contended that race could be used as one criterion in the admissions decisions of institutions of higher education. Although the ruling legalized the use of affirmative action, in subsequent decisions during the next several decades the court limited the scope of such programs, and several U.S. states prohibited affirmative action programs based on race.

Bollinger Decisions

The *Bollinger* decisions were a pair of legal cases addressing the issue of affirmative action in which, on June 23, 2003, the U.S. Supreme Court ruled that the undergraduate admissions policy of the University of Michigan violated the equal-protection clause of the Fourteenth Amendment to the U.S. Constitution (*Gratz* v. *Bollinger*) and that the admissions policy of the University of Michigan Law School did not (*Grutter* v. *Bollinger*).

In 1995 and 1997, respectively, Jennifer Gratz and Patrick Hamacher, both of whom were white, were denied admission to the University of Michigan's School of Literature, Science, and the Arts (LSA) despite being qualified or well-qualified according to the university's academic standards. The two filed a class-action suit alleging racial discrimination in violation of the equal-protection clause and Title VI of the Civil Rights Act (1964), which assures nondiscrimination in the distribution of funds under federally assisted programs. The admissions policy then used by the LSA, which was aimed at achieving racial diversity within the student body, automatically awarded points to candidates whose race was African American, Hispanic, or Native American. In *Gratz* v. *Bollinger*, the court ruled by a 6–3 majority that the LSA's use of race or ethnicity in its admissions policy was not "narrowly tailored" and thus too closely approximated the racial quotas that the court had determined were inconsistent with the equal-protection clause in *Regents of the University of California* v. *Bakke* (1978). The court's opinion was written by Chief Justice William Rehnquist.

In 1997 Barbara Grutter, who was white, was denied admission to the University of Michigan Law School despite being well-qualified according to the school's academic standards; she then filed suit alleging violation of the equal-protection clause and Title VI. The admissions policy then used by the school took the race of the candidate into account but did not grant an automatic and significant advantage to certain candidates on the basis of race or ethnicity. In *Grutter* v. *Bollinger*, the court ruled by a 5–4 majority that the school's admissions policy, unlike that of the LSA, did not violate the equal-protection clause or Title VI because it used race in a "narrowly tailored" and "holistic" manner within a system of highly individualized interviews, treating race or ethnicity as merely a "'plus' in a particular applicant's file," as recommended by Justice Lewis F. Powell in his concurring opinion in *Bakke*. The court's opinion in *Gratz* was written by Justice Sandra Day O'Connor.

Issues and Cases in Constitutional History

Chapter 6

Due Process

The Meaning of Due Process

Due process is a course of legal proceedings according to rules and principles that have been established in a system of jurisprudence for the enforcement and protection of private rights. In each case, due process contemplates an exercise of the powers of government as the law permits and sanctions, under recognized safeguards for the protection of individual rights.

Principally associated with one of the fundamental guarantees of the United States Constitution, due process derives from early English common law and constitutional history. The first concrete expression of the due-process idea embraced by Anglo-American law appeared in the 39th article of Magna Carta (1215) in the royal promise that "No freeman shall be taken or (and) imprisoned or disseised or exiled or in any way destroyed . . . except by the legal judgment of his peers or (and) by the law of the land." In subsequent English statutes, the references to "the legal judgment of his peers" and "laws of the land" are treated as substantially synonymous with due process of law. Drafters of the U.S. federal Constitution adopted the due-process phraseology in the Fifth Amendment, ratified in 1791, which provides that "No person shall . . . be deprived of life, liberty, or property, without due process of law." Because this amendment was held inapplicable to state

PRIMARY SOURCE: THE CONSTITUTION OF THE UNITED STATES: AMENDMENT V

No person shall be held to answer for a capital, or otherwise infamous crime, unless on a presentment or indictment of a Grand Jury, except in cases arising in the land or naval forces, or in the Militia, when in actual service in time of War or public danger; nor shall any person be subject for the same offence to be twice put in jeopardy of life or limb; nor shall be compelled in any criminal case to be a witness against himself, nor be deprived of life, liberty, or property, without due process of law; nor shall private property be taken for public use without just compensation.

actions that might violate an individual's constitutional rights, it was not until the ratification of the Fourteenth Amendment in 1868 that the several states became subject to a federally enforceable due-process restraint on their legislative and procedural activities.

The meaning of due process as it relates to substantive enactments and procedural legislation has evolved over decades of controversial interpretation by the Supreme Court. Today, if a law may reasonably be deemed to promote the public welfare and the means selected bear a reasonable relationship to the legitimate public interest, then the law has met the due-process standard. If the law seeks to regulate a fundamental right, such as the right to travel or the right to vote, then this enactment must meet a stricter judicial scrutiny, known as the compelling interest test. Economic legislation is generally upheld if the state can point to any conceivable public benefit resulting from its enactment.

In determining the procedural safeguards that should be obligatory upon the states under the due-process clause of the Fourteenth Amendment, the Supreme Court has exercised considerable supervision over the administration of criminal justice in state courts, as well as occasional influence upon state civil and administrative proceedings. Its decisions have been vigorously criticized, on the one hand, for unduly meddling with state judicial administration and, on the other hand, for not treating all of the specific procedural guarantees of the first 10 amendments as equally applicable to state and to federal proceedings.

Some justices have adhered to the proposition that the framers of the Fourteenth Amendment intended the entire Bill of Rights to be binding on the states. They have asserted that this position would provide an objective basis for reviewing state activities and would promote a desirable uniformity between state and federal rights and sanctions. Other justices, however, have contended that states should be allowed considerable latitude in conducting their affairs, so long as they comply with a fundamental fairness standard. Ultimately, the latter position substantially prevailed, and due process was recognized as embracing only those principles of justice that are "so rooted in the traditions and conscience of our people as to be ranked as fundamental." In fact, however, almost all of the Bill of Rights has by now been included among those fundamental principles.

The due-process clause has been interpreted and applied by the U.S. Supreme Court in a number of landmark cases. Two of the most significant of these decisions were the Slaughterhouse Cases (1873) and *Adair* v. *United States* (1908).

The Slaughterhouse Cases

The Slaughterhouse Cases were a set of legal cases that resulted in 1873 in a landmark U.S. Supreme Court decision limiting the protection of the privileges and immunities clause of the Fourteenth Amendment to the U.S. Constitution.

In 1869 the Louisiana state legislature granted a monopoly of the New Orleans slaughtering business to a single corporation. Other slaughterhouses brought suit, contending that the monopoly abridged their privileges and immunities as U.S. citizens and deprived them of property without due process of law. When the suit reached the Supreme Court in 1873, it presented the first test of the Fourteenth Amendment, ratified in 1868.

By a 5–4 majority, the Court ruled against the other slaughterhouses. Associate Justice Samuel F. Miller, for the majority, declared that the Fourteenth Amendment had "one pervading purpose": protection of the newly emancipated African Americans. The amendment did not, however, shift control over all civil rights from the states to the federal government. States still retained legal jurisdiction over their citizens, and federal protection of civil rights did not extend to the property rights of businessmen.

Dissenting justices held that the Fourteenth Amendment protected all U.S. citizens from state violations of privileges and immunities and that state impairment of property rights was a violation of due process.

The Slaughterhouse Cases represented a temporary reversal in the trend toward centralization of power in the federal government. More importantly, in limiting the protection of the privileges and immunities clause, the court unwittingly weakened the power of the Fourteenth Amendment to protect the civil rights of African Americans.

Adair v. United States

In its *Adair* v. *United States* ruling, issued on Jan. 27, 1908, the U.S. Supreme Court upheld so-called "yellow dog" contracts forbidding workers from joining labour unions. William Adair of the Louisville and Nashville Railroad fired O.B. Coppage for belonging to a labour union, an action in direct violation of the Erdman Act of 1898, which prohibited railroads engaged in interstate commerce from requiring workers to refrain from union membership as a condition of employment. In 1908 the Supreme Court decided in a 6–2 vote that the Erdman Act was unconstitutional. The court held that the act represented an unreasonable violation of the due process clause of the Fifth Amendment, which guaranteed freedom of contract and property rights; moreover, according to the majority, Congress's constitutional authority over interstate commerce did not extend to matters of union membership.

FREEDOM OF SPEECH AND FREEDOM OF THE PRESS

Freedom of speech is the right to express information, ideas, and opinions free of government restrictions based on content. It encompasses freedom of the press, which is the right of individuals, companies, or other organizations to publish, broadcast, or otherwise disseminate information without prior (prepublication) restraint or censorship or postpublication sanction by the government. In the United States the freedoms of speech and of the press are guaranteed by the First Amendment to the Constitution:

> *Congress shall make no law respecting an establishment of religion, or prohibiting the free exercise thereof; or abridging the freedom of speech, or of the press; or the right of the people peaceably to assemble, and to petition the Government for a redress of grievances.*

These freedoms are not absolute. Since the early 20th century, the Supreme Court has permitted restrictions on speech and the press in cases in which there is a risk or threat to safety or other public interests that is serious and imminent.

Schenck v. United States

Schenck v. *United States* was a legal case in which, on March 3, 1919, the U.S. Supreme Court ruled that the freedom of speech protection afforded in the U.S. Constitution's First Amendment could be restricted if the words spoken or printed represented to society a "clear and present danger."

In June 1917, shortly after U.S. entry into World War I, Congress passed the Espionage Act, which made it illegal during wartime to

> *willfully make or convey false reports or false statements with intent to interfere with the operation or success of the military or naval forces of the United States or to promote the success of its enemies . . . [or] willfully cause or attempt to cause insubordination, disloyalty, mutiny, or refusal of duty, in the military or naval forces of the United States, or shall willfully obstruct the recruiting or enlistment service of the United States, to the injury of the service or of the United States.*

Charles T. Schenck was general secretary of the U.S. Socialist Party, which opposed the implementation of a military draft in the country. The party printed and distributed some 15,000 leaflets that called for men who were drafted to resist military service. Schenck was subsequently arrested for having violated the Espionage Act; he was convicted on three counts and sentenced to 10 years in prison for each count.

Oral arguments at the Supreme Court were heard on Jan. 9, 1919, with Schenck's counsel arguing that the Espionage Act was unconstitutional and that his client was simply exercising his freedom of speech guaranteed by the First Amendment. On March 3 the court issued a unanimous ruling upholding the Espionage Act and Schenck's conviction. Writing for the court, Justice Oliver Wendell Holmes, Jr., argued:

> *The character of every act depends upon the circumstances in which it is done. The most stringent protection of free speech would not protect a man in falsely shouting fire in a theatre and causing a panic. [The] question in every case is whether the words used are used in such circumstances and are of such a nature as to create a clear and present danger that they will bring about the substantive evils that Congress has a right to prevent.*

Throughout the 1920s, however, the court abandoned the clear and present danger rule and instead utilized an earlier-devised "bad [or dangerous] tendency" doctrine, which enabled speech to be limited even more broadly (as seen in, for example, *Gitlow* v. *New York* [1925]).

Gitlow v. *New York*

The Supreme Court's *Gitlow* v. *New York* ruling of June 8, 1925, held that the U.S. Constitution's First Amendment protection of free speech, which states that the federal "Congress shall make no law . . . abridging the freedom of speech," applied also to state governments. The decision was the first in which the Supreme Court held that the Fourteenth Amendment's due-process clause required state and federal governments to be held to the same standards in regulating speech.

The case arose in November 1919 when Benjamin Gitlow, who had served as a local assemblyman, and an associate, Alan Larkin, were arrested by New York City police officers for criminal anarchy, an offense under New

York state law. Gitlow and Larkin were both Communist Party members and publishers of the *Revolutionary Age*, a radical newspaper in which they printed "The Left Wing Manifesto" (modeled on *The Communist Manifesto* by Karl Marx and Friedrich Engels), which advocated the violent overthrow of the U.S. government. Although Gitlow argued at trial that no violent action was precipitated by the article, he was convicted, and the conviction was subsequently upheld by the state appellate court.

Oral arguments before the Supreme Court took place in April and November 1923, and the Supreme Court issued its ruling, written by Justice Edward T. Sanford, in June 1925. The court upheld Gitlow's conviction, but perhaps ironically the ruling expanded free speech protections for individuals, since the court held that the First Amendment was applicable to state governments through the due-process clause of the Fourteenth Amendment. The majority opinion stipulated that the court "assume[s] that freedom of speech and of the press which are protected by the First Amendment from abridgment by Congress are among the fundamental personal rights and 'liberties' protected by the due process clause of the Fourteenth Amendment from impairment by the States." In ruling that the conviction was constitutional, however, the court rejected the "clear and present danger" test established in *Schenck* v. *United States* (1919) and instead used the "bad (or dangerous) tendency" test. The New York state law was constitutional because the state "cannot reasonably be required to defer the adoption of measures for its own peace and safety until the revolutionary utterances lead to actual disturbances of the public peace or imminent and immediate danger of its own destruction; but it may, in the exercise of its judgment, suppress the threatened danger in its incipiency." In an eloquent dissenting opinion, Justices Oliver Wendell

Holmes, Jr., and Louis Brandeis held to the clear and present danger test, arguing that

> *there was no present danger of an attempt to overthrow the government by force on the part of the admittedly small minority who shared the defendant's views . . . . Every idea is an incitement. It offers itself for belief and if believed it is acted on unless some other belief outweighs it or some failure of energy stifles the movement at its birth . . . . If the publication of this document had been laid as an attempt to induce an uprising against government at once and not at some indefinite time in the future it would have presented a different question . . . . But the indictment alleges the publication and nothing more.*

The ruling, which enabled prohibitions on speech that simply advocated potential violence, was eventually dismissed by the Supreme Court in the 1930s and later as the court became more restrictive in the types of speech that government could permissibly suppress.

Dennis v. United States

On June 4, 1951, in *Dennis* v. *United States*, the U.S. Supreme Court upheld the constitutionality of the Smith Act (1940), which made it a criminal offense to advocate the violent overthrow of the government or to organize or be a member of any group or society devoted to such advocacy.

The case originated in 1948 when Eugene Dennis, general secretary of the American Communist Party, along with several other high-ranking communists, was arrested and convicted of having violated the Smith Act. The conviction was upheld by lower courts, despite the fact that no evidence existed that Dennis and his colleagues had encouraged any of their followers to commit specific violent acts, and was appealed to the Supreme Court, which agreed to hear the case.

Against the backdrop of the case was a growing fear in the United States during the Cold War of a communist takeover of the country. Oral arguments were held on Dec. 1, 1950, and on the following June 4 the Supreme Court issued a 6–2 ruling upholding the convictions, in essence finding that it was constitutional to restrict the guarantee of freedom of speech found in the U.S. Constitution's First Amendment when an individual's speech was so grave that it represented a vital threat to the security of the country. The court's plurality opinion was written by Chief Justice Fred M. Vinson, joined by Justices Harold Burton, Sherman Minton, and Stanley Reed, who argued: "Certainly an attempt to overthrow the Government by force, even though doomed from the outset because of inadequate numbers or power of the revolutionists, is a sufficient evil for Congress to prevent." The ruling further maintained that government need not wait to prohibit speech "until the putsch is about to be executed, the plans have been laid and the signal is awaited. If Government is aware that a group aiming at its overthrow is attempting to indoctrinate its members and to commit them to a course whereby they will strike when the leaders feel the circumstances permit, action by the Government is required." Two other justices, Felix Frankfurter and Robert H. Jackson, voted with the majority but wrote special concurrences that deviated somewhat from the ruling's overall logic. Frankfurter, in particular, argued that Congress needed to balance free speech protections against the threat of that speech. The court's opinion ran somewhat contrary to the clear and present danger rule of Justice Oliver Wendell Holmes, Jr., in *Schenck* v. *United*

States in 1919, which required that immediate violence or danger be present for speech to be lawfully limited.

Dissenting from the majority were Justices Hugo L. Black, who had developed a literal interpretation of the Bill of Rights and an absolutist position on First Amendment rights, and William O. Douglas. Black's eloquent opinion both captured the tenor of the times and was a strong defense of freedom of speech:

> *So long as this Court exercises the power of judicial review of legislation, I cannot agree that the First Amendment permits us to sustain laws suppressing freedom of speech and press on the basis of Congress' or our own notions of mere 'reasonableness.' Such a doctrine waters down the First Amendment so that it amounts to little more than an admonition to Congress. The Amendment as so construed is not likely to protect any but those 'safe' or orthodox views which rarely need its protection .... Public opinion being what it now is, few will protest the conviction of these Communist petitioners. There is hope, however, that, in calmer times, when present pressures, passions and fears subside, this or some later Court will restore the First Amendment liberties to the high preferred place where they belong in a free society.*

In *Yates* v. *United States* (1957), the court later amended its ruling to make parts of the Smith Act unenforceable, and though the law remained on the books, no prosecutions took place under it thereafter.

The Pentagon Papers and the *Progressive*

One of the most dramatic 20th-century attempts by the government of the United States to exercise prior restraint occurred in connection with the Pentagon Papers, a top secret multivolume history of the U.S. role in Indochina from World War II until May 1968 that was commissioned in 1967 by U.S. Secretary of Defense Robert S. McNamara. The papers were turned over (without authorization) to the *New York Times* by Daniel Ellsberg, a senior research associate at the Massachusetts Institute of Technology's Center for International Studies.

The 47-volume history, consisting of approximately 3,000 pages of narrative and 4,000 pages of appended documents, took 18 months to complete. Ellsberg, who worked on the project, had been an ardent early supporter of the U.S. role in Indochina but, by the project's end, had become seriously opposed to U.S. involvement. He felt compelled to reveal the nature of U.S. participation and leaked major portions of the papers to the press.

On June 13, 1971, the *New York Times* began publishing a series of articles based on the study. After the third daily installment appeared in the *Times*, the U.S. Department of Justice obtained in U.S. District Court a temporary restraining order against further publication of the classified material, contending that further public dissemination of the material would cause "immediate and irreparable harm" to U.S. national-defense interests.

The *Times*—joined by the *Washington Post*, which also was in possession of the documents—fought the order through the courts for the next 15 days, during which time publication of the series was suspended. On June 30, 1971, the U.S. Supreme Court, in a 6–3 decision, freed the newspapers to resume publishing the material. The court held that the government had failed to justify restraint of publication.

The Pentagon Papers revealed that Pres. Harry S. Truman's administration gave military aid to France in its colonial war against the communist-led Viet Minh, thus directly involving the United States in Vietnam; that in

1954 Pres. Dwight D. Eisenhower decided to prevent a communist takeover of South Vietnam and to undermine the new communist regime of North Vietnam; that Pres. John F. Kennedy transformed the policy of "limited-risk gamble" that he had inherited into a policy of "broad commitment"; that Pres. Lyndon B. Johnson intensified covert warfare against North Vietnam and began planning to wage overt war in 1964, a full year before the depth of U.S. involvement was publicly revealed; and that Johnson ordered the bombing of North Vietnam in 1965 despite the judgment of the U.S. intelligence community that it would not cause the North Vietnamese to cease their support of the Viet Cong insurgency in South Vietnam.

The release of the Pentagon Papers stirred nationwide and, indeed, international controversy because it occurred after several years of growing dissent over the legal and moral justification of intensifying U.S. actions in Vietnam. The disclosures and their continued publication despite top-secret classification were embarrassing to the administration of Pres. Richard M. Nixon, who was preparing to seek reelection in 1972. So distressing were these revelations that Nixon authorized unlawful efforts to discredit Ellsberg, efforts that came to light during the investigation of the Watergate scandal. The papers were subsequently published in book form as *The Pentagon Papers* (1971).

Another attempt at prior restraint occurred in 1979, when the U.S. government sued the *Progressive* magazine (*United States* v. *Progressive, Inc.*) in federal district court to prevent the publication of an article purporting to reveal the operating principles of a thermonuclear bomb. The author and the magazine argued that the article should not be suppressed because it was based on information that was already in the public domain; the government insisted that publication of the article would make it significantly easier for unfriendly governments or terrorist organizations to obtain a nuclear weapon. Although the court issued a preliminary injunction, the government dropped the case on appeal after newspapers in two states published a letter containing approximately the same information. The magazine published the original article two months later.

Texas v. Johnson

Most uses of language, whether written or spoken, are clearly understood to be speech. But what about a symbolic act, such as burning a national flag as an expression of protest? In its controversial *Texas* v. *Johnson* decision, issued on June 21, 1989, the U.S. Supreme Court ruled that the burning of the U.S. flag was a constitutionally protected form of speech under the U.S. Constitution's First Amendment.

The case originated during the Republican National Convention in Dallas in August 1984, when the party had gathered to nominate Pres. Ronald Reagan as its candidate in that year's presidential election. Gregory Lee Johnson, part of a group that had gathered to protest Reagan's policies, doused an American flag with kerosene and lit it on fire in front of the Dallas City Hall. He was arrested for violating Texas's state law that prohibited desecration of the U.S. flag and eventually was convicted; he was fined and sentenced to one year in jail. His conviction subsequently was overturned by the Texas Court of Criminal Appeals (the state's highest appeals court for criminal cases), which argued that symbolic speech was protected by the First Amendment.

The case was accepted for review by the U.S. Supreme Court, and oral arguments were heard in March 1989. In June the Supreme Court released a controversial 5–4 ruling in which it upheld the appeals court decision that desecration of the U.S. flag was constitutionally protected, calling the First Amendment's protection of speech a "bedrock principle" and stating that the government could not prohibit "expression of an idea simply because society finds the idea itself offensive or disagreeable." Justice William J. Brennan, Jr., noted for his liberal jurisprudence, wrote the majority opinion and was joined by fellow liberals Thurgood Marshall and Harry Blackmun, as well as by conservatives Anthony Kennedy and Antonin Scalia.

HABEAS CORPUS

History of Habeas Corpus

Another bedrock principle in jurisprudence—dating back centuries—is that of habeas corpus, meaning "you should have the body." Habeas corpus is an ancient common-law writ, or written order, issued by a court or a judge that directs someone who holds another person in his custody to produce the body of that person before the court for some specified purpose. Although there have been and are many varieties of the writ, the most important is that used to correct violations of personal liberty by directing judicial inquiry into the legality of a detention. The habeas corpus remedy is recognized in the

Henry VII, painting by an unknown artist, 1505, in the National Portrait Gallery, London. Courtesy of the National Portrait Gallery, London

countries of the common-law system but is generally not found in civil-law countries, although some of the latter have adopted comparable procedures.

The origins of the writ cannot be stated with certainty. Before the Magna Carta (1215), a variety of writs performed some of the functions of habeas corpus. During the Middle Ages habeas corpus was employed to bring cases from inferior tribunals into the king's courts. The modern history of the writ as a device for the protection of personal liberty against official authority may be said to date from the reign of Henry VII (1485–1509), when efforts were made to employ it on behalf of persons imprisoned by the Privy Council. By the reign of Charles I, in the 17th century, the writ was fully established as the appropriate process for checking the illegal imprisonment of people by inferior courts or public officials.

Many of the procedures that made for effective assertion of these rights were provided by the Habeas Corpus Act of 1679, which authorized judges to issue the writ when courts were on vacation and provided severe penalties for any judge who refused to comply with it. Its use was expanded during the 19th century to cover those held under private authority. In 1960 legislation was enacted limiting the instances in which habeas corpus could be denied and establishing new lines of appeal.

In the British colonies in North America, by the time of the American Revolution, the rights to habeas corpus were popularly regarded as among the basic protections of individual liberty. The U.S. Constitution guarantees that the privilege "shall not be suspended, unless when in cases of rebellion or invasion the public safety may require it." In England such suspension had occurred during the wars with France at the time of the French Revolution. In the United States, Pres. Abraham Lincoln suspended the writ by executive proclamation at the outbreak of the Civil War in 1861. The presidential act was challenged by Chief Justice Roger Taney who, in the case of *Ex Parte Merryman*, vigorously contended that the power of suspension resided only in Congress. Lincoln ignored the order of the court, but the weight of modern opinion appears to support the view that suspension of the writ requires the consent of Congress.

The current uses of habeas corpus in the United States are quite varied. The Supreme Court's liberal interpretation of the constitutional rights of those accused of crime led in the mid-20th century to the filing of many habeas corpus petitions by prisoners, challenging their convictions. A writ frequently is requested on behalf of one in police custody for the purpose of requiring the police to either charge the arrested person with an offense or release him. Habeas corpus proceedings may be employed to obtain release of the accused prior to trial on the ground that the bail set is excessive. On occasion habeas corpus relief has been granted a prisoner who is unlawfully detained after expiration of his sentence. In cases of one arrested on a warrant of extradition, a proceeding in habeas corpus may be instituted to challenge the validity of the warrant.

The writ may also be employed in a wide variety of situations not involving criminal proceedings. Thus competing claims to the custody of a minor may be adjudicated in habeas corpus. One confined to a mental hospital may in some jurisdictions bring about his release by showing at a habeas corpus hearing that he has recovered his sanity.

Ex Parte Merryman

Ex Parte Merryman was a legal case at the start of the American Civil War in 1861 in which the president's power to suspend the writ of habeas corpus during a national emergency was contested.

On May 25, 1861, a secessionist named John Merryman was imprisoned by military order at Fort McHenry, Baltimore, Md., for his alleged pro-Confederate activities. Supreme Court Chief Justice Roger B. Taney, sitting as a federal circuit court judge, issued a writ of habeas corpus on the grounds that Merryman was illegally detained. General George Cadwalader, in command of Fort McHenry, refused to obey the writ, however, on the basis that Pres. Abraham Lincoln had suspended habeas corpus.

Taney cited Cadwalader for contempt of court and then wrote an opinion about Article I, Section 9, of the Constitution, which allows suspension of habeas corpus "when in cases of rebellion or invasion the public safety may require it." Taney argued that only Congress—not the president—had the power of suspension.

Pres. Lincoln justified his action in a message to Congress in July 1861. More importantly, he ignored Taney's opinion and adhered to the suspension of habeas corpus throughout the Civil War. Merryman, however, was later released. The constitutional question of who has the right to suspend habeas corpus, Congress or the president, has never been officially resolved.

Korematsu v. United States

On Dec. 18, 1944, in *Korematsu* v. *United States*, the U.S. Supreme Court upheld the conviction of Fred Korematsu—a son of Japanese immigrants who was born in Oakland, Calif.—for having violated an exclusion order requiring him to submit to forced relocation during World War II.

On Feb. 19, 1942, two months after the Pearl Harbor attack by Japan's military against the United States and

Sign marking the entrance to the Manzanar War Relocation Center near Lone Pine, Calif.; photograph by Ansel Adams, 1943. Library of Congress, Washington D.C. (neg. no. LC-DIG-ppprs-00226 DLC)

U.S. entry into World War II, Pres. Franklin D. Roosevelt issued Executive Order 9066, which enabled his secretary of war and military commanders "to prescribe military areas in such places and of such extent as he or the appropriate Military Commander may determine, from which any or all persons may be excluded." Although the order mentioned no group in particular, it subsequently was applied to most of the Japanese American population on the West Coast. Soon thereafter, the Nisei (U.S.-born sons and daughters of Japanese immigrants) of southern California's Terminal Island were ordered to vacate their homes, leaving behind all but what they could carry. On March 18 Roosevelt signed another executive order, creating the War Relocation Authority, a civilian agency charged with speeding the process of relocating Japanese

Americans. A few days later, the first wave of "evacuees" arrived at Manzanar War Relocation Center, a collection of tar-paper barracks in the California desert, and most spent the next three years there.

On May 3, Exclusion Order Number 34 was issued, under which 23-year-old Fred Korematsu and his family were to be relocated. Although his family followed the order, Fred failed to submit to relocation. He was arrested on May 30 and eventually was taken to Tanforan Relocation Center in San Bruno, south of San Francisco. He was convicted of having violated military order and received a sentence of five years' probation. He and his family were subsequently relocated to Topaz Internment Camp in Utah.

Korematsu appealed his conviction to the U.S. Court of Appeals, which upheld the conviction and the exclusion order. The Supreme Court agreed to hear his appeal, and oral arguments were held on Oct. 11, 1944. In a 6–3 ruling issued on December 18, the court upheld Korematsu's conviction. Writing for the majority, Justice Hugo L. Black argued:

> *Compulsory exclusion of large groups of citizens from their homes, except under circumstances of direst emergency and peril, is inconsistent with our basic governmental institutions. But when, under conditions of modern warfare, our shores are threatened by hostile forces, the power to protect must be commensurate with the threatened danger.*

Dissenting from the majority were Justices Owen Roberts, Frank Murphy, and Robert H. Jackson. Jackson's dissent is particularly critical:

> *Korematsu was born on our soil, of parents born in Japan. The Constitution makes him a citizen of the United States by*

nativity, and a citizen of California by residence. No claim is made that he is not loyal to this country. There is no suggestion that, apart from the matter involved here, he is not law-abiding and well disposed. Korematsu, however, has been convicted of an act not commonly a crime. It consists merely of being present in the state whereof he is a citizen, near the place where he was born, and where all his life he has lived.

IN FOCUS: NISEI

Nisei, a Japanese term meaning "second-born," refers to second-generation Japanese people in the United States. During World War II all persons of Japanese ancestry on the U.S. West Coast were forcibly evacuated from their homes and relocated in inland detention centres as a result of mass hysteria following the Japanese attack on Pearl Harbor (Dec. 7, 1941). The U.S. government claimed that it was forced by public hysteria, agitation by the press and radio, and military pressure to establish the War Relocation Authority by executive order (March 18, 1942); this agency administered the mass evacuation.

Under the jurisdiction of the Western Defense Command, during the spring and summer of 1942 110,000 Japanese Americans (including a number who were still aliens) were placed in 10 war relocation centres located in isolated areas from the Sierra Nevada to the Mississippi River. The sparsely furnished military barracks in these camps afforded meagre "work opportunities" for adults and a minimal education for children. By the time the evacuation was complete, U.S. forces were largely in command of the Pacific and all danger of a possible Japanese invasion had passed. After individual screening at the centres to prove their loyalty, 17,600 Nisei were accepted for service in the U.S. armed forces; many of their units were later cited for bravery.

Demands for redress for the losses and injury suffered by the evacuees during the war were met in 1988 when the U.S. government apologized for the internments and passed legislation providing partial monetary payments to the approximately 60,000 surviving Japanese Americans who had been interned.

On the same day as the *Korematsu* decision, in *Ex Parte Endo*, the court sidestepped the constitutionality of internment as a policy, but it forbade the government to detain a U.S. citizen whose loyalty was recognized by the U.S. government.

Rasul v. Bush

The habeas corpus rights of foreign nationals have been debated in relation to prisoners of the United States held at the Guantánamo Bay detention camp on the U.S. naval base at Guantánamo Bay, Cuba. On June 28, 2004, in *Rasul* v. *Bush*, the U.S. Supreme Court ruled that U.S. courts have jurisdiction to hear habeas corpus petitions filed on behalf of foreign nationals imprisoned at Guantánamo because the base, which the United States has held under lease from Cuba since 1899, is effectively within U.S. territory. The implication of the decision was that hundreds of foreign nationals held at the camp had a legal right to challenge their imprisonment.

The case originally concerned four British and Australian citizens, Shafiq Rasul, Asif Iqbal, Mamdouh Habib, and David Hicks, who had been seized in Pakistan and Afghanistan in 2001–02 and eventually turned over to U.S. authorities. The four men were transferred to the Guantánamo Bay detention camp, where they were held without charge, trial, or access to counsel. In 2002, Rasul, Iqbal, and Hicks challenged their detentions in U.S. district court, arguing that they had not engaged in combat against the United States or in any terrorist acts and that their detention amounted to a violation of the due-process clause of the Fifth Amendment. Habib filed a similar suit three months later. Hearing the first case, *Rasul* v. *Bush*, together with a similar case involving 12 Kuwaiti citizens, *al Odah* v. *Bush*, the district court dismissed the challenges, holding on the basis of *Johnson* v. *Eisentrager* (1950) that foreign nationals imprisoned abroad may not file habeas corpus petitions in U.S. courts because the jurisdictions of such courts are limited to territory within the United States. The court later dismissed *Habib* v. *Bush* on the same grounds. After these decisions were affirmed by a court of appeals, the Supreme Court granted a writ of certiorari to hear the consolidated cases as *Rasul* v. *Bush*, and oral arguments were heard on April 20, 2004. (While the case was pending, the petitioners Shafiq Rasul and Asif Iqbal were released from detention at Guantánamo and set free in the United Kingdom upon their arrival there.) In a 6–3 ruling, issued on June 28, the court overturned the lower courts' decisions. Writing for the majority, Justice John Paul Stevens held that, although Cuba retains "ultimate sovereignty," the "plenary and exclusive" jurisdiction exercised by the United States over the territory of the Guantánamo Bay naval base was sufficient to guarantee habeas corpus rights to foreign nationals held there.

Boumediene v. Bush

In *Boumediene* v. *Bush*, issued on June 12, 2008, the U.S. Supreme Court held that the Military Commissions Act (MCA) of 2006, which barred foreign nationals held by the United States as "enemy combatants" from challenging their detentions in U.S. federal courts, was an unconstitutional suspension of the writ of habeas corpus guaranteed in the U.S. Constitution.

In 2002 six Algerians were arrested in Bosnia and Herzegovina on suspicion of plotting to attack the U.S. embassy in Sarajevo; designated enemy combatants, they were imprisoned at the Guantánamo Bay detention camp on the U.S. naval base at Guantánamo Bay, Cuba. One of the detainees, Lakhdar Boumediene, petitioned in federal district court for a writ of habeas corpus, which was denied on the grounds that the camp was outside U.S. territory and therefore not within the court's jurisdiction. In 2004, however, the Supreme Court held in *Rasul* v. *Bush* that the "plenary and exclusive" jurisdiction of the United States over the Guantánamo Bay naval base entitled foreign nationals held there to habeas corpus privileges. Foreseeing a rash of habeas corpus petitions by hundreds of foreign detainees in the camp, Congress passed the MCA, which stripped the federal courts of jurisdiction to hear habeas corpus petitions on behalf of foreign detainees who had been designated enemy combatants according to procedures established in the Detainee Treatment Act (DTA) of 2005. On the basis of the MCA, the United States Court of Appeals for the District of Columbia Circuit denied Boumediene's second appeal. The Supreme Court granted a writ of certiorari, and oral arguments were heard on Dec. 5, 2007.

The main issue to be decided was whether the MCA violated the Suspension Clause of Article I of the Constitution, which states: "The Privilege of the Writ of Habeas Corpus shall not be suspended, unless when in Cases of Rebellion or Invasion the public Safety may require it." In a 5–4 ruling issued on June 12, 2008, the court held that the MCA did violate the Suspension Clause. Writing for the majority, Justice Anthony M. Kennedy argued that "because the DTA's procedures for reviewing detainees' status are not an adequate and effective substitute for the habeas writ, [the] MCA . . . operates as an unconstitutional suspension of the writ." Detainees "are not barred from seeking the writ or invoking the Suspension Clause's protections because they have been designated as enemy combatants or because of their presence at Guantánamo." In his separate dissenting opinion, Justice Antonin Scalia memorably warned that the court's decision "will almost certainly cause more Americans to be killed."

OBSCENITY

The Legal Concept of Obscenity

Obscenity is a legal concept used to characterize certain (particularly sexual) material as offensive to the public sense of decency. A wholly satisfactory definition of obscenity is elusive, however, largely because what is considered obscene is often, like beauty, in the eye of the beholder. Although the term originally referred to things considered repulsive, it has since acquired a more specifically sexual meaning.

Legal restrictions on the content of literature and works of visual art have existed since ancient times. Traditionally, however, governments were much more concerned with sedition, heresy, and blasphemy, and it was not until relatively modern times that sexuality became a major preoccupation of political and religious authorities. One of the first systematic efforts to regulate literature was undertaken by the Roman Catholic Church, which banned heretical works as early as the 4th century. By the Middle Ages the list of banned works had grown dramatically. In 1542 Pope Paul III established the Sacred Congregation of the Roman Inquisition—the precursor of the modern Congregation for the Doctrine of the Faith—one of whose responsibilities was the suppression of heretical and immoral books. In 1559 Pope Paul IV published the *Index Auctorum et Librorum Prohibitorum*, a comprehensive list of forbidden books that went through numerous editions before it was abolished in 1966. Immoral works also were suppressed in Protestant countries such as England, where, prior to the 18th century, restrictions were applied almost exclusively to antireligious or seditious acts or publications, rather than to obscene material in the modern sense.

Modern obscenity law emerged as a direct response to social and technological changes—particularly the development of the printing press in the 15th century—that permitted the wide and easy distribution of what was then considered sexually explicit material. By the 17th century such books and prints had become widely available throughout Europe; governments and church authorities responded by arresting and prosecuting publishers and distributors. A similar sequence of events occurred in Japan, where the development of colour woodblock printing ended up soon creating a sizable industry in erotic pictures. In 1722 the Japanese government introduced the first of several edicts against unlicensed materials, whether erotic or political.

In the early 18th century the temporal courts of England failed to pass judgment on defendants charged with obscenity because there was no law against the publication of such material. The offense of obscene libel subsequently developed to enable the prosecution of people of "wicked and depraved mind and disposition" for publishing materials that corrupted the morals of society by creating "lustful desires." In the 1720s bookseller Edmund Curll became the first person to be convicted on a charge of obscenity in England in the common-law (as opposed to the ecclesiastical) courts, for his publication of a new edition of *Venus in the Cloister; or, The Nun in Her Smock*, a mildly pornographic work that had been written several decades earlier; his sentence, a fine and one hour in the pillory, was delayed because no punishment was then specified in the law. Thereafter obscenity was recognized as an indictable misdemeanour under common law. (Because the charge of obscene libel applied only to publications, obscene acts were prosecuted on the charges of conspiracy to corrupt public morals and conspiracy to outrage public decency.)

Not surprisingly, it was often difficult to draw a sharp distinction between the suppression of published materials for moral reasons and for reasons of political control or repression. Thus, the 18th-century English laws that regulated indecent or suggestive materials were also used to suppress criticism of government ministers and other favoured political figures. In the 1760s the journalist and politician John Wilkes, a leading government critic, was charged with seditious libel for his periodical *North Briton* and with obscene libel for his poem "An Essay on Woman," a parody of Alexander Pope's "An Essay on Man." Prosecutions for obscenity in other European countries also betrayed a merging of moral and political concerns. Perhaps the most celebrated obscenity trial in 19th-century France was that of Gustave Flaubert, who was charged with "outrage to public morals and religion" for his novel *Madame Bovary* (1857). Although the book was indeed sexually frank by the standards of the day, the prosecution, which was unsuccessful, was motivated primarily by the government's desire to close down *Revue de Paris*, the magazine in which the work first appeared.

By the mid-19th century the spread of Victorian notions of morality resulted in harsher legislation against the publication and distribution of sexually explicit material. In Great Britain such material was prohibited on purely sexual grounds for the first time by the Obscene

Publications Act of 1857. The legislation, which failed to define obscenity, faced strong opposition but was passed after the lord chief justice guaranteed that it would be used to prosecute individuals for works "written for the single purpose of corrupting the morals of youth and of a nature calculated to shock the common feelings of decency." A legal definition of obscenity was subsequently established in Britain in *Regina* v. *Hicklin* (1868), in which the court held that obscene material is marked by a tendency "to deprave and corrupt those whose minds are open to such immoral influences and into whose hands a publication of this sort may fall." It was understood that this test could be applied to isolated passages of a work, and the ruling made it possible to label a work obscene not on the basis of the intended readership but on how it might influence anyone in society (e.g., women and children). This perspective later formed the basis of antiobscenity laws in legal systems influenced by British law, particularly in countries that were at one time part of the British Empire.

Beginning in the 1820s, state governments in the United States began passing obscenity laws, and in 1842 the federal government enacted legislation that allowed the seizure of obscene pictures. The most comprehensive federal legislation of the era was the Comstock Act (1873)—named for its chief proponent, Anthony Comstock—which provided for the fine and imprisonment of any person mailing or receiving "obscene," "lewd," or "lascivious" publications. The act became notorious as the basis for the widespread suppression not merely of pornographic books and pictures but also of publications containing legitimate medical information about contraception and abortion, as well as contraceptive devices themselves.

The variability of legal definitions of obscenity is well illustrated by court cases in the United States. Until the middle of the 20th century, the standard definition used by U.S. courts was the one articulated in the British *Hicklin* case. On this basis several novels, including Theodore Dreiser's *An American Tragedy* (1925) and D.H. Lawrence's *Lady Chatterley's Lover* (published privately in 1928), were banned. In 1934 a New York circuit court of appeals abandoned the *Hicklin* standard in legalizing the publication of James Joyce's novel *Ulysses*, holding that the proper standard for judging obscenity was not the content of isolated passages but rather "whether a publication taken as a whole has a libidinous effect." Two decades later, in *Roth* v. *United States* (1957), the U.S. Supreme Court held that the standard of obscenity should be "whether, to the average person, applying contemporary community standards, the dominant theme of the material taken as a whole appeals to prurient interest." In subsequent years the court struggled to develop a more adequate definition. The difficulty of the task was reflected in Associate Supreme Court Justice Potter Stewart's concurring opinion in *Jacobellis* v. *Ohio* (1964), which dealt with the alleged obscenity of a motion picture: he wrote that, though he could not define obscenity, "I know it when I see it." In a 1966 ruling on John Cleland's novel *Fanny Hill* (1748–49), the court declared that, in order to be pornographic, a work must be "utterly without redeeming social value."

In the 1970s the Supreme Court began to move in a more conservative direction. In *Miller* v. *California* (1973), it devised a three-part test to determine whether a work was obscene: (1) "the average person, applying contemporary community standards," would judge that the work appeals primarily to prurient interests; (2) "the work depicts or describes, in a patently offensive way, sexual

PRIMARY SOURCE: MILLER V. CALIFORNIA (EXCERPTS)

Mr. Chief Justice Burger delivered the opinion of the Court. ...

This case involves the application of a State's criminal obscenity statute to a situation in which sexually explicit materials have been thrust by aggressive sales action upon unwilling recipients who had in no way indicated any desire to receive such materials. This Court has recognized that the States have a legitimate interest in prohibiting dissemination or exhibition of obscene material when the mode of dissemination carries with it a significant danger of offending the sensibilities of unwilling recipients or of exposure to juveniles. ...

Apart from the initial formulation in the *Roth* case, no majority of the Court has at any given time been able to agree on a standard to determine what constitutes obscene, pornographic material subject to regulation under the States' police power. ...

This much has been categorically settled by the Court, that obscene material is unprotected by the First Amendment. ...We acknowledge, however, the inherent dangers of undertaking to regulate any form of expression. State statutes designed to regulate obscene materials must be carefully limited. As a result, we now confine the permissible scope of such regulation to works which depict or describe sexual conduct. That conduct must be specifically defined by the applicable state law, as written or authoritatively construed. A state offense must also be limited to works which, taken as a whole, appeal to the prurient interest in sex, which portray sexual conduct in a patently offensive way, and which, taken as a whole, do not have serious literary, artistic, political, or scientific value. ...

Under a national Constitution, fundamental First Amendment limitations on the powers of the States do not vary from community to community, but this does not mean that there are, or should or can be, fixed, uniform national standards of precisely what appeals to the "prurient interest" or is "patently offensive." These are essentially questions of fact, and our nation is simply too big and too diverse for this Court to reasonably expect that such standards could be articulated for all 50 States in a single formulation, even assuming the prerequisite consensus exists. ...

We conclude that neither the State's alleged failure to offer evidence of "national standards," nor the trial court's charge that the jury consider state community standards, were constitutional errors. Nothing in the First Amendment requires that a jury must consider hypothetical and unascertainable "national standards" when attempting to determine whether certain materials are obscene as a matter of fact. ...

In sum we (a) reaffirm the *Roth* holding that obscene material is not protected by the First Amendment, (b) hold that such material can be regulated by the States, subject to the specific safeguards enunciated above, without a showing that the material is "utterly without redeeming social value," and (c) hold that obscenity is to be determined by applying "contemporary community standards," ... not "national standards." The judgment of the Appellate Department of the Superior Court, Orange County, California, is vacated and the case remanded to that court for further proceedings not inconsistent with the First Amendment standards established by this opinion.

conduct specifically defined by the applicable state law"; and (3) the work "lacks serious literary, artistic, political, or scientific value." Although the *Miller* decision expanded the legal basis for suppressing many sexually explicit books and motion pictures, the public's increasingly permissive attitude toward issues related to sex and marriage made such prosecutions difficult to pursue in the late 20th and early 21st century.

Reflecting this shift in sexual morality, obscenity laws in Australia, Canada, the United States, and western European countries were gradually relaxed beginning in the 1960s. Similar developments occurred in countries in eastern Europe following the collapse of communism there in 1989. For example, in the Czech Republic and Poland in the 1990s, sizable pornography industries developed, and they faced little legal intervention or censorship from the government. Generally, the new legal environment in North America and Europe favoured greater sexual permissiveness and the right to individual privacy. Perhaps the most significant development in this regard was the decriminalization of homosexuality in many countries and the removal of proscriptions against depictions and discussions of homosexual relationships in books, motion pictures, and other media. (Countries in Africa and Asia generally were slower to liberalize such laws, and former British colonies, such as India, often maintained the older British obscenity laws and definitions.)

An important exception to the general trend toward greater permissiveness were laws against the sexually explicit depiction of minors (the definition of which varies from country to country). Indeed, such restrictions were strengthened, especially in the English-speaking world; in the United Kingdom, for example, the Protection of Children Act (1978), which was designed to safeguard children from sexual exploitation, effectively outlawed child pornography. Beginning in the late 1970s, a series of increasingly strict laws in the United States criminalized the possession of photographs of nude children or of children in sexually suggestive poses, though similar pictures of adults would have been deemed merely indecent rather than obscene. In *New York* v. *Ferber* (1982), the Supreme Court upheld the use of strict standards of obscenity in cases involving children, maintaining that the government's interest in protecting children was "compelling" and "surpassing." In *Osborne* v. *Ohio* (1990), the court upheld a law that criminalized the private possession of a photograph of a nude adolescent.

Throughout the 1980s, feminist groups campaigned against pornography not because it offended traditional sexual morality but because, in their view, it degraded women, violated their human rights, and encouraged sex crimes. Feminist arguments had some influence on obscenity laws in certain countries, notably Canada, which in the 1980s clamped down on pornography (in particular, those materials imported by businesses catering to homosexuals). The implementation of such laws pitted feminist reformers against those supporting a more libertarian approach. The feminist approach prompted some U.S. cities to pass local ordinances against pornography. However, many of these regulations were struck down by U.S. federal courts in the 1990s.

Although most countries suppress obscene material through the criminal law, many also attempt to control it through administrative or regulatory agencies such as customs, the postal service, and national or local boards for the licensing of motion pictures or stage performances. In some countries, notably those that grant a privileged position to Islamic concepts of law (e.g., Saudi Arabia and Iran), special religious agencies play a powerful role in defining and suppressing obscenity.

In the late 20th and early 21st century, differences between countries regarding legal definitions and cultural conceptions of obscenity became increasingly important with the development of the Internet, which enabled anyone with a computer to view materials—including texts, images, and motion pictures—originating from virtually anywhere in the world. The ease with which sexually explicit material could be viewed over the Internet complicated the regulation of child pornography in many jurisdictions, in particular because of differences between countries regarding the legal definition of childhood, the legal age of sexual consent, and tolerance of suggestive or indecent images of children. Various solutions were attempted, particularly in the United States, to limit access to what were considered obscene Internet sites (e.g., by requiring that libraries deny access to Web sites of a sexual nature). However, the courts in the United States showed little sympathy toward such efforts. Particularly problematic was that material considered obscene by some may be considered to have social merit by others (e.g., information about breast-cancer prevention or sex education). Countries that had some success in reducing access to Internet pornography (e.g., China and Saudi Arabia) adopted stringent restrictions on most Internet access. Despite these problems, there were moves in Western countries to adopt consistent policies toward child pornography, often along the lines of the relatively strict laws of the United States.

Ashcroft v. Free Speech Coalition

On April 16, 2002, in *Ashcroft* v. *Free Speech Coalition*, the U.S. Supreme Court upheld a lower court's decision that provisions of the Child Pornography Prevention Act (CPPA) of 1996 were vague and overly broad and thus violated the free-speech protection contained in the First Amendment to the U.S. Constitution. The act specifically proscribed computer-generated or -altered depictions of minors engaging in explicit sexual conduct (so-called "virtual" child pornography) and images of explicit sexual conduct by adults who resemble minors. The court ruled that the law's expanded definition of child pornography as including any image that "appears to be" of a minor engaging in sexually explicit conduct or that is "presented . . . in such a manner that conveys the impression" that it is of a minor engaging in sexually explicit conduct would criminalize images that are not obscene and images that were not produced with any real children.

The CPPA was introduced in the U.S. Congress in response to the development of computer technology that allowed the creation of electronic images that appeared in every way to be photographs of real subjects but in fact were entirely artificial. Other technology enabled genuine photographs to be digitally altered so as to introduce fictional elements that were virtually undetectable. The sponsors of the legislation argued that the existing legal definition of child pornography as images of minors engaged in explicit sexual conduct needed to be broadened to include computer-generated or -altered images that only appeared to depict such activity. They reasoned that such images could be used as easily as real images by pedophiles to seduce children into sexual conduct, that they were just as effective as real images in whetting the pedophile's desire to exploit children sexually, and that their exact similarity to real images would make it difficult to identify and prosecute those who possessed or distributed child pornography involving real children. The CCPA accordingly defined child pornography as "any visual depiction, including any photograph, film, video, picture, or computer or computer-generated image or picture...of sexually explicit conduct," in which

> *(A) the production of such visual depiction involves the use of a minor engaging in sexually explicit conduct; (B) such visual depiction is, or appears to be, of a minor engaging in sexually explicit conduct; (C) such visual depiction has been created, adapted, or modified to appear that an identifiable minor is engaging in sexually explicit conduct; or (D) such visual depiction is advertised, promoted, presented, described, or distributed in such a manner that conveys the impression that the material is or contains a visual depiction of a minor engaging in sexually explicit conduct.*

The Free Speech Coalition, a trade association of the adult entertainment industry, filed suit in federal district court, which found for the government. Its decision was

PRIMARY SOURCE: THE CHILD PORNOGRAPHY PREVENTION ACT, SECTION 121, SUBSECTION 1 (EXCERPTS)

Subsection 1. Findings.
Congress finds that—

(1) the use of children in the production of sexually explicit material, including photographs, films, videos, computer images, and other visual depictions, is a form of sexual abuse which can result in physical or psychological harm, or both, to the children involved;

(2) where children are used in its production, child pornography permanently records the victim's abuse, and its continued existence causes the child victims of sexual abuse continuing harm by haunting those children in future years;

(3) child pornography is often used as part of a method of seducing other children into sexual activity; ...

(4) child pornography is often used by pedophiles and child sexual abusers to stimulate and whet their own sexual appetites, and as a model for sexual acting out with children; ...

(5) new photographic and computer imagining technologies make it possible to produce by electronic, mechanical, or other means, visual depictions of what appear to be children engaging in sexually explicit conduct that are virtually indistinguishable to the unsuspecting viewer from unretouched photographic images of actual children engaging in sexually explicit conduct; ...

(8) the effect of visual depictions of child sexual activity on a child molester or pedophile using that material to stimulate or whet his own sexual appetites, or on a child where the material is being used as a means of seducing or breaking down the child's inhibitions to sexual abuse or exploitation, is the same whether the child pornography consists of photographic depictions of actual children or visual depictions produced wholly or in part by electronic, mechanical, or other means, including by computer, which are virtually indistinguishable to the unsuspecting viewer from photographic images of actual children;

(9) the danger to children who are seduced and molested with the aid of child sex pictures is just as great when the child pornographer or child molester uses visual depictions of child sexual activity produced wholly or in part by electronic, mechanical, or other means, including by computer, as when the material consists of unretouched

photographic images of actual children engaging in sexually explicit conduct; ...

(13) the elimination of child pornography and the protection of children from sexual exploitation provide a compelling governmental interest for prohibiting the production, distribution, possession, sale, or viewing of visual depictions of children engaging in sexually explicit conduct, including both photographic images of actual children engaging in such conduct and depictions produced by computer or other means which are virtually indistinguishable to the unsuspecting viewer from photographic images of actual children engaging in such conduct. ...

later reversed by the Ninth Circuit Court of Appeals. The Supreme Court granted a writ of certiorari, and oral arguments were heard on Oct. 30, 2001. In a 6–3 ruling issued on April 16, 2002, the court upheld the Ninth Circuit's decision. Writing for the majority, Justice Anthony M. Kennedy argued that the CPPA would prohibit speech that is clearly not obscene by the definition established in *Miller* v. *California* (1973)—viz., that a work is obscene if, taken as a whole, it appeals to prurient sexual interests, is patently offensive by community standards, and is devoid of literary, artistic, political, or scientific value. He also rejected the government's analogy with *Ferber* v. *New York*, in which the court found that even speech that was not obscene could be banned in order to protect children from being sexually exploited in its production. Unlike the real child pornography proscribed in *Ferber*, the virtual child pornography banned by the CPPA "records no crime and creates no victims by its production . . . . While the Government asserts that the images can lead to actual instances of child abuse, the causal link is contingent and indirect. The harm does not necessarily follow from the speech, but depends upon some unquantified potential for subsequent criminal acts." Moreover, "the mere tendency of speech to encourage unlawful acts is not a sufficient reason for banning it."

Chief Justice William Rehnquist dissented from the majority and was joined by Justice Antonin Scalia. (Justice Sandra Day O'Connor concurred in part and dissented in part.) Rehnquist argued that the majority had construed the CCPA too broadly and that it was not the intention of Congress that the law should be used to prohibit speech of genuine merit, such as that of a modern film portraying the teenage lovers in *Romeo and Juliet*. "We should be loath to construe a statute as banning film portrayals of Shakespearian tragedies, without some indication—from text or legislative history—that such a result was intended. In fact, Congress explicitly instructed that such a reading of the CPPA would be wholly unwarranted."

PRIVACY AND REPRODUCTIVE RIGHTS

Rights of Privacy

Although the U.S. Constitution does not explicitly protect privacy, the right is commonly regarded as created by certain provisions, particularly the First, Fourth, and Fifth amendments. The Fourth Amendment prohibits unreasonable searches and seizures; the First and Fifth include privacy protections in that they focus not on what the government may do but rather on the individual's freedom to be autonomous.

Rights of privacy are an amalgam of principles in U.S. law, embodied in the federal Constitution or recognized by courts or lawmaking bodies, concerning what Supreme Court Justice Louis Brandeis described in 1890 as "the right to be left alone." The right of privacy is a legal concept in both the law of torts and U.S. constitutional law. The tort concept is of 19th-century origin. Subject to limitations of public policy, it asserts a right of persons to recover damages or obtain injunctive relief for unjustifiable invasions of privacy prompted by motives of gain, curiosity, or malice. In torts law, privacy is a right not to be disturbed emotionally by conduct designed to subject the victim to great tensions by baring his intimate life and affairs to public view or by humiliating and annoying invasions of his solitude. Less broad protections of privacy are afforded public officials and other prominent persons considered to be "public figures," as defined by law.

The rights of privacy were initially interpreted to include only protection against tangible intrusions resulting in measurable injury. After publication of an influential article by Justice Brandeis and Samuel Warren, "The Right to Privacy," in the *Harvard Law Review* in 1890, however, the federal courts began to explore various constitutional principles that today are regarded as constituent elements of a constitutional right to privacy. For example, in 1923 the Supreme Court struck down a Nebraska law prohibiting schools from teaching any language other than English, saying the law interfered with the rights of personal autonomy. In 1965 the Supreme Court held that the federal Constitution included an implied right of privacy. In that case, *Griswold* v. *Connecticut*, the court invalidated a law prohibiting the use of contraceptives, even by married persons. Justice William O. Douglas, writing for the court, stated that there is a "zone of privacy" within a "penumbra" created by fundamental constitutional guarantees, including the First, Fourth, and Fifth amendments. The Supreme Court extended this right to privacy to sexual relationships in 2003, striking down a Texas law criminalizing sodomy.

The "right to be left alone" also has been extended to provide the individual with at least some control over information about himself, including files kept by schools, employers, credit bureaus, and government agencies. Under the U.S. Privacy Act of 1974, individuals are guaranteed access to many government files pertaining to themselves, and the agencies of government that maintain such files are prohibited from disclosing personal information except under court order and certain other limited circumstances. In 2001 the USA PATRIOT Act (formally, the Uniting and Strengthening America by Providing Appropriate Tools Required to Intercept and Obstruct Terrorism Act of 2001) granted federal police agencies the authority to search the business records of individuals it suspected of involvement in terrorism, including their library records. Modern technology, giving rise to electronic eavesdropping, and the practices of industrial espionage have complicated the problem of maintaining a right of privacy in both tort and constitutional law.

Griswold v. State of Connecticut

On June 7, 1965, in *Griswold* v. *State of Connecticut*, the U.S. Supreme Court found in favour of the constitutional right of married persons to use birth control.

The state case was originally ruled in favour of the plaintiff, the state of Connecticut. Estelle Griswold, the executive director of the Planned Parenthood League of Connecticut, and Lee Buxton, a physician and professor at Yale Medical School who served as Medical Director for the League, were convicted as accessories to the crime of providing married couples information about contraception and in some cases writing prescriptions for contraceptive devices for the woman. At the time of their arrests (1961), Connecticut law made it a crime for any person to use a device or drug to prevent conception, and it was also a crime for any person to assist, abet, counsel, cause, or command another to do the same. The defendants were found guilty of such assistance and fined $100 each.

In its judgment the Supreme Court ruled that Connecticut's birth control law was unconstitutional based on rights set down in the Fourth and Fifth amendments that protect an individual's home and private life from interference by the government. Judging marriage to be a sacred and private bond that lies within a zone of privacy guaranteed by several provisions within the constitution, namely the concept of liberty implied in the Bill of Rights, the Court found that the original decision against Griswold and Buxton should be overturned, and that citizens in the state of Connecticut should enjoy the freedom to use birth control within the bonds of marriage.

This particular privacy case has been cited in other important Supreme Court judgments, including *Roe* v. *Wade* and *Planned Parenthood of Southeastern Pennsylvania et al.* v. *Casey, governor of Pennsylvania, et al.*

Abortion

Abortion is the expulsion of a fetus from the uterus before it has reached the stage of viability (in human beings, usually about the 20th week of gestation). An abortion may occur spontaneously, in which case it is also called a miscarriage, or it may be brought on purposefully, in which case it is often called an induced abortion.

Induced abortions may be performed for reasons that fall into four general categories: to preserve the life or physical or mental well-being of the mother; to prevent the completion of a pregnancy that has resulted from rape or incest; to prevent the birth of a child with serious deformity, mental deficiency, or genetic abnormality; or to prevent a birth for social or economic reasons (such as the extreme youth of the pregnant female or the sorely strained resources of the family unit).

Whether and to what extent induced abortions should be permitted, encouraged, or severely repressed is a social issue that has divided theologians, philosophers, and legislators for centuries. Abortion was apparently a common and socially accepted method of family limitation in the Greco-Roman world. Although Christian theologians early and vehemently condemned abortion, the application of severe criminal sanctions to deter its practice became common only in the 19th century. In the 20th century such sanctions were modified in one way or another in various countries; in some countries the unavailability of birth-control devices was a factor in the acceptance of abortion. In the late 20th century China used abortion on a large scale as part of its population-control policy. In the early 21st century some jurisdictions with large Roman Catholic populations decriminalized abortion despite strong opposition from the church, while others increased restrictions on it.

A broad social movement for the relaxation or elimination of restrictions on the performance of abortions resulted in the passing of liberalized legislation in several states in the United States during the 1960s. The U.S. Supreme Court ruled in *Roe* v. *Wade* (1973) that unduly restrictive state regulation of abortion was unconstitutional, in effect legalizing abortion for any reason for women in the first three months of pregnancy. A countermovement for the restoration of strict control over the circumstances under which abortions might be permitted soon sprang up, and the issue became entangled in social and political conflict. In rulings in 1989 and 1992 a more conservative Supreme Court upheld the legality of new state restrictions on abortion, though it proved unwilling to overturn *Roe* v. *Wade* itself. In 2007 the court also upheld a federal ban on a rarely used abortion method known as intact dilation and evacuation.

The public debate of the issue has demonstrated the enormous difficulties experienced by political institutions in grappling with the complex and ambiguous ethical problems raised by the question of abortion. Opponents of abortion, or of abortion for any reason other than to save the life of the mother, argue that there is no rational basis for distinguishing the fetus from a newborn infant; each is totally dependent and potentially a member of society, and each possesses a degree of humanity. Proponents of liberalized regulation of abortion hold that only a woman herself, rather than the state, has the right to manage her pregnancy and that the alternative to legal, medically supervised abortion is illegal and demonstrably dangerous, if not deadly, abortion.

Roe v. Wade

On Jan. 22, 1973, in *Roe* v. *Wade*, the U.S. Supreme Court issued one of its most controversial decisions of the past several decades, holding unduly restrictive state regulation of abortion to be unconstitutional. In a 7–2 vote the Supreme Court upheld the lower court's decision that a Texas statute criminalizing abortion in most instances violated a woman's constitutional right of privacy, which the court found implicit in the liberty guarantee of the due-process clause of the Fourteenth Amendment. The case began in 1970 when Jane Roe (a fictional name used to protect the identity of Norma McCorvey) instituted federal action against Henry Wade, the district attorney of Dallas county, Texas, where Roe resided. The court disagreed with Roe's assertion of an absolute right to terminate pregnancy in any way and at any time and attempted to balance a woman's right of privacy with a state's interest in regulating abortion. The court stated that only a "compelling state interest" justifies regulations limiting "fundamental rights," such as privacy, and that legislators must therefore draw statutes narrowly "to express the legitimate state interests at stake." The court then attempted to balance the state's distinct compelling interests in the health of pregnant women and in the potential life of fetuses. It placed the point after which a state's compelling interest in the pregnant woman's health would allow it to regulate abortion "at approximately the end of the first trimester" of pregnancy. With regard to fetuses, the court located that point at "capability for meaningful life outside the mother's womb," or viability. The court held that the Texas statute was unconstitutional because of its breadth. Repeated challenges since 1973, such as *Planned Parenthood* v. *Casey* (1992), have narrowed the scope of *Roe* v. *Wade* but have yet to overturn it. In *Gonzales* v. *Carhart* (2007), the Supreme Court upheld the federal Partial-Birth Abortion Ban Act (2003), which prohibited a rarely used abortion procedure known as intact dilation and evacuation.

Planned Parenthood of Southeastern Pennsylvania v. Casey

In 1992, in *Planned Parenthood of Southeastern Pennsylvania* v. *Casey*, the U.S. Supreme Court redefined several provisions regarding abortion rights as established in *Roe* v. *Wade*.

In 1988 and 1989 the Commonwealth of Pennsylvania, led by Governor Robert Casey, enacted new abortion statutes that required that a woman seeking an abortion give her informed consent, that a minor seeking an abortion obtain parental consent (the provision included a judicial waiver option), that a married woman notify her husband of her intended abortion, and, finally, that clinics provide certain information to a woman seeking an abortion and wait 24 hours before performing the abortion. Before any of these laws could take effect, Planned Parenthood of Southeastern Pennsylvania brought suit against the governor, protesting the constitutionality of the statutes.

In a 1992 plurality opinion, the U.S. Supreme Court affirmed the "essential holding" (i.e., the basic principle) of *Roe* v. *Wade*, that women have a right to choose abortion prior to fetal viability, but rejected *Roe*'s trimester-based framework for allowing states to curb the availability of abortion in favour of a more flexible medical definition of viability. The decision restated that the source of the privacy right that undergirds women's right to choose abortion derives from the "due-process" clause of the Fourteenth Amendment, placing individual decisions about abortion, family planning, marriage, and education within "a realm of personal liberty which the government may not enter." The judgment also revised the test that courts use to scrutinize laws relating to abortion, moving to an "undue burden" standard: a law is invalid if its "purpose or effect is to place substantial obstacles in the path of a woman seeking an abortion before the fetus attains viability." Ultimately, the court upheld all the provisions of the Pennsylvania statute under attack except for the requirement of spousal notification. Many suits brought since *Planned Parenthood* v. *Casey* have centred on the meaning of "undue burden."

SAME-SEX MARRIAGE

Same-sex marriage is the practice of marriage between two males or two females. Although the institution of marriage between male and female partners has been regulated through law, religion, and custom in most countries of the world, the legal and social responses to same-sex marriage have ranged from celebration on the one hand to criminalization on the other.

Some scholars, most notably the Yale professor and historian John Boswell (1947–94), have argued that same-sex unions were recognized by the Roman Catholic Church in medieval Europe, although others have disputed this claim. Scholars and the general public became increasingly interested in the issue during the late 20th century, a period when attitudes toward homosexuality and laws regulating homosexual behaviour were liberalized, particularly in western Europe and the United States.

The issue of same-sex marriage frequently sparked emotional and political clashes between supporters and opponents. By the early 21st century, several jurisdictions, both at the national and subnational levels, had legalized same-sex marriage; in other jurisdictions, constitutional measures were adopted to prevent same-sex marriages from being sanctioned, or laws were enacted that refused to recognize such marriages performed elsewhere. That the same act was evaluated so differently by various groups indicates its importance as a social issue in the early 21st century; it also demonstrates the extent to which cultural diversity persisted both within and among countries.

Same-Sex Marriage and the Law

Societies have resolved the intertwined issues of sexuality, reproduction, and marriage in myriad ways. Their responses regarding the morality, desirability, and administrative perquisites of same-sex partnerships have been equally diverse. Notably, however, by the beginning of the 21st century most countries opted for one of only three legal resolutions to these intersecting problems: to ignore same-sex partnerships, to criminalize them, or to grant them a status similar or equal to that of heterosexual marriage. Many countries, including the United States, have yet to reach a consensus on these issues.

As noted above, many societies traditionally chose to ignore the issue of same-sex marriage by treating same-sex intimacy as a subject unsuitable for discussion. Many of these jurisdictions, as well as those that actively criminalize same-sex unions, contended that homosexuality and lesbianism are mental disorders and built their public policies on this premise. In treating same-sex desire as a psychiatric illness, these cultures moved same-sex intimacy and marriage from the realm of civil regulations (the domain of contract law) to that of public safety (the domain of criminal law). In such societies, the possibility of arrest or institutionalization further reinforced taboos on same-sex intimacy and discussions thereof, typically driving such activities underground.

In the early 21st century the countries that most seriously penalized same-sex relations tended to be in deeply conservative regions of the world, particularly Islamic theocracies and some parts of Asia and Africa. They often proscribed behaviours that other countries viewed as subject to moral, rather than legal, regulation. The judicial systems of many predominantly Muslim countries, for instance, invoke Islamic law (Sharīʿah) in a wide range of contexts. A variety of sexual or quasi-sexual acts, usually including same-sex intimacy, were criminalized in these countries, and the penalties for these acts could be as severe as execution. However, in a notable show of support for transgender individuals in the late 20th century, Iranian Ayatollah Ruhollah Khomeini issued a legal decree, or *fatwa*, supporting gender reassignment surgery when undertaken by individuals who wished to "fix" their physiology and thus become heterosexual in the eyes of the law.

In contrast, the acceptance of same-sex partnerships was particularly apparent in northern Europe and in countries with cultural ties to that region. In 1989 Denmark became the first country to establish registered partnerships—an attenuated version of marriage—for same-sex couples. Soon thereafter Norway (1993), Sweden (1994), Greenland (1994), Iceland (1996), The Netherlands (1997), and Finland (2001) established similar laws, generally using specific vocabulary (e.g., civil union, civil partnership, domestic partnership, registered partnership) to differentiate same-sex unions from heterosexual marriages. By the early 21st century other European countries with such legislation included Croatia, France, Germany, Great Britain, Hungary, Luxembourg, Portugal, and Switzerland. Interestingly—and perhaps as a reflection of tensions between the marriage-for-procreation and marriage-for-community-good positions discussed above—many European countries initially prevented same-sex couples from adoption and artificial insemination; by 2007, however, most of these restrictions had been removed. Outside Europe, some jurisdictions also adopted some form of same-sex partnership rights; Israel recognized common-law same-sex marriage in the mid-1990s (the Israeli Supreme Court further ruled in 2006 that same-sex marriages performed abroad should be recognized), while same-sex civil unions were legalized in New Zealand in 2004, in the Brazilian state of Rio Grande do Sul also in 2004, and in Mexico City in 2006. In 2007 Uruguay became the first Latin American country to legalize same-sex civil unions; the legislation became effective in 2008.

Some jurisdictions opted to specifically apply the honorific of "marriage" to same-sex as well as heterosexual unions. In 2001 The Netherlands revised its same-sex partnership law and became the first country to replace civil unions with marriages. It was followed in 2003 by Belgium; in the same year, the European Union mandated that all of its members pass laws recognizing the same-sex marriages of fellow EU countries. In 2005 Spain and Canada enacted full marriage legislation; soon afterward South Africa (2006), Norway (2008), and Sweden (2009) followed suit. As countries began to legalize same-sex partnerships, public opinion, particularly in Europe, began to shift in favour of full marriage rights for same-sex unions. For example, by the mid-2000s a Eurobarometer poll (carried out by the European Commission) found that four-fifths of the citizens of The Netherlands felt that same-sex marriage should be legal throughout Europe; in a further seven countries (Sweden, Denmark, Belgium, Luxembourg, Spain, Germany, and the Czech Republic), a majority held a similar view. Nevertheless, in other parts of Europe, particularly central and southern Europe, support for same-sex marriage was quite low, often with less than one-fifth of those polled favouring legalization. In the United States, though a majority opposed same-sex marriage rights, polls found nearly two-fifths of the population supporting legalization by the mid-2000s.

In the United States the question of whether couples of the same sex should be allowed to marry has roiled politics since at least 1993. In that year the Supreme Court of Hawaii heard a case in which the plaintiffs claimed that the state's refusal to issue marriage licenses to same-sex couples abrogated those individuals' rights to equal treatment under the law. The state, in turn, argued that it had a compelling interest in preventing same-sex marriage, as that practice would inherently damage the public good. The court found for the plaintiffs, basing its argument on the law's absence of a clear definition of who might or might not participate in such a partnership. Soon after this finding, Hawaiian legislators added such a definition to the state constitution and thus made moot the issuing of marriage licenses to same-sex partners.

Many Americans felt that the Hawaii court decision represented a serious threat to social stability, and in 1996 the U.S. Congress enacted the Defense of Marriage Act. This legislation declared that same-sex marriages would not be recognized for federal purposes, such as the award of Social Security benefits normally afforded to a surviving spouse, or employment-based benefits for the partners of federal employees. The act also restated existing law by providing that no U.S. state or territory was required to recognize marriages from elsewhere when it had strong policies to the contrary. Within a decade of the federal act's passage, almost all of the states had enacted laws or constitutional amendments declaring variously that marriage was legally defined as a heterosexual institution, that same-sex marriages from other states would not be recognized, or that same-sex marriage was contrary to the public policies of the state.

Nonetheless, some states moved toward the legal recognition of same-sex partnerships. In 1999 the Vermont Supreme Court declared that same-sex couples were entitled under the state constitution to the same legal rights as married heterosexual couples; shortly thereafter the state legislature enacted the Vermont Civil Union Act, a law creating "civil unions," which conferred all the rights and responsibilities of marriage but not the name. In 2003

PRIMARY SOURCE: SUMMARY OF THE VERMONT CIVIL UNION ACT (EXCERPTS)

The purpose of the act is "to respond to the constitutional violation found by the Vermont Supreme Court in *Baker* v. *State*, and to provide eligible same-sex couples the opportunity to 'obtain the same benefits and protections afforded by Vermont law to married opposite-sex couples' as required by Chapter I, Article 7th of the Vermont Constitution." ...

Civil union status is available to two persons of the same sex who are not related to one another. Parties to the civil union must be at least 18 years old and competent to enter a contract. To enter a civil union, a person may not already be a party to another civil union or a marriage.

Parties to a civil union will have all of the same benefits, protections and responsibilities under law, whether they derive from statute, administrative or court rule, policy, common law or any other source of civil law, as are granted to spouses in a marriage.

The family court will have jurisdiction over all proceedings relating to the dissolution of civil unions. The dissolution of civil unions will follow the same procedures, and be subject to the same substantive rights and obligations that are involved in the dissolution of marriage, including any residency requirements. ...

Insurers must make available dependent coverage to parties to a civil union that is equivalent to that provided to married persons. An individual or group health insurance policy which provides coverage for a spouse or family member of the insured shall also provide the equivalent coverage for a party to a civil union.

Employers are not required to provide coverage to parties to a civil union. Insurers will be required to offer equivalent coverage, but the employer then decides whether to purchase the group health insurance for its employees and which employees are eligible for the insurance. ...

"Marriage" is defined as the legally recognized union of one man and one woman in both the marriage chapter and the civil union chapter in the domestic relations title.

California enacted a similar statute, calling the relationships "domestic partnerships."

Also in 2003, the Massachusetts Supreme Court ruled that the denial of marriage licenses to same-sex couples violated the state constitution; the court gave the state six months to comply with its order to remedy the situation. The state soon began to issue marriage licenses for same-sex couples, but these were quickly challenged and their legal status over the long term remained uncertain. Officials in some smaller jurisdictions, notably San Francisco, joined the controversy in early 2004 by issuing marriage licenses in defiance of local prohibitions; these licenses were later found to be invalid. In 2005–07 several other states, including Connecticut, New Jersey, and New Hampshire (the latter effective from 2008), also established same-sex civil unions, while other states (Hawaii, Maine, and Washington) and Washington, D.C., adopted jurisdiction-wide policies that accorded some spousal rights to same-sex couples. In 2008 and 2009, respectively, the supreme courts of Connecticut and Iowa ruled that their state's ban on same-sex marriage was unconstitutional. In 2009 the Vermont legislature, which had approved civil unions for gay couples in 2000, legalized same-sex marriage. Thus Connecticut, Iowa, and Vermont joined Massachusetts as the only U.S. states to allow gay marriage.

Broadly reflecting the community-benefit rhetoric noted above, many American legal scholars and same-sex marriage advocates developed arguments that the equal protection clause of the U.S. Constitution guaranteed the fundamental right to marry. Opposition arguments broadly reflected the procreative position and frequently invoked biblical exegeses or other religious doctrine to support claims that marriage, strictly defined, should be available only to heterosexual couples. Advocates of both perspectives cited various and conflicting sociological studies in defense of their claims. In the early 21st century a majority of the U.S. population opposed same-sex marriage, but many were also open to the creation of legally recognized partnerships for same-sex couples.

The Complexity of the Debate

Part of the complexity of the issue of same-sex marriage is that it really involves two different debates. The first is a normative debate about what relationships to value or even to sanctify. The second is a debate about administration—that is, which relationships ought to have legal consequences.

The normative debate, which contains religious dimensions for many people, concerns what relationships are intrinsically valuable. The key question is one about objective moral reality: are same-sex relationships as such morally equal to heterosexual relationships, or do heterosexual relationships partake of a good that homosexual relationships cannot possibly share?

On this issue, Americans are divided, with different groups adhering to two very different moral visions. According to the anti-same-sex-marriage vision, sex can be morally worthy precisely and only because of its place in procreation. Even the marriages of infertile heterosexual couples take their meaning from the fact that they form a union of the procreative kind. From this perspective the movement for same-sex marriage is a misguided attempt to deny fundamental moral distinctions. According to the other moral vision, sex is valuable, either in itself or because it draws people toward friendship of a singular degree and kind. This bringing together of persons has intrinsic worth, whether or not it leads to childbearing or child rearing. On this account, sexuality is linked to the flourishing of the next generation only to the extent that it is one of a number of factors that can bond adults together into stable familial units in which children are likely to thrive. From this perspective it is the devaluation of same-sex intimacy that is immoral, because it reflects arbitrary and irrational discrimination.

The administrative debate concerns what relationships between persons ought to be given legal recognition. Here the issue is more mundane: how should resources be allocated and unfair disruption of people's lives be prevented? Households, of whatever kind, and relationships of dependency exist, and members of those households have wants and needs if some unprovided-for contingency arises, such as the illness or death of one member. Financial issues, such as inheritance rights and employer benefits for dependents of employees, also come into play.

Because the moral and the administrative questions are distinct, many jurisdictions have opted to grant same-sex couples some or all of the rights of married couples without the honorific of "marriage." Civil unions, however, are also controversial. Many conservatives believe that same-sex relationships are morally wrong and should not be given any recognition at all by the state, while gay rights advocates object that withholding the name of "marriage" implies an inferior status. Finally, gay men and lesbians are not unanimous in support of same-sex marriage. Some gay rights proponents contend that their movement should focus instead on AIDS prevention, HIV and health care, antigay violence, immigration, employment discrimination, and the military's exclusion of gay service members.

Many legal scholars have developed defensible arguments that same-sex marriage should be protected under the federal constitution, under either the guarantee of equal protection of the laws or the fundamental right to marry. It seems unlikely, however, that the U.S. Supreme

Court will adopt these arguments in the near future. In *Lawrence* v. *Texas*, a 2003 decision that struck down laws criminalizing homosexual sex, the Court made clear that it was not about to touch the marriage question. Even if the court is inclined to support same-sex marriage—which is far from clear—it appears to understand that any such decision would almost certainly be overruled by a constitutional amendment.

SELF-INCRIMINATION

The Concept of Self-Incrimination

Supreme Court renderings on the issue of self-incrimination, the giving of evidence that might tend to expose the witness to punishment for crime, have also caused controversy. The term is generally used in relation to the right to refuse to give such evidence. In some continental European countries (Germany, for example, but not France), a person fearing self-incrimination may make his own decision as to whether or not he will testify. In Anglo-American practice, on the other hand, a person other than an accused cannot refuse to testify; he may only cite his privilege against self-incrimination, and the judge decides whether he must testify. If required to testify, he must answer all questions except those he considers to be self-incriminating.

Miranda v. Arizona

In its *Miranda* v. *Arizona* decision of June 13, 1966, the U.S. Supreme Court specified a code of conduct for police interrogations of criminal suspects held in custody. Chief Justice Earl Warren, writing for the 5–4 majority of the justices, declared that the prosecution may not use statements made by a person under questioning in police custody unless certain minimum procedural safeguards were followed. The court established new guidelines to ensure "that the individual is accorded his privilege under the Fifth Amendment" not to be compelled to incriminate himself. Known as the Miranda warnings, these guidelines include informing arrested persons prior to questioning that they have the right to remain silent, that anything they say may be used against them as evidence, and that they have the right to the counsel of an attorney.

The *Miranda* decision was one of the most controversial decisions of the Warren court, which under Chief Justice Warren had become increasingly concerned about the methods used by local police to obtain confessions. In an earlier (1964) case, *Escobedo* v. *Illinois*, 378 U.S. 478, the court had ruled that criminal suspects must be advised of their right to consult an attorney. But that decision had failed to specify the precise procedures police must follow to ensure that the suspect's rights in this regard are not violated.

In *Miranda* v. *Arizona* the court reversed an Arizona court's conviction of Ernesto Miranda on charges of kidnapping and rape. After being identified in a police lineup, Miranda had been questioned by police; he confessed and then signed a written statement without first being told that he had the right to have a lawyer present to advise him or that he had the right to remain silent. Miranda's confession was later used at his trial to obtain his conviction. The court held that the prosecution could not use his statements obtained by the police while the suspect was in custody unless the police had complied with several procedural safeguards to secure the Fifth Amendment privilege against self-incrimination.

The *Miranda* ruling shocked the law-enforcement community and was hotly debated. Critics of the *Miranda* decision said that the court, in seeking to protect the rights of individuals, had seriously weakened law-enforcement agencies. Under Chief Justice Warren Burger, a more conservative Supreme Court later issued several decisions that limited the scope of the Miranda safeguards. In a decision in 2009 (*Herring* v. *United States*), the Supreme Court ruled that evidence resulting from the unlawful arrest of a defendant is admissible in trial if the arrest occurred because of an innocent error in record keeping by police.

SEPARATION OF CHURCH AND STATE

The Concept of Church and State

Church and state is the belief, largely Christian in origin, that the religious and political powers in society are or should be clearly distinct, though both claim the people's loyalty.

Before the advent of Christianity, separate religious and political orders were not clearly defined in most civilizations. People worshipped the gods of the particular state in which they lived, religion in such cases being but a department of the state. In the case of the Jewish people, the revealed Law of the Scripture constituted the Law of Israel. The Christian concept of the secular and the spiritual is founded on the words of Jesus: "Render to Caesar the things that are Caesar's, and to God the things that are God's" (Mark 12:17). Two distinct, but not altogether separate, areas of human life and activity had to be distinguished; hence, a theory of two powers came to form the basis of Christian thought and teaching from earliest times.

During the 1st century CE the Apostles, living under a pagan empire, taught respect for and obedience to the governing powers so long as such obedience did not violate the higher, or divine, law, which superseded political jurisdiction. Among the Church Fathers, who lived in a period when Christianity had become the religion of the Roman Empire, the emphasis on the primacy of the spiritual was even stronger. They insisted upon the independence of the church and the right of the church to judge the actions of the secular ruler.

With the decline of the Roman Empire in the West, civil authority fell into the hands of the only educated class that remained—the churchmen. The church, which formed the only organized institution, became the seat of temporal as well as spiritual power. In the East the civil authorities, centred in Constantinople, dominated the ecclesiastical throughout the Byzantine period.

In 800, under Charlemagne, the empire was restored in the West, and by the 10th century many secular rulers held power throughout Europe. A period of political manipulation of the church hierarchy and a general decline in clerical zeal and piety brought vigorous action from a line of reforming popes, the most famous of whom was Gregory VII.

The following centuries were marked by a dramatic struggle of emperors and kings with the popes. During the 12th and 13th centuries, papal power greatly increased. In the 13th century, however, the greatest scholar of the age, St. Thomas Aquinas, borrowing from Aristotle, aided in raising the dignity of the civil power by declaring the state a perfect society (the other perfect society was the church) and a necessary good. The medieval struggle between secular and religious power came to a climax in the 14th century with the rise of nationalism and the increased prominence of lawyers, both royalist and canon. Numerous theorists contributed to the atmosphere of controversy, and the papacy finally met with disaster, first in the removal of the popes to Avignon under French influence and second with the Great Schism attendant upon an effort to bring the popes back to Rome. Church discipline was relaxed, and church prestige fell in all parts of Europe.

The immediate effect of the Reformation was to diminish the power of the church even further. Christianity in its fractured condition could offer no effective opposition to strong rulers, who now claimed divine right for their positions as head of church and state. John Calvin's assertion of ecclesiastical supremacy in Geneva was an exception of the day. Many Lutheran churches became, in effect, arms of the state. In England Henry VIII ended ties with Rome and assumed the headship of the Church of England.

In the 17th century there were few who believed that diversity of religious belief and a church unconnected with the civil power were possible in a unified state. Common religious standards were looked upon as a principal support of the political order. When the notions of diversity of belief and toleration of dissent did start to grow, they were not generally seen to conflict with the concept of a state church. The Puritans, for example, who fled religious persecution in England in the 17th century, enforced rigid conformity to church ideas among settlers in the American colonies.

The concept of secular government as expressed in the First Amendment to the U.S. Constitution reflected both the influence of the French Enlightenment on colonial intellectuals and the special interests of the established churches in preserving their separate and distinct identities. The Baptists, notably, held the separation of church and state powers as a principle of their creed.

The great wave of migration to the United States by Roman Catholics in the 1840s prompted a reassertion of the principle of secular government by state legislatures fearing allocation of government funds to parochial educational facilities. The 20th century saw the First and Fourteenth amendments to the Constitution applied with considerable strictness by the courts in the field of education. Late in the century, conservative Christian groups in the United States generated considerable controversy by seeking textbook censorship, reversal of court prohibition of school prayer, and requirements that certain Biblical doctrines be taught alongside scientific theories, in particular the theory of human evolution.

West Virginia State Board of Education v. Barnette

In *West Virginia State Board of Education* v. *Barnette*, decided on June 14, 1943, the U.S. Supreme Court ruled that compelling children in public schools to salute the U.S. flag was an unconstitutional violation of their freedom of speech and religion.

On the heels of *Minersville School District (Pennsylvania)* v. *Gobitis* (1940), in which the Supreme Court upheld (8–1) the school district's expulsion of two students for refusing to salute the flag on the basis of religious grounds (the children were Jehovah's Witnesses), West Virginia enacted a rule in 1942 that required students to salute the U.S. flag. Walter Barnette, a Jehovah's Witness in West Virginia, sued in U.S. district court and won an injunction against state enforcement of the rule. The state school board appealed to the U.S. Supreme Court, which agreed to hear the case.

Oral arguments were held on March 11, 1943, and the ruling was issued on June 14. In a 6–3 decision the court overturned the *Gobitis* ruling. The majority opinion was written by Justice Robert H. Jackson, who had voted with the majority in *Gobitis*. While the earlier decision had focused primarily on claims of freedom of religion protections in the U.S. Constitution's First Amendment, the *Barnette* ruling invoked both freedom of religion and an individual's freedom of speech—and that freedom of speech included the right not to be forced to speak against one's will. Jackson's opinion underscored the rights of minorities against the tyranny of the majority: "If there is any fixed star in our constitutional constellation, it is that no official, high or petty, can prescribe what shall be orthodox in politics, nationalism, religion, or other matters of opinion, or force citizens to confess by word or act their faith therein." And, attempting to capture the essence of the Bill of Rights protections, Jackson wrote:The very purpose of a Bill of Rights was to withdraw certain subjects from the vicissitudes of political controversy, to place them beyond the reach of majorities and officials and to establish them as legal principles to be applied by the courts. One's right to life, liberty, and property, to free speech, a free press, freedom of worship and assembly, and other fundamental rights may not be submitted to vote; they depend on the outcome of no elections.

Engel v. Vitale

In *Engel* v. *Vitale*, on June 25, 1962, the U.S. Supreme Court ruled that voluntary prayer in public schools violated the U.S. Constitution's First Amendment prohibition of a state establishment of religion.

New York state's Board of Regents wrote and authorized a voluntary nondenominational prayer that could be recited by students at the beginning of each school day. In 1958–59 a group of parents that included Steven Engel in

Hyde Park, N.Y., objected to the prayer, which read, "Almighty God, we acknowledge our dependence upon Thee, and beg Thy blessings upon us, our teachers, and our country," and sued the school board president, William Vitale. The prayer, which proponents argued was constitutional because it was voluntary and promoted the free exercise of religion (also protected in the First Amendment), was upheld by New York's courts, prompting the petitioners to file a successful appeal to the U.S. Supreme Court. Engel et al. were supported by the American Civil Liberties Union, and briefs were filed on their behalf by the American Ethical Union and the American Jewish Committee, while the governments of some 20 states called on the U.S. Supreme Court to uphold the prayer.

Oral arguments took place on April 3, 1962. The Supreme Court's ruling was released on June 25 and found New York's law unconstitutional by a margin of 6–1 (two justices did not participate in the decision). Hugo L. Black wrote the Supreme Court's opinion, in which the majority argued "that, by using its public school system to encourage recitation of the Regents' prayer, the State of New York has adopted a practice wholly inconsistent with the Establishment Clause." The lone dissent came from Potter Stewart, who argued that the majority had "misapplied a great constitutional principle" and could not understand "how an 'official religion' is established by letting those who want to say a prayer say it. On the contrary, I think to deny the wish of these school children to join in reciting this prayer is to deny them the opportunity of sharing in the spiritual heritage of our Nation." The decision, the first in which the Supreme Court had ruled unconstitutional public school sponsorship of religion, was unpopular with a broad segment of the American public.

Justices and Jurists

Chapter 7

The Supreme Court of the United States is a bastion of tradition. As is the custom in American courts, Justices are seated by seniority on the Bench, with the Chief Justice occupying the centre chair. In keeping with the tradition of the Court, at each station Justices find a quill pen at the ready. In addition, as has been customary since at least 1800, Justices wear black robes while in Court.

Over the past more than 200 years, the Supreme Court has been variously constituted. The Warren court (1953–69) is regarded as having expanded the range of civil rights and civil liberties, to the delight of some and the consternation of others. The Rehnquist court (1986–2006) handed down a number of decisions redefining the relationship between the federal government and the states. What follows is a list of the men, and later women, who have shaped the nation's understanding of the Constitution, and thereby determined the scope and limits of lawmaking at the federal, state, and local levels.

THE CURRENT SUPREME COURT

The current court is led by Chief Justice John G. Roberts, Jr., who was appointed by Republican Pres. George W. Bush. Five of his eight colleagues—Samuel Alito, Clarence Thomas, Antonin Scalia, Anthony Kennedy, and John Paul Stevens—were also appointed by Republicans. But, the party affiliation of a president is not always a good indicator of how a justice he appoints will vote—Stevens's decisions, for example, have generally been firmly in the liberal camp. Still, Roberts, Alito, Thomas, and Scalia are consistent votes for the more conservative position in cases, while Stephen Breyer and Ruth Bader Ginsburg (both appointed by Democrats), are liberal. Justice Anthony Kennedy (appointed by a Republican) has often served as the "swing vote" in split decisions. How Democratic Pres. Barack Obama's appointment of Sonia Sotomayor, the first Hispanic and the third woman to serve, will affect the balance of the court is a subject of interest to parties that will bring cases to the court as well as to all other Americans.

John Roberts, Jr.

(b. Jan. 27, 1955, Buffalo, N.Y.)

John Glover Roberts, Jr., became the 17th chief justice of the United States in 2005. Roberts was raised in Indiana and received undergraduate (1976) and law (1979) degrees from Harvard University, where he was the managing editor of the *Harvard Law Review*. From 1980 to 1981 he served as a law clerk to Supreme Court Justice William H. Rehnquist, who later became chief justice. Pres. Ronald Reagan appointed Roberts special assistant to Atty. Gen. William French Smith in 1981, and the following year he became associate counsel to the president. He later worked at the law firm of Hogan & Hartson LLP in Washington, D.C., from 1986 to 1989, when he became deputy solicitor general in the administration of Pres. George H.W. Bush. In 1992 Bush nominated him to the U.S. Court of Appeals for the District of Columbia Circuit. His nomination, however, died in the Senate, and the following year he returned to Hogan & Hartson. In his various roles, Roberts argued nearly 40 cases before the Supreme Court, winning 25 of them.

With wife Jane Roberts at his side, John G. Roberts, Jr., is sworn in as chief justice of the United States by Associate Justice John Paul Stevens, Sept. 29, 2005. Paul Morse/The White House

In 2001 Roberts was reappointed to the D.C. Circuit Court of Appeals, this time by Pres. George W. Bush, and his bid again stalled. Bush resubmitted his name in 2003, and later that year he was finally confirmed by the Senate. Among Roberts's noted opinions was his dissent in *Rancho Viejo* v. *Norton Gale* (2003), in which a real-estate developer had been ordered to remove a fence that threatened an endangered species of toad. The court declined to hear the case, but Roberts questioned whether the Constitution's commerce clause, which ostensibly gave the federal government the authority to enforce such an order, applied. Some legal scholars interpreted Roberts's opinion as a challenge to the Endangered Species Act and other environmental protection laws. Roberts served on the circuit court until 2005, when Bush nominated him to fill the vacancy left on the Supreme Court by the retirement of Justice Sandra Day O'Connor, whom he had helped prepare for her confirmation hearings in 1981. Shortly before Roberts's confirmation hearings began, Rehnquist died, prompting Bush to appoint Roberts chief justice. Roberts received bipartisan support, though some senators were troubled by his apparent advocacy of strongly conservative legal viewpoints as counsel in the Reagan and Bush administrations and by his refusal to provide specific answers to questions about his positions on various issues, including civil rights and abortion. The latter issue was a matter of particular concern to those who wondered whether Roberts's judicial decisions would be inappropriately influenced by his strong Roman Catholic faith. Quickly confirmed by the Senate (78–22), he was sworn in on Sept. 29, 2005.

John Paul Stevens

(b. April 20, 1920, Chicago, Ill.)

John Paul Stevens has been an associate justice of the Supreme Court of the United States since 1975.

Stevens, who traced his American ancestry to the mid-17th century, attended the University of Chicago, where he graduated with a Bachelor of Arts degree in 1941. During World War II he served in the navy, winning a Bronze Star. After the war, he attended the Northwestern University School of Law, graduating in 1947. He clerked for Wiley B. Rutledge (1947–48), an associate justice of the Supreme Court, before joining a Chicago law firm to specialize in antitrust law. He also taught law part-time at the University of Chicago and Northwestern University and served on various public commissions, including as counsel for a House of Representatives subcommittee that investigated the power of monopolies. In 1970 Pres. Richard M. Nixon appointed

Stevens circuit judge of the United States Court of Appeals for the Seventh circuit, where he gained a reputation for his scholarly acumen and well-written decisions. After Justice William O. Douglas retired in 1975, Stevens was appointed to the U.S. Supreme Court by Pres. Gerald R. Ford, winning unanimous approval by the U.S. Senate.

John Paul Stevens, 1976. Library of Congress, Washington, D.C. (neg. no. LC-USZC6-29)

Although he was expected to serve as a conservative counterbalance to the remnants of the liberal court of Chief Justice Earl Warren, Stevens proved to be an independently minded justice who occupied a moderately liberal position on the court. Indeed, as the court became more conservative after appointments by Ronald Reagan and George Bush, Stevens increasingly found himself amid the court's liberal bloc. On pivotal issues—such as minority rights—that defined the court's shift from moderately liberal in the 1970s to more conservative in the 1980s and '90s, Stevens exhibited a profound commitment to establishing durable legal standards designed to protect individual rights. For example, his dissents in cases involving gay rights and race-conscious districting (the practice of creating electoral districts in which racial minorities, especially African Americans and Hispanics, constitute a majority of the voting population) represented a defense of the rights of groups that historically had been disenfranchised or discriminated against. Stevens was usually a strong defender of free speech, though he vigorously dissented from the court's 1989 ruling in *Texas* v. *Johnson* that flag burning is protected under the First Amendment. Although he coauthored the majority opinion in *Jurek* v. *Texas* (1976), which reinstated the death penalty in the United States, he remained suspicious of capital punishment, opposing it for convicted rapists and for those under age 18 at the time their crimes were committed. Eventually he concluded that adequate protections against bias and error in capital cases no longer existed, and in 2008 he renounced the death penalty as unconstitutional.

Stevens's tenure on the court must be understood in light of the ideological changes that swept through the institution after his appointment in 1975. He remained committed to the legal right to abortion established in *Roe* v. *Wade* (1973), arguing in 1992 that the ruling is "an integral part of a correct understanding of both the concept of liberty and the basic equality of men and women." In the multifaceted controversy over the proper balance between the powers of the federal and state governments, Stevens found himself routinely dissenting from his more recently appointed conservative peers, who supported greater limitations on the powers of the federal government. In the final analysis, Stevens can be considered not so much a liberal as a centrist who was increasingly isolated by a newer and more conservative bloc.

Antonin Scalia

(b. March 11, 1936, Trenton, N.J.)

Antonin Scalia has been an associate justice of the Supreme Court of the United States since 1986, when he became the first Supreme Court justice of Italian ancestry.

Scalia's father, a Sicilian immigrant, taught Romance languages at Brooklyn College, and his Italian American mother taught elementary school. Scalia received a Roman Catholic parochial education in New York City and graduated at the top of his class from Georgetown University (A.B., 1957) in Washington, D.C. He attended Harvard Law School, where he edited the prestigious *Harvard Law Review*, graduating in 1960. He then worked for a law firm in Cleveland, Ohio (1961–67), before moving to Charlottesville, Va., where he taught at the University of Virginia Law School (1967–74). During his tenure at Virginia, he served the federal government as counsel to the Office of Telecommunications Policy (1971–72) and as chairman of the Administrative Conference of the United States (1972–74). In 1974 Scalia left academia to serve as assistant attorney general in the Office of Legal Counsel of the U.S. Department of Justice.

Scalia resumed his academic career at the University of Chicago Law School, where he taught from 1977 to 1982. During that period he was editor of *Regulation*, a review published by the conservative American Enterprise Institute. In 1982 Pres. Ronald Reagan appointed him to the U.S. Court of Appeals for the District of Columbia Circuit. Appointed by Reagan to the Supreme Court in 1986, he won unanimous confirmation in the U.S. Senate.

Among the court's most passionate and outspoken justices, Scalia quickly earned a reputation for aggressiveness in oral argument and scathing criticism in written opinions, especially when expressing dissenting views. This tendency was especially apparent in cases involving abortion, which Scalia vehemently opposed. In *Webster* v. *Reproductive Health Services* (1989), for example, he admonished his fellow conservatives for failing to strike down *Roe* v. *Wade* (1973), which had established the right to abortion; and in a dissent to *Madsen* v. *Women's Health Center*

(1994), in which the court ruled 6–3 that "buffer zones" around abortion clinics did not violate the free-speech rights of abortion opponents, he asserted that the court's ruling "departs so far from the established course of our jurisprudence that in any other context it would have been regarded as a candidate for summary reversal."

Scalia was unwavering in his opinions as well as in his general approach to constitutional law. An opponent of "judicial activism," the alleged tendency of some judges to usurp the power of elected legislatures by making the law rather than merely interpreting it, Scalia favoured a restrained judiciary, deference to the original intent of the framers in constitutional interpretation, and a limited role for the federal government. His originalism was illustrated by his view of the Eighth Amendment's prohibition of cruel and unusual punishment, which he claimed must be understood relative to the standards of justice applicable in the late 18th century. Although sometimes portrayed as unusual, his decisions also were noted for their logic and consistency. According to Scalia, the same freedom of speech that belongs to abortion opponents also extends to those who would desecrate the American flag. In his dissent in *Edwards* v. *Aguillard* (1987), in which the court struck down Louisiana's Balanced Treatment for Creation-Science and Evolution-Science in Public School Instruction Act, Scalia argued that original or legislative intent should govern judicial decisions when it is discoverable and apparently unambiguous, as he believed it was in this case. On the limited role of government, Scalia led a sharply divided court in striking down key provisions of the Brady Handgun Violence Prevention Act, arguing on the basis of states' rights in *Printz* v. *United States* (1997) that the federal government could not require state and local law-enforcement agencies to perform background checks on prospective gun owners. His credentials as a conservative justice were illustrated in *Lawrence* v. *Texas* (2003), in which the court struck down a Texas antisodomy law as an unconstitutional invasion of privacy; in a dissent read from the bench, Scalia criticized his colleagues for taking "sides in the culture war" and for signing on to "the so-called homosexual agenda."

Although Scalia's views often elicited fierce criticism from scholars of constitutional law, he was nevertheless regarded as one of the court's leading intellects, and his opinions were considered among the best written in the Supreme Court's long history.

Anthony Kennedy

(b. July 23, 1936, Sacramento, Calif.)

Anthony McLeod Kennedy has been an associate justice of the Supreme Court of the United States since 1988.

Kennedy received a bachelor's degree from Stanford University in 1958 and a law degree from Harvard University in 1961. He was admitted to the bar in 1962 and subsequently practiced law in San Francisco and Sacramento, Calif. In 1965 he was appointed professor of constitutional law at the University of the Pacific's McGeorge School of Law, where he taught until 1988. In 1975 Kennedy was appointed by Pres. Gerald R. Ford to the U.S. Court of Appeals for the Ninth Circuit, and in that capacity he established himself as a distinguished candidate to fill the vacant seat on the U.S. Supreme Court created by the retirement of Justice Lewis Powell in 1987. Instead, Pres. Ronald Reagan nominated Robert H. Bork, whose outspoken demeanour and sharply conservative views on constitutional law and social policy led to his rejection by the Senate. The quieter Kennedy was eventually nominated and was unanimously confirmed.

Early in his tenure, Kennedy proved to be markedly conservative. In his first term, he voted with Chief Justice William H. Rehnquist and Justice Antonin Scalia, two of the court's most conservative members, more than 90 percent of the time. With Justice Sandra Day O'Connor, Kennedy contributed critical votes that led to winning conservative majorities in cases limiting congressional authority under the commerce clause of the Constitution of the United States and striking down portions of gun-control legislation. In subsequent years, however, his decisions were more independent. Parting ways with his conservative colleagues, Kennedy rejected congressional term limits. In 1992 he coauthored (with O'Connor and Justice David Souter) the court's majority opinion in *Planned Parenthood of Southeastern Pennsylvania* v. *Casey*, which held that legal restrictions on access to abortion must not constitute an "undue burden" on a woman's exercise of her right to abortion as established in *Roe* v. *Wade* (1973).

Kennedy's episodic departure from conservative jurisprudence reflected a civil-libertarian perspective on certain individual rights. For example, although he was generally deferential to the government on criminal law and related matters, he voted, along with Scalia and the court's liberals, to declare unconstitutional a Texas law that prohibited the desecration of the American flag, on the grounds that the Constitution protects such acts as symbolic speech. He also wrote the court's decision in *Romer, Governor of Colorado* v. *Evans* (1996), which voided an amendment to the Colorado state constitution that prohibited laws barring discrimination against homosexuals, and in *Lawrence* v. *Texas* (2003), which declared unconstitutional Texas's law criminalizing sodomy between two consenting adults of the same sex.

Clarence Thomas

(b. June 23, 1948, Pinpoint, near Savannah, Ga.)

Clarence Thomas has been an associate justice of the Supreme Court of the United States since 1991. The second African American to serve on the court, Thomas was appointed to replace Justice Thurgood Marshall, the court's first African American member.

Thomas's father abandoned the family when Thomas was two years old. After the family house was destroyed by fire, Thomas's mother, a maid, remarried, and Thomas, then age seven, and his brother were sent to live with their grandfather. He was educated in Savannah, Georgia, at an all-African American Roman Catholic primary school run by white nuns and then at a boarding-school seminary, where he graduated as the only African American in his class. He attended Immaculate Conception Abbey in his freshman year of college and then transferred to Holy Cross College in Worcester, Mass., where he graduated with a bachelor's degree in 1971. He received a law degree from Yale University in 1974.

Thomas was successively assistant attorney general in Missouri (1974–77), a lawyer with the Monsanto Company (1977–79), and a legislative assistant to Republican Sen. John C. Danforth of Missouri (1979–81). In the Republican presidential administrations of Ronald Reagan and George Bush, Thomas served as assistant secretary in the U.S. Department of Education (1981–82), chairman of the Equal Employment Opportunity Commission (EEOC; 1982–90), and judge on the U.S. Court of Appeals for the Federal District in Washington, D.C. (1990–91), a post to which he was appointed by Bush.

Marshall's retirement gave Bush the opportunity to replace one of the court's most liberal members with a conservative. The president was under significant political pressure to appoint another African American, and Thomas's service under Republican senators and presidents made him an obvious choice. Despite his appeal to Republican partisans, however, his nomination engendered controversy for several reasons: he had little experience as a judge; he had produced little judicial scholarship; and he refused to answer questions about his position on abortion (he claimed during his confirmation hearings that he had never discussed the issue). Nevertheless, Thomas seemed headed for easy confirmation until a former aide stepped forward to accuse him of sexual harassment, a subject that dominated the latter stages of the hearings. The aide, Anita Hill, an African American law professor at the University of Oklahoma who had worked for Thomas at the EEOC and the Department of Education, alleged in televised hearings that Thomas had made sexually offensive comments to her in an apparent campaign of seduction. Thomas denied the charge and accused the Senate Judiciary Committee of engineering a "high-tech lynching." A deeply divided Senate only narrowly confirmed Thomas's nomination by a vote of 52 to 48.

On the Supreme Court, Thomas maintained a relatively quiet presence but evidenced a strong conservatism in his votes and decisions, frequently siding with fellow conservative Justice Antonin Scalia. This alliance was forged in Thomas's first major case, *Planned Parenthood of Southeastern Pennsylvania* v. *Casey* (1992), in which he joined Scalia's dissent, which argued that *Roe* v. *Wade* (1973), the ruling that established the legal right to abortion, should be reversed. Thomas's conservative ideology also was apparent in his opinions on the issue of school desegregation; in *Missouri* v. *Jenkins* (1995), for example, he wrote a 27-page concurring opinion that condemned the extension of federal power into the states and tried to establish a legal justification for reversing the desegregation that had begun in 1954 with *Brown* v. *Board of Education of Topeka*. Because "desegregation has not produced the predicted leaps forward in black educational achievement," Thomas argued, "there is no reason to think that black students cannot learn as well when surrounded by members of their own race as when they are in an integrated environment."

Although the controversy surrounding his appointment dissolved shortly after he joined the bench, Thomas will perhaps always be measured against the justice he succeeded. Ideologically, Thomas and Marshall were stark contrasts, and throughout his career Thomas worked against many of the causes championed by his predecessor. As one of the most reliable conservatives appointed by Republican presidents, Thomas generally followed a predictable pattern in his opinions—conservative, restrained, and suspicious of the reach of the federal government into the realm of state and local politics.

Ruth Bader Ginsburg

(b. March 15, 1933, Brooklyn, N.Y.)

Ruth Bader Ginsburg (née Ruth Joan Bader) has been an associate justice of the Supreme Court of the United States since 1993. She was only the second woman to serve on the Supreme Court.

Ginsburg graduated from Cornell University in 1954, finishing first in her class. She attended Harvard Law School, where she was elected president of her class, for two years before transferring to Columbia Law School to join her husband, who had been hired by a prestigious law firm in New York City. She was elected to the law reviews of both schools and graduated tied for first in her class at Columbia in 1959. Despite her outstanding academic record, Ginsburg was turned down for numerous jobs after graduation because she was a woman.

After clerking for U.S. District Judge Edmund L. Palmieri (1959–61), she taught at Rutgers University Law School (1963–72) and at Columbia (1972–80), where she became the school's first female tenured professor. During the 1970s she also served as the director of the Women's Rights Project of the American Civil Liberties Union, for which she argued six landmark cases on gender equality before the Supreme Court. She won five of those cases and thereby helped establish the unconstitutionality of unequal treatment of men and women.

In 1980 Pres. Jimmy Carter appointed Ginsburg to the U.S. Court of Appeals for the District of Columbia Circuit. She served there until she was appointed to the Supreme Court in 1993 by Pres. Bill Clinton to fill the seat vacated by Justice Byron White; she was easily confirmed by the Senate (96–3).

As a lawyer, Ginsburg had been known for her pioneering advocacy of the rights of women. As a judge, she favoured caution, moderation, and restraint. She was considered part of the Supreme Court's minority moderate-liberal bloc.

In 1996 Ginsburg wrote the Supreme Court's landmark decision in *United States* v. *Virginia*, which held that the state-supported Virginia Military Institute could not refuse to admit women. Despite her reputation for restrained writing, she gathered considerable attention for her dissenting opinion in the case of *Bush* v. *Gore*, which effectively decided the 2000 presidential election between George W. Bush and Al Gore. Objecting to the court's majority opinion favouring Bush, Ginsburg deliberately and subtly concluded her decision with the words, "I dissent"—a significant departure from the tradition of including the adverb *respectfully*.

Stephen Breyer

(b. Aug. 15, 1938, San Francisco, Calif.)

Stephen Gerald Breyer has been an associate justice of the Supreme Court of the United States since 1994.

Breyer received bachelor's degrees from Stanford University (1959) and the University of Oxford (1961), which he attended on a Rhodes scholarship, and a law degree from Harvard University (1964). In 1964–65 he clerked for U.S. Supreme Court Justice Arthur J. Goldberg. He taught law at Harvard University from 1967 to 1994.

Breyer took leave from Harvard in 1973 to serve as an assistant prosecutor in the Watergate investigation. In 1974–75 he was special counsel to the U.S. Senate Judiciary Committee, and from 1979 to 1981 he was its chief counsel, working on projects ranging from the federal criminal code to airline and trucking deregulation. In 1980 he was appointed by Pres. Jimmy Carter to the United States Court of Appeals for the First Circuit, becoming its chief judge in 1990. In 1994 Pres. Bill Clinton nominated Breyer to fill the seat of the retiring justice Harry Blackmun. As a pragmatic moderate acceptable to Democrats and Republicans alike, Breyer was easily confirmed by the Senate (87–9).

More liberal than most other members of the court, Breyer was highly regarded, even by conservatives, for his analytic rather than ideological approach to the Constitution. In the area of civil rights, Breyer consistently sided with efforts to dismantle historical and symbolic vestiges of racial segregation. In *Bush* v. *Gore* (2000), which settled that year's controversial presidential election between George W. Bush and Al Gore, he issued a passionate yet precise dissent. He argued that, by failing to refuse the case under the rubric of the political-question doctrine (which the court often had invoked in order to sidestep controversial issues that it thought were best handled by the legislature) and by deciding the case on the basis of equal protection (i.e., it ruled that manual recounts of certain votes in Florida violated the rights of voters whose ballots were not manually reviewed), the court had undermined its integrity and authority. In *McConnell* v. *Federal Election Commission* (2003), he joined a majority in holding that limits on campaign advertisements and contributions imposed by the Bipartisan Campaign Reform Act of 2002, popularly known as the McCain-Feingold Act, did not violate the First Amendment's guarantee of freedom of speech.

Breyer is the author of *Breaking the Vicious Circle: Toward Effective Risk Regulation* (1993), an analysis of government environmental and health regulations, and *Active Liberty: Interpreting Our Democratic Constitution* (2005), an outline of his judicial philosophy.

Samuel A. Alito, Jr.

(b. April 1, 1950, Trenton, N.J.)

Samuel Anthony Alito, Jr., has been an associate justice of the Supreme Court of the United States since 2006.

Alito earned a bachelor's degree (1972) from Princeton University and a law degree (1975) from Yale University, where he served as an editor of the *Yale Law Journal*. In the Republican administrations of Presidents Ronald Reagan and George Bush, he served as assistant to the U.S. solicitor general (1981–85), deputy assistant to the U.S. attorney general (1985–87), and U.S. attorney for the district of New Jersey (1987–90). During his time in the attorney general's office, Alito argued several cases before the Supreme Court. In 1990 he was appointed by Bush to serve as a judge on the U.S. Court of Appeals for the Third Circuit. His judicial philosophy was generally considered conservative—many

Samuel A. Alito, Jr., (centre) *being sworn in as associate justice of the Supreme Court by Chief Justice John Roberts (right), Feb. 1, 2006. Pres. George W. Bush looks on.* Shealah Craighead/The White House

referred to him by the nickname "Scalito," a reference to similarities with conservative associate justice Antonin Scalia. Alito voted in favour of restrictions on abortion rights and in favour of the right of local governments to display religious symbols (such as a nativity scene) during holidays and voted against federal gun-control legislation. In 2005 he was appointed associate justice of the U.S. Supreme Court by Pres. George W. Bush to fill the seat of retiring justice Sandra Day O'Connor; he was confirmed (58–42) by the U.S. Senate the following year.

Sonia Sotomayor

(b. June 25, 1954, Bronx, N.Y.)

An American lawyer and judge, Sonia Sotomayor was nominated associate justice of the Supreme Court of the

United States in 2009 by Pres. Barack Obama. Confirmed that August by the U.S. Senate, she became the first Hispanic and the third woman to serve on the Supreme Court.

The daughter of parents who moved to New York City from Puerto Rico, Sotomayor was raised in a housing project in the Bronx. After the death of her father, her mother worked long hours as a nurse to support the family. Sotomayor credits the episodes of the television crime show *Perry Mason* (1957–66) that she watched as a child with influencing her decision to become a lawyer. She graduated summa cum laude from Princeton University (B.A., 1976) before attending Yale Law School, where she worked as an editor of the *Yale Law Journal*. She graduated in 1979 and worked for five years as an assistant district attorney in New York county before pursuing private practice in a New York firm, where she worked on intellectual property and copyright cases.

In 1992 Pres. George H.W. Bush appointed Sotomayor a federal judge in the U.S. District Court, Southern District of New York. As a federal judge, Sotomayor received national attention in 1995 when she ruled in favour of Major League Baseball players, then on strike, who were suing because of changes to the free agent system and salary arbitration rules. Sotomayor issued an injunction against the team owners, effectively bringing the eight-month strike to an end.

When Pres. Bill Clinton nominated Sotomayor to be a judge of the U.S. Court of Appeals for the Second Circuit in 1997, Republican senators delayed her appointment for more than a year because of their concerns that the position might lead to a Supreme Court nomination. After her appointment to the court in 1998, Sotomayor was known for her candid, direct speaking style and for her carefully reasoned decisions. Some of her decisions provoked controversy. In 2001 she ruled in favour of a woman with dyslexia who wanted more accommodations under the Americans with Disabilities Act in order to take the bar exam. In 2003 in *Ricci* v. *DeStefano*, a group of white firefighters from New Haven, Conn., sued the city for discarding a test, the results of which had in effect barred all African American firefighters from promotion. Sotomayor and two other judges in 2008 accepted the lower court's decision against the white firefighters with little further comment, but in June 2009 the Supreme Court reversed their decision.

Justice Sonia Sotomayor, a few months prior to her confirmation as the nation's first Hispanic and third female Supreme Court justice, 2009. The White House/Getty Images

In May 2009 President Obama nominated Sotomayor to the Supreme Court in order to fill the vacancy left by departing justice David Souter. Sotomayor faced initial criticism for once stating that policy was made in the Court of Appeals (as opposed to the legislative branch) and, in a different speech, that a Latina judge was better equipped to make judgments than a white man. Her diabetes also brought questions about her potential longevity on the court. Sotomayor's confirmation hearings before the Senate Judiciary Committee in July 2009 went smoothly, and the following month she was confirmed (68–31) by the Senate.

PAST CHIEF JUSTICES OF THE SUPREME COURT

John Jay

(b. Dec. 12, 1745, New York City—d. May 17, 1829, Bedford, N.Y.)

John Jay was a founding father of the United States who served the new nation in both law and diplomacy. He established important judicial precedents as first chief justice of the United States (1789–95) and negotiated the Jay Treaty of 1794, which settled major grievances with Great Britain and promoted commercial prosperity.

A successful New York attorney, Jay deplored the growing estrangement between the colonies and the mother country, fearing that independence might stir up violence and mob rule. Nevertheless, once the revolution was launched, he became one of its staunchest supporters. As a delegate to the First Continental Congress (1774) in Philadelphia, he drafted *The Address to the People of Great Britain*, stating the claims of colonists. He helped assure the approval of the Declaration of Independence (1776) in New York, where he was a member of the provincial Congress. The following year he helped draft New York's first constitution, was elected the state's first chief justice, and in 1778 was chosen president of the Continental Congress.

In 1779 Jay was appointed minister plenipotentiary to Spain, which had joined France in openly supporting the revolutionaries against Britain. His mission—to borrow money and to gain access to the Mississippi River—proved abortive, and he was sent in May 1782 to join Benjamin Franklin in Paris as joint negotiator for peace with Great Britain. In undercover talks with the British he won surprisingly liberal terms, which were later included essentially intact in the Treaty of Paris (Sept. 3, 1783), which concluded the war.

On his return from abroad, Jay found that Congress had elected him secretary for foreign affairs (1784–90). Frustrated by the limitations on his powers in that office, he became convinced that the nation needed a more strongly centralized government than was provided for by the Articles of Confederation, and he plunged into the fight for ratification of the new federal Constitution, framed in 1787. Using the pseudonym Publius, he collaborated with Alexander Hamilton and James Madison by writing five essays for *The Federalist*—the classic defense of the new governmental structure. In 1789 Pres. George Washington appointed Jay the country's first chief justice, in which capacity he was instrumental in shaping Supreme Court procedures in its formative years. His most notable case was *Chisholm* v. *Georgia*, in which Jay and the court affirmed the subordination of the states to the federal government. Unfavourable reaction to the decision led to adoption of the Eleventh Amendment, denying federal courts authority in suits by citizens against a state.

In 1794 Washington sent Jay as a special envoy to Great Britain to help avert war over accumulated grievances. The commercial agreement, called the Jay Treaty (November 19), aroused a storm of protest among the Jeffersonian Republicans, who denounced it as a sellout by pro-British Federalists. Mobs burned Jay in effigy, and opponents denounced him as a traitor. Before the negotiations, Jay at one time had been considered a leading candidate to succeed Washington, but the unpopular treaty ruined whatever chances he had for the presidency. New York Federalists, however, elected him governor (1795–1801), an office from which he retired to spend the remainder of his life on his farm.

John Rutledge

(b. September 1739, Charleston, S.C.—d. July 18, 1800, Charleston, S.C.),

John Rutledge was an American legislator who, as a delegate to the Constitutional Convention of 1787, strongly supported the protection of slavery and the concept of a strong central government, a position then possible, but paradoxical in later times when slavery's defenders sheltered behind the bastion of states' rights.

After studying in England, Rutledge returned to Charleston to practice law. Reflecting views acceptable to both planters and merchants in his area, he was chosen as a delegate to the Stamp Act Congress (1765) and to the Continental Congress (1774–77, 1782–83). After chairing the committee that framed the South Carolina constitution (1776), he was elected president of the state's General Assembly, but he resigned in 1778 when the constitution was amended to include provisions he considered too democratic. In 1779 he was elected South Carolina's governor, and, after the state was invaded by the British in that year, he held the skeleton colonial government together until the end of the war.

John Rutledge. Library of Congress, Washington, D.C. (neg. no. LC-USZ62-91143)

At the Constitutional Convention in 1787,

Rutledge spoke for Southern planters by supporting slavery. He argued in favour of dividing society into classes as a basis for representation and also postulated high property qualifications for holding office. As chairman of the Committee on Detail, he recommended the granting of indefinite powers of legislation to the national government for the purpose of promoting the general welfare.

From 1789 to 1791 he served as an associate justice of the U.S. Supreme Court and for the next four years as chief justice of the South Carolina Supreme Court. Nominated Chief Justice of the United States in 1795, he failed to win Senate confirmation because of his outspoken opposition to the Jay Treaty of the previous year.

His brother Edward Rutledge was a signer of the Declaration of Independence (1776), fought against the British in South Carolina during the American Revolution, and served in the South Carolina legislature (1782–98) and as governor (1798–1800) of the state.

Oliver Ellsworth

(b. April 29, 1745, Windsor, Conn.—d. Nov. 26, 1807, Windsor, Conn.)

Oliver Ellsworth was an American statesman and jurist and chief author of the 1789 act establishing the U.S. federal court system. He was the third chief justice of the United States.

Ellsworth attended Yale and the College of New Jersey (now Princeton), graduating from the latter in 1766. After pursuing theological and legal studies, he was admitted to the bar in Hartford, which he represented in the Connecticut General Assembly. He was subsequently state's attorney for Hartford county (1777), a member of the Continental Congress (1777–83) and of the Governor's Council of Connecticut (1780–85), and a judge on the state superior court (1785–89).

In 1787 Ellsworth, together with Roger Sherman and William Samuel Johnson, represented Connecticut at the Constitutional Convention in Philadelphia, serving as a member of the important committee on detail. At the convention, he proposed with Sherman the decisive "Connecticut compromise," by which the federal legislature was made to consist of two houses, the upper having equal representation from each state, the lower being chosen on the basis of population. This bargain is a keystone of the U.S. federal system. To secure Southern support for the Constitution, Ellsworth supported free international trade in slaves. He also vigorously defended the Constitution at the Connecticut ratifying convention. His *Letters to a Landholder*, printed in the *Connecticut Courant* and the *American Mercury*, had a broad influence during the ratification debates, much as the Federalist Papers did in New York.

In 1789 Ellsworth became one of Connecticut's first U.S. senators and the acknowledged Federalist leader in the U.S. Senate. He reported the first Senate rules and suggested a plan for printing the journals, shaped the conference report on the Bill of Rights, framed the measure of admission for North Carolina, helped devise the government of the territory south of the Ohio River, and drafted the first bill regulating the consular service. He was chairman of the committee to establish the federal court system and the chief author of the Federal Judiciary Act of 1789, the principal basis ever since of the U.S. court structure.

In 1796 Pres. George Washington appointed him chief justice of the Supreme Court of the United States, after John Rutledge had failed to receive Senate confirmation and William Cushing, the senior associate justice, had declined. Ellsworth's service on the high court was cut short in 1800 by ill health. In the 1790s Supreme Court justices also served in the circuit courts, and some of Ellsworth's most important decisions were given on circuit. His most controversial opinion was *United States* v. *Isaac Williams* (1799), which applied in the United States the common-law rule that a citizen may not expatriate himself without the consent of his government.

In 1799 he accepted Pres. John Adams's request to join William Vans Murray and William R. Davie as commissioners to France to negotiate a new treaty. In October 1800 Ellsworth persuaded Napoleon to accept a compromise convention that provided for freedom of commerce between the two nations and in effect concluded the undeclared war between the United States and France.

From France he sent his resignation as chief justice. Until his death in 1807, he lived in Windsor, Conn. Though his career included few acts of genius and little public acclaim, Ellsworth's political skill, balanced judgment, and clarity of purpose entitle him to recognition as a founder of the highest stature.

Ellsworth lacked the intellectual brilliance of some of his contemporaries, but, in the arena of practical politics, none of the founders was superior to—and perhaps none even equaled—him in the pragmatic art of effectively wielding power in legislative assemblies. In particular, Ellsworth had an extraordinary ability to fashion workable compromises. He had a clear, sophisticated, and detailed political philosophy and psychology, but he was not a member of the secular Enlightenment. Instead, he was a strict Calvinist who claimed that, as a young man, he had personally experienced his election by God for salvation. His entire personal and public life was ordered by a rigorous Calvinism founded upon a belief in absolute predestination. He firmly believed that everything he did was part of God's plan for mankind. In the political realm, he enthusiastically embraced compromise as long as he was convinced of the overall righteousness of a particular project.

Like all Connecticut Calvinists, Ellsworth firmly opposed slavery on religious grounds. Because he had an abiding faith that, as part of God's plan, slavery inevitably would wither away, he had no qualms about firmly supporting the Southern states' right to import slaves in order to gain Southern support for the Constitution at the Constitutional Convention.

By the time of his mission to France in 1800, he had reluctantly concluded that the federal government was unworkable. He cherished order, but the emergence of Thomas Jefferson's Republican Party and rifts within Ellsworth's Federalist Party presaged disorder and even chaos. Ellsworth resigned from the national government and returned to Connecticut, where he was an active participant in state politics for the rest of his life.

John Marshall

(b. Sept. 24, 1755, near Germantown [now Midland], Va.—d. July 6, 1835, Philadelphia, Pa.),

John Marshall was the fourth chief justice of the United States and the principal founder of the U.S. system of constitutional law. As perhaps the Supreme Court's most influential chief justice, Marshall was responsible for constructing and defending both the foundation of judicial power and the principles of American federalism. The first of his great cases in more than 30 years of service was *Marbury* v. *Madison* (1803), which established the Supreme Court's right to expound constitutional law and exercise judicial review by declaring laws unconstitutional. His defense of federalism was articulated in *McCulloch* v. *Maryland* (1819), which upheld the authority of Congress to create the Bank of the United States and declared unconstitutional the right of a state to tax an instrument of the federal government. In his ruling on *McCulloch*, Marshall at once explained the authority of the court to interpret the constitution, the nature of federal-state relations inherent in a federal system of government, and the democratic nature of the U.S. government. During his tenure as chief justice, Marshall participated in more than 1,000 decisions, writing more than 500 of them himself.

John Marshall (1755–1835). MPI/Hulton Archive/Getty Images

Born in a log cabin, John Marshall was the eldest of 15 children of Thomas Marshall, a sheriff, justice of the peace, and land surveyor who came to own some 200,000 acres (80,000 ha) of land in Virginia and Kentucky and who was a leading figure in Prince William county (from 1759 Fauquier county), Va., and Mary Keith Marshall, a clergyman's daughter whose family was related to both the Randolphs and the Lees (two of Virginia's most prominent families). Marshall's childhood and youth were spent in the near-frontier region of Fauquier county, and he later lived in the Blue Ridge mountain area where his father had acquired properties. His schooling was primarily provided by his parents, supplemented only by the instruction afforded by a visiting clergyman who lived with the family for about a year and by a few months of slightly more formal training at an academy in Westmoreland county.

When political debate with England was followed by armed clashes in 1775, Marshall, as lieutenant, joined his father in a Virginia regiment of minutemen and participated in the first fighting in that colony. Joining the Continental Army in 1776, Marshall served under George Washington for three years in New Jersey, New York, and Pennsylvania, his service including the harsh winter of 1777–78 at Valley Forge. He eventually rose to the rank of captain, and when the term of service of his Virginia troops expired in 1779, Marshall returned to Virginia and thereafter saw little active service prior to his discharge in 1781.

Marshall's only formal legal training was a brief course of lectures he attended in 1780 at William and Mary College given by George Wythe, an early advocate of judicial review. Licensed to practice law in August 1780, Marshall returned to Fauquier county and was elected to the Virginia House of Delegates in 1782 and 1784. Attending the sessions of the legislature in the state capital at Richmond, he established a law practice there and made the city his home after his marriage to Mary Ambler in January 1783.

For the next 15 years Marshall's career was marked by increasing stature at the bar of Virginia and within Virginia politics. Although by 1787 he had not achieved a public position that would have sent him as a delegate to the Constitutional Convention in Philadelphia, he was an active, if junior, proponent of the new Constitution of the United States in the closely contested fight for ratification. That year Marshall was elected to the legislature that would take the first step toward ratification by issuing a call for a convention in Virginia to consider ratifying; he was also elected a delegate to the convention. His principal effort on the floor of the convention was, perhaps prophetically, a defense of the judiciary article. He then used his acknowledged popularity to gain or build the narrow margin by which Virginia's ratification of the Constitution was won.

Shortly after the new constitution came into force, Pres. George Washington offered Marshall appointment as U.S. attorney for Virginia, a post Marshall declined. In 1789, however, he sought and obtained a further term in Virginia's House of Delegates as a supporter of the national government. As party lines emerged and became defined in the 1790s, Marshall was recognized as one of the leaders of the Federalist Party in Virginia. In 1795 Washington tendered him an appointment as attorney general. This, too, was declined, but Marshall returned to the state legislature as a Federalist leader.

In 1797 Marshall accepted an appointment by Pres. John Adams to serve as a member of a commission, with Elbridge Gerry and Charles C. Pinckney, that unsuccessfully sought to improve relations with the government of France. After the mission, reports were published that disclosed that certain intermediaries, some shadowy figures known as X, Y, and Z, had approached the commissioners and informed them that they would not be received by the French government unless they first paid large bribes; the reports further revealed that these advances had been rebuffed in a memorandum prepared by Marshall. Marshall subsequently became a popular figure, and the conduct of his mission was applauded by one of the earliest American patriotic slogans, "Millions for defense, but not one cent for tribute."

Upon his return from France, Marshall declined appointment to the Supreme Court to succeed Justice James Wilson, but he was persuaded by Washington to run for Congress and was elected in 1799 as a Federalist. His service in the House of Representatives was brief,

British engraving satirizing Franco-American relations after the XYZ Affair. Frenchmen plunder female "America," while five figures (lower right) representing other European countries look on. John Bull (England) sits laughing on "Shakespeare's Cliff." British Cartoon Prints Collection, Library of Congress, Washington, D.C. (Digital File Number: cph 3g02711)

however. His chief accomplishment there was the effective defense of the president against a Republican attack for having honoured a British request under the extradition treaty for the surrender of a seaman charged with murder on a British warship on the high seas.

In May 1800 Pres. John Adams requested the resignation of his secretary of war and offered the post to Marshall and again Marshall declined. Adams then dismissed his secretary of state and offered Marshall the vacant position. In an administration harassed by dissension and with uncertain prospects in the forthcoming election, the appeal of the invitation must have been addressed principally to Marshall's loyalty. After some initial hesitation, Marshall accepted. In the autumn of 1800, Chief Justice

Oliver Ellsworth resigned because of ill health. Adams, defeated in the November election, tendered reappointment to John Jay, the first chief justice, but Jay declined. Adams then turned to Marshall, and in January 1801 Adams sent to the Senate the nomination of John Marshall to be chief justice. The last Federalist-controlled Senate confirmed the nomination on Jan. 27, 1801. On February 4, Marshall was sworn in, but at Adams's request Marshall continued to act as secretary of state for the last month of the Adams presidential administration. (Marshall also served briefly, at Jefferson's request, as secretary of state in Jefferson's administration.)

Under Marshall's leadership for more than 34 years—the longest tenure for any chief justice—the Supreme Court set forth the main structural lines of the government. Initially, there was no consensus as to whether the Constitution had created a single country or a federation of independent states, and although judicial decisions could not alone dispel differences of opinion, they could create a body of coherent, authoritative, and disinterested doctrine around which opinion could mass and become effective. To the task of creating such a core of agreement Marshall brought qualities that were admirably adapted for its accomplishment. His own mind had apparently a clear and well-organized concept of the effective government that he believed was needed and was provided by the Constitution. He wrote with a lucidity, a persuasiveness, and a vigour that gave to his judicial opinions a quality of reasoned inevitability that more than offset an occasional lack in precision of analysis. His tenure gave opportunity for the development of a unified body of constitutional doctrine. It was the first aspect of Marshall's accomplishment that he and the court he headed did not permit this opportunity to pass unrecognized.

Marshall distinguished himself from his colleagues by wearing a plain black robe, in stark contrast to the scarlet and ermine robes worn by the other justices. Prior to Marshall's appointment, it had been the custom of the Supreme Court, as it was in England, for each justice to deliver an opinion in each significant case. This method may be effective where a court is dealing with an organized and existing body of law, but with a new court and a largely unexplored body of law, it created an impression of tentativeness, if not of contradiction, which lent authority neither to the court nor to the law it expounded. With Marshall's appointment—and presumably at his instigation—this practice changed. Thereafter, for some years, it became the general rule that there was only a single opinion from the Supreme Court. Indeed, Marshall's term was marked by great consensus and stability on the court; Marshall only dissented formally once during his tenure, and between 1811 and 1823 the Supreme Court's personnel did not change—the longest such period in history. This change of practice alone would have contributed to making the court a more effective institution. And when the opinions were cast in the mold of Marshall's clear and compelling statement, the growth of the court's authority was assured.

Marbury v. *Madison* (1803) was the first of Marshall's great cases and the case that established for the court its power to invalidate federal laws and acts found to be in conflict with the Constitution. The foundation of the case and the significance of its ruling must be understood within the historical and strategic context of the time. Shortly before the expiration of Pres. John Adams's term, the Federalist-controlled Congress created and Adams filled a number of federal judicial positions. The commissions of the judges had been signed and the seal of the United States affixed in the office of the secretary of state

(Marshall's office), but some of them, including that of William Marbury, remained undelivered. (Ironically, Marshall, as secretary of state, was responsible for delivering these appointments.) Offended by what he perceived to be a Federalist court-packing plan, Pres. Thomas Jefferson ordered his secretary of state, James Madison, to halt delivery of the remaining commissions.

Marbury unsuccessfully petitioned the Department of State for his commission, and subsequently he instituted suit in the Supreme Court against Madison. Although the matter was not beyond question, the court found that Congress had, under the authority of Section 13 of the Judiciary Act of 1789, authorized that such suits be started in the Supreme Court rather than in a lower court. The court faced a dilemma of historic proportions. If it issued a writ of mandamus ordering Madison to deliver the commission, it was clear that such a command would be ignored, thereby undermining the court's influence for generations, but if it failed to issue the writ the Supreme Court would be seen as cowering in the face of presidential power. Under Marshall's direction, the Supreme Court altered the issue at hand, and, speaking through Marshall, the court held that Article III of the Constitution did not permit this expansion of the court's original jurisdiction and that the court could not follow a statute that was in conflict with the Constitution. It thereby confirmed for itself its most controversial power—the function of judicial review, of finding and expounding the law of the Constitution.

Throughout Marshall's tenure as chief justice, the Supreme Court held only one term each year, lasting about seven or eight weeks (slightly longer after 1827). Each justice, however, also conducted a circuit court—Marshall in Richmond, Va., and Raleigh, N.C. Marshall's conflict with the Jefferson administration erupted once more in 1807 in

Richmond, where Marshall presided at the treason trial of former Vice Pres. Aaron Burr, successfully frustrating President Jefferson's efforts toward a runaway conviction; as a result, Burr was freed. With hardly more than three months annually engaged in judicial duties (at that time, the court's docket was much smaller than it is today), Marshall had much time to devote to personal endeavours. In 1807 he completed the five-volume *The Life of George Washington*. He also served (1812) as chair of a commission charged with finding a land and water route to link eastern and western Virginia, and in 1829 he was part of the Virginia state constitutional convention.

Once the power of judicial review had been established, Marshall and the court followed with decisions that assured that it would be exercised and that the whole body of federal law would be determined in a unified judicial system with the Supreme Court at its head. *Martin* v. *Hunter's Lessee* (1816) and *Cohens* v. *Virginia* (1821) affirmed the Supreme Court's right to review and overrule a state court on a federal question, and in *McCulloch* v. *Maryland* (1819) the Supreme Court asserted the doctrine of "implied powers" granted Congress by the Constitution (in this instance, that Congress could create a bank of the United States, even though such a power was not expressly given by the Constitution).

McCulloch v. *Maryland* well illustrated that judicial review could have an affirmative aspect as well as a negative; it may accord an authoritative legitimacy to contested government action no less significant than its restraint of prohibited or unauthorized action. The ruling, which nearly precipitated a constitutional crisis, upheld the authority of the federal government and denied to the states the right to impose a tax on the federal government. Faced with the daunting task of explaining where the authority of the

Congress to create a bank is located in the Constitution, Marshall turned to Article I, Section 8, Paragraph 18, which grants to the federal government the power to "make all laws which shall be necessary and proper" for carrying out the powers it was explicitly granted in the Constitution. The ruling infuriated states' rights advocates, leading several to admonish Marshall and the court through the press. In an unprecedented move, Marshall replied under an assumed name, writing as "A Friend to the Constitution."

In commerce law Marshall led the court in deciding a number of cases brought in response to the emerging American economy and the government's attempts to regulate it. *Fletcher* v. *Peck* (1810) and the Dartmouth College case (1819) established the inviolability of a state's contracts, and *Gibbons* v. *Ogden* (1824) affirmed the federal government's right to regulate interstate commerce and to override state law in doing so. Many of Marshall's decisions dealing with specific restraints upon government have turned out to be his less-enduring ones, however, particularly in later eras of increasing governmental activity and control; indeed, it has been in this area that judicial review has evoked its most vigorous critics.

Outside the court, Marshall spent much of his time caring for an invalid wife. He also enjoyed companionship, drinking, and debating with friends in Richmond. In general, for the first 30 years of his service as chief justice, his life was largely one of contentment. In late 1831, at age 76, Marshall underwent the rigours of surgery for the removal of kidney stones and appeared to make a rapid and complete recovery. But the death of his wife on Christmas of that year was a blow from which his spirits did not so readily recover. In 1835 his health declined rapidly, and on July 6 he died in Philadelphia. He was buried alongside his wife in Shockoe Cemetery in Richmond.

ROGER TANEY

(b. March 17, 1777, Calvert County, Md.—d. Oct. 12, 1864, Washington, D.C.)

Roger Brooke Taney was the fifth chief justice of the Supreme Court of the United States. The first Roman Catholic member of the Supreme Court and the first to hold the office of chief justice, he is remembered principally for the *Dred Scott* decision (1857).

Taney was the son of Michael and Monica (Brooke) Taney. Of English ancestry, Michael Taney had been educated in France and was a prosperous tobacco grower in Calvert County, Md. After graduation from Dickinson College in Pennsylvania, in 1795, Taney studied law with Judge Jeremiah Chase of the Maryland General Court. He was admitted to the bar in 1799 at Annapolis and served one year in the Maryland House of Delegates before settling down in Frederick, Md., to practice law. In 1806 he married Anne Key, whose brother, Francis Scott Key, later wrote "The Star-Spangled Banner."

Roger B. Taney, photograph by Mathew Brady. Library of Congress, Washington, D.C.

Taney was a member of the conservative, property-conscious Federalist Party until 1812, when the party opposed the war against England. He returned to the Maryland House of Delegates in 1816, when, as a political maverick, he was elected to the state senate.

Two years after his term expired in 1821, he moved his family to Baltimore where he was soon recognized as an excellent lawyer. Juries were impressed with his sense of fair play and his courtesy toward opposing attorneys. In 1827 he was appointed attorney general of Maryland. By this time he had aligned himself with Andrew Jackson, the leader of the Democratic Party, and when Jackson, elected president in 1828, reorganized his cabinet in 1831, he appointed Taney attorney general of the United States.

Throughout his tenure in Washington, Taney had been an outspoken leader in the Democrats' fight against the central bank, the Bank of the United States, which was widely regarded as a tool of Eastern financial interests. Taney believed it had abused its powers, and he strongly advised the president to veto the congressional bill that would renew the bank's charter and wrote much of the veto message; he also recommended that government funds be withdrawn from the bank and be deposited in a number of state banks.

As a result of his role in the fight over the Bank of the United States, Taney had become a national figure, and in 1833 President Jackson appointed him secretary of the treasury. But opposition to Taney and his financial program was so strong that the Senate rejected him in June 1834, marking the first time that Congress had refused to confirm a presidential nominee for a cabinet post.

Taney returned to Baltimore to rebuild his law practice. A year later, Jackson nominated him to the Supreme Court of the United States as an associate justice. Taney's enemies stalled the nomination indefinitely. Then, on July 6, 1835, Chief Justice John Marshall died, and Taney was nominated to fill his place on the bench.

Despite powerful resistance, led by such prominent politicians as Henry Clay, John C. Calhoun, and Daniel

Webster, Taney was sworn in as chief justice in March 1836. Although he had inherited the conservative tradition of the Southern aristocracy and had supported states' rights, the Taney court did not discard John Marshall's ideas of federal supremacy. Taney believed firmly in divided sovereignty, but he also believed it was the Supreme Court's role to decide which powers should be shared. Eventually many of those who had opposed Taney's appointment came to respect him.

One of the most important decisions for which the Taney court is noted concerned rights granted by charters. The majority opinion in *Charles River Bridge* v. *Warren Bridge* (1837) declared that rights not specifically conferred could not be inferred from the language of a document. In this decision Taney rejected the claim of a bridge company that the subsequent grant by the state legislature of a charter to another bridge company impaired the legislature's charter to the first company.

The majority opinion that Taney delivered on March 6, 1857, in *Dred Scott* v. *Sanford* is the one for which he is best known. In essence, the decision argued that Scott was a slave and as such was not a citizen and could not sue in a federal court. Taney's further opinion that Congress had no power to exclude slavery from the territories and that Negroes could not become citizens was bitterly attacked in the Northern press. The *Dred Scott* decision probably created more disagreement than any other legal opinion in U.S. history; it became a violently divisive issue in national politics and dangerously undermined the prestige of the Supreme Court.

Whenever state authorities threatened or interfered with the execution of federal power, however, Taney upheld federal supremacy. His opinion in *Ableman* v. *Booth* (1858), denying state power (in this case the courts of the state of Wisconsin) to obstruct the processes of the federal courts, remains a magnificent statement of constitutional federalism. Under Taney's leadership federal judicial power was expanded over corporations, the federal government was held to have paramount and exclusive authority over foreign relations, and congressional authority over U.S. property and territory was vigorously upheld. His conflict with Pres. Abraham Lincoln over the president's suspension of a citizen's petition for a writ of habeas corpus in time of war made him an object of bitter criticism, although, eventually, many jurists came to agree with Taney's defense of an individual's constitutional rights.

Taney, a deeply religious Roman Catholic, considered slavery an evil. He had freed the slaves he had inherited before he came to the Supreme Court. It was his belief, however, that slavery was a problem to be resolved gradually and chiefly by the states in which it existed. As an adherent of the South, he could do nothing but watch the defeat of his cause. Even though his thinking ran counter to the dominant historical trends of his time, he had an enduring influence on the substance and evolution of U.S. constitutional law.

Morrison Remick Waite

(b. Nov. 29, 1816, Lyme, Conn.—d. March 23, 1888, Washington, D.C.)

Morrison Remick Waite was the seventh chief justice of the United States (1874–88). He frequently spoke for the Supreme Court in interpreting the post–Civil War constitutional amendments and in redefining governmental jurisdiction over commerce in view of the great expansion of American business. Reacting against the extreme nationalism predominant during the Civil War and in the early Reconstruction years, the Waite court did much to rehabilitate the idea of states' rights.

The son of a justice of the Connecticut Supreme Court, Waite practiced law in Toledo, Ohio. In 1871–72 he became nationally prominent as one of the U.S. counsels to the *Alabama* arbitration commission at Geneva, dealing with Great Britain's liability to the United States for permitting Confederate warships to be built and serviced in British ports. The favourable impression he made on Pres. Ulysses S. Grant at that time led to his appointment as chief justice by Grant on Jan. 19, 1874.

Waite's most famous opinion was *Munn* v. *Illinois*, 94 U.S. 113 (1877), one of a group of six Granger cases involving Populist-inspired state legislation to fix maximum rates chargeable by grain elevators and railroads. Against the assertion that the Granger laws constituted deprivation of private property without due process of law and conflicted with the Fourteenth Amendment, Waite borrowed a phrase from Sir Matthew Hale, lord chief justice of England (1671–76), to hold that, when a business or private property was "affected with a public interest," it was subject to governmental regulation.

Morrison Remick Waite. Courtesy of the Library of Congress, Washington, D.C.

In several cases concerning the recently freed and supposedly enfranchised African

Morrison Remick Waite. Library of Congress, Washington, D.C.

Americans, Waite held that the privileges and immunities of U.S. citizens had not been increased by the Fourteenth Amendment and that neither it nor the Fifteenth Amendment had given Congress extensive power to safeguard civil rights. In *United States* v. *Cruikshank*, 92 U.S. 542 (1876), he stated that, despite its apparently plain language, the Fifteenth Amendment had not conferred a federal right of suffrage on African Americans, because "the right to vote comes from the states." In *Hall* v. *De Cuir*, 95 U.S. 485 (1878), he struck down, as a "direct burden" on interstate commerce, a Louisiana statute requiring full racial integration of passengers by common carriers. In *Reynolds* v. *United States*, 98 U.S. 145 (1878), in upholding the application of antipolygamy laws to Mormons, Waite distinguished between the freedom to hold a religious belief and the freedom to engage in religious practices (polygamy) that had been outlawed by legislative act.

Waite tried to establish a nonpolitical conception of the chief justiceship. In 1876 he might have had the Republican Party's nomination for president, but he rejected it because, in his view, his candidacy would detract from the court's prestige.

Melville Weston Fuller

(b. Feb. 11, 1833, Augusta, Maine—d. July 4, 1910, Sorrento, Maine)

Melville Weston Fuller was the eighth chief justice of the Supreme Court of the United States (1888–1910). His amiability, impartiality, and rare administrative skill enabled him to manage court conferences efficiently and to resolve or forestall serious disputes among the justices whom he superintended. Justices Oliver Wendell Holmes and Samuel F. Miller, two outstanding members of the Fuller court, called him the best presiding judge they had ever known.

Graduated from Bowdoin College, Brunswick, Maine (1853), Fuller attended Harvard Law School briefly, was a newspaperman in Augusta for a time, was admitted to the bar in 1855, and from 1856 practiced law in Chicago. He was elected as a Democrat to the Illinois Constitutional Convention of 1861 and to the State House of Representatives in 1862.

Melville Weston Fuller, 1902. Courtesy of the Library of Congress, Washington, D.C.

Prominent at the Chicago bar but unknown nationally, Fuller was appointed chief justice by Pres. Grover Cleveland in 1888. He successfully administered a court that comprised such justices as Holmes, Miller, Stephen J. Field, Joseph P. Bradley, and John Marshall Harlan, all of whom overshadowed him in either intelligence or forcefulness. He wrote two important opinions, both in 1895: *U.S.* v. *E.C. Knight Co.*, in which he construed the Sherman Anti-Trust Act of 1890 so narrowly as to prevent its application to almost any business except transportation; and *Pollock* v. *Farmers' Loan and Trust Co.*, in which he declared the federal income tax law of 1894 unconstitutional.

While serving as chief justice, Fuller also was an arbitrator of the Venezuelan boundary dispute between that nation and Great Britain (1897–99) and a member of the Hague Court of International Arbitration (1900–10).

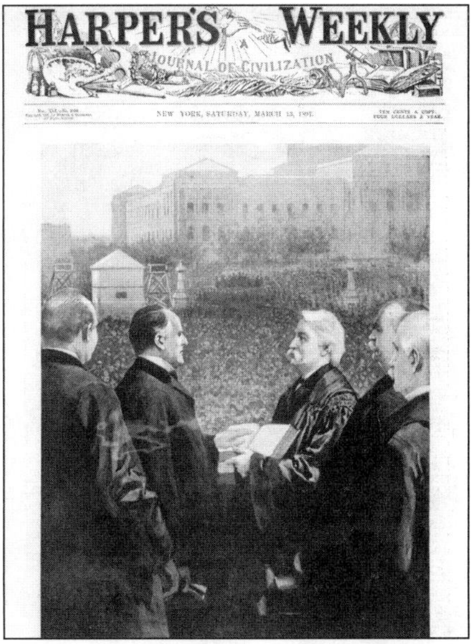

Chief Justice Fuller administers the oath of office at the inauguration of President McKinley, as depicted in Harper's Weekly, *March 13, 1897.* Library of Congress Prints and Photographs Division

Edward Douglass White

(b. Nov. 3, 1845, near Thibodaux, La.—d. May 19, 1921, Washington, D.C.)

Edward Douglass White was the ninth chief justice of the United States (1911–21). His major contribution to U.S. jurisprudence was his "rule of reason" decision in 1911, which federal courts have since applied to antitrust cases.

The son of a judge, U.S. congressman, and Louisiana governor, White received a Roman Catholic Jesuit education and fought briefly for the Confederacy in the Civil War, after which he was trained in a New Orleans law office. Entering Louisiana politics as a Democrat, he was elected a

Edward Douglass White. Courtesy of the National Archives, Washington, D.C.

state senator in 1874 and was appointed to the state Supreme Court in 1878. Elected to the U.S. Senate in 1890, he was elevated to the U.S. Supreme Court by Pres. Grover Cleveland in 1894.

As an associate justice, he formulated the concept of the "incorporation" of territories that the United States had acquired in 1898 by the Spanish-American War. In a concurring opinion in *Downes* v. *Bidwell* (1901), one of a group called the Insular cases, White argued that "incorporation" into the United States, by treaty or statute, determined the availability of constitutional safeguards to residents of a new U.S. possession. This vague criterion was adopted by a majority of the court in 1905 and was invoked to deny constitutional protection in Hawaii and the territories won from Spain, which were held to be "unincorporated."

Promoted to the chief justiceship by Pres. William Howard Taft in 1910, White assumed office early the next year. In *Standard Oil Company of New Jersey* v. *United States* and *United States* v. *American Tobacco Company* (both 1911) he promulgated the idea that a restraint of trade by a monopolistic business must be "unreasonable" to be illegal under the Sherman Act. His failure to define a "reasonable" restraint, coupled with the imprecise brevity of the

Sherman Act, made subsequent antitrust decisions very difficult to predict.

During World War I, White wrote two important decisions in favour of federal emergency powers. *Wilson* v. *New* (1917) sustained the Adamson Act of 1916, fixing minimum wages and maximum hours for railroad workers. Military conscription was upheld in the Selective Draft Law Case (*Arver* v. *United States*; 1917).

William Howard Taft

(b. Sept. 15, 1857, Cincinnati, Ohio—d. March 8, 1930, Washington, D.C.)

William Howard Taft was the 27th president of the United States (1909–13) and the 10th chief justice of the United States (1921–30). As the choice of Pres. Theodore Roosevelt to succeed him and carry on the progressive Republican agenda, Taft as president alienated the progressives—and later Roosevelt—thereby contributing greatly to the split in Republican ranks in 1912, to the formation of the Bull Moose Party (also known as the Progressive Party), and to his humiliating defeat that year in his bid for a second term.

William Howard Taft, 1909. Library of Congress, Washington, D.C.

The son of Alphonso Taft, secretary of war and attorney general (1876–77) under Pres. Ulysses S. Grant, and Louisa Maria

Torrey, Taft graduated second in his Yale class of 1878, studied law, and was admitted to the Ohio bar in 1880. Drawn to politics in the Republican Party, he served in several minor appointive offices until 1887, when he was named to fill the unfinished term of a judge of the superior court of Ohio. The following year he was elected to a five-year term of his own, the only time he ever attained office via popular vote other than his election to the presidency. From 1892 to 1900 he served as a judge of the United States Sixth Circuit Court of Appeals, where he made several decisions hostile to organized labour. He upheld the use of an injunction to stop a strike by railroad workers, and he declared illegal the use of a secondary boycott. On the other hand, he upheld the rights of workers to organize, to join a union, and to strike, and he extended the power of the injunction to enforce antitrust laws.

Secretary of War William Howard Taft and Alice Roosevelt on a goodwill mission to Japan and the Philippines in 1905. Library of Congress, Washington, D.C.

Taft resigned his judgeship on March 15, 1900, to accept appointment by Pres. William McKinley to serve as chairman of the Second Philippine Commission. Charged with organizing civil government in the islands following the Spanish-American War (1898), Taft displayed considerable talent as an executive and administrator. In 1901 he became the first civilian governor of the Philippines, concentrating in that post on the economic development of the islands. Fond of and very popular among the Philippine people, Taft twice refused to leave the islands when offered appointment to the Supreme Court by Pres. Theodore Roosevelt. In 1904 he agreed to return to Washington to serve as Roosevelt's secretary of war, with the stipulation that he could continue to supervise Philippine affairs.

Although dissimilar in both physique and temperament, the rotund, easygoing Taft and the muscular, almost-manic Roosevelt nonetheless became close friends; the president regarded his secretary of war as a trusted adviser. When Roosevelt declined to run for reelection, he threw his support to Taft, who won the 1908 Republican nomination and defeated Democrat William Jennings Bryan in the electoral college by 321 votes to 162. Progressive Republicans, who had found their champion in Theodore Roosevelt, now expected Roosevelt's handpicked successor to carry forward their reform agenda.

However, progressives soon found abundant reason to be disappointed with Taft. Temperamentally, he lacked Roosevelt's compelling leadership qualities, which had inspired people to charge into battle against all that was wrong in American society. Politically, Taft offended progressives when he failed to appoint any from their ranks to his cabinet. He further angered progressives when he backed the Payne-Aldrich Tariff of 1909, a highly protectionist measure that ironically was the product of a special session of Congress called (by Taft) to revise tariff rates downward. Progressives, who favoured lower tariffs, expected a veto. When Taft not only signed the tariff but called it "the best bill that the party has ever passed," the rupture in Republican ranks seemed unlikely to be mended.

Despite his close relationship with Roosevelt, Taft as president aligned himself with the more conservative members in the Republican Party. He did prove to be a vigorous trustbuster, however, launching twice as many antitrust prosecutions as had his progressive predecessor. He also backed conservation of natural resources, another key component of the progressive reform program. But when he fired Gifford Pinchot—head of the Bureau of Forestry, ardent conservationist, and close friend of Roosevelt—Taft severed whatever support he still had among Republican progressives.

Roosevelt returned from an African safari in 1910, and progressives quickly urged him to come out publicly in opposition to his political protégé. At first Roosevelt declined to criticize Taft by name, but by 1912 a breach between the former friends was clearly evident. When Roosevelt decided to challenge Taft for the Republican presidential nomination, the two attacked each other mercilessly in the Republican primary elections. The primary results proved beyond doubt that Republican voters wanted Roosevelt to be the party's standard-bearer in 1912, but Taft's forces controlled the convention and secured the nomination for the incumbent. Believing that the convention had been rigged and that their man had been cheated out of the nomination he deserved, Republican progressives bolted their party to form the Bull Moose (or Progressive) Party and nominated Roosevelt as their presidential candidate.

The split in Republican ranks assured the election of Democrat Woodrow Wilson. Roosevelt came in a distant

MUTUAL SOLACE.

Messrs. Taft and Roosevelt (*to one another*). "CHEER UP! IT MIGHT HAVE BEEN WORSE. *I* MIGHT HAVE WON."

Cartoon depicting William Howard Taft and Theodore Roosevelt lying exhausted after the 1912 presidential campaign and saying, "Cheer up! I might have won." Library of Congress, Washington, D.C.

second, and Taft, capturing less than a quarter of the popular vote, won just two states—Utah and Vermont. In the electoral college, Taft set a record for the poorest performance by an incumbent president seeking reelection: He won a mere 8 electoral votes compared with 88 for Roosevelt and 435 for Wilson.

As president, Taft frequently claimed that "politics makes me sick." Never eager for the office, he had been prodded to pursue it by his wife, Helen Herron Taft, whom he had married in 1886. As first lady she was a key political adviser to her husband.

On his departure from the White House Taft returned to Yale, where he became a professor of constitutional law.

With the entry of the United States into World War I, he served on the National War Labor Board, and at the war's conclusion he strongly supported American participation in the League of Nations. In 1921 Pres. Warren G. Harding appointed Taft chief justice of the United States, launching what was probably the happiest period in Taft's long career in public service. He promptly took steps to improve the efficiency of the Supreme Court, which had fallen far behind in its work. His influence was decisive in securing passage of the Judge's Act of 1925, which gave the Supreme Court greater discretion in choosing its cases so that it could focus more attention on constitutional questions and other issues of national importance.

Although generally conservative in his judicial philosophy, Taft was no rigid ideologue. His approval of court injunctions, for example, was limited by his insistence that injunctions could not be employed to interfere with the rights of workers to organize and strike. His most important contribution to constitutional law was his opinion in *Myers* v. *United States* (1926) upholding the authority of the president to remove federal officials, a much-belated endorsement of the position taken by Pres. Andrew Johnson with respect to the Tenure of Office Act in his impeachment trial in 1868.

William Howard Taft, Kent professor of constitutional law at Yale University between 1913 and 1921. Library of Congress, Washington, D.C.

Suffering from heart disease, Taft resigned as chief justice on Feb. 3, 1930, and he died a little more than a month later.

Charles Evans Hughes

(b. April 11, 1862, Glens Falls, N.Y.—d. Aug. 27, 1948, Osterville, Mass.)

Charles Evans Hughes was a jurist and statesman who served as an associate justice of the Supreme Court of the United States (1910–16), U.S. secretary of state (1921–25), and 11th chief justice of the United States (1930–41). As chief justice he led the Supreme Court through the great controversy arising over the New Deal legislation of Pres. Franklin D. Roosevelt.

Hughes was the son of David Charles Hughes, an immigrant from England (1855) and a Baptist minister, and Mary Catherine Connelly Hughes. He received much of his early education at home, before attending Madison University (now Colgate University) from 1876 to 1878. He then transferred to Brown University, where he graduated in 1881, and he received a law degree with honours from Columbia University School of Law in 1884. After passing the bar he joined Chamberlain, Carter, and Hornblower, a prominent New York City law firm; stress caused him to take a sabbatical in the 1890s, during which time he served as visiting professor at Cornell University Law School (he returned to his legal practice after only two years for financial reasons).

Hughes gained prominence in 1905 as counsel to New York state legislative committees investigating abuses in the gas and electric power industries and the life insurance business. Reluctant to enter the political arena, Hughes was enticed by the support of Pres. Theodore Roosevelt to run for governor of New York in 1906, and he won a close election over the flamboyant newspaper publisher

William Randolph Hearst, becoming the only Republican to win statewide office in New York that year. Hughes served with a profound sense of responsibility, endorsing reform measures, and he was skeptical and terse with regard to politically motivated and populist policies, even in the form of legislation. Because of his preference for merit over favouritism in the appointments process and his rejection of certain popular policy proposals (e.g., equal pay for women), he only narrowly won reelection in 1908. Indeed, his appointment to the U.S. Supreme Court in 1910 by Pres. William Howard Taft arguably spared him the likelihood of losing his bid for a third term in office.

Hughes's first period of service on the Supreme Court was relatively unremarkable. Ideologically moderate, he supported federal governmental responsibility in regulating commerce and favoured First and Fourteenth amendment rights.

In the absence of controversy on the bench—and insulated from the split in the Republican Party (i.e., the Bull Moose revolt of 1912)—Hughes emerged as a leading candidate for the Republican presidential nomination in 1916. After receiving the Republican nomination, he resigned from the Supreme Court (he also won the endorsement of the Progressives—the Bull Moose Party). Hughes was narrowly defeated (277 electoral votes to 254), however, by Pres. Woodrow Wilson. He then returned to the private practice of law.

In 1921 Hughes was appointed secretary of state by Pres. Warren G. Harding (and following Harding's death, he continued to serve in that position under Pres. Calvin Coolidge). Hughes negotiated a separate peace treaty with Germany after the U.S. Senate failed to ratify the Treaty of Versailles, supported attempts to secure the entry of the United States into the League of Nations, and planned and then served as chairman of the Washington Conference

(1921–22) on disarmament. He also insisted that the United States refrain from recognizing the government of the Soviet Union until it recognized property rights and other elements central to capitalism. In 1925 Hughes resigned as secretary of state and returned to private law practice.

In 1930 Pres. Herbert Hoover nominated Hughes to become chief justice of the Supreme Court. His nomination elicited opposition within the Senate, however, particularly from Democrats who found that his representation and support of corporate interests appeared at variance with concern for the economic crisis precipitated by the Great Depression; nevertheless, he was confirmed by the Senate 52–26 on February 13. In several cases involving problems raised by the Great Depression, Hughes generally favoured the exercise of federal power. On May 27, 1935 ("Black Monday" to critics of the court), however, there was a flurry of judicial activity regarding the constitutionality of several New Deal proposals; declared unconstitutional by the court were the National Industrial Recovery Act of 1933 (in *Schechter Poultry Corporation* v. *United States*), in which Hughes wrote the majority opinion, the Frazier–Lemke Act (which had provided debt relief to farmers), and the Federal Home Owner's Loan Act of 1933. As the 1930s also marked a period of jurisprudential transition—a movement away from economic questions and toward issues of individual rights—Hughes found himself and the court supporting the doctrine of selective incorporation, under which some elements of the Bill of Rights (e.g., freedom of speech, the press, and religion) were made applicable to the states under the rubric of the due-process clause of the Fourteenth Amendment to the Constitution of the United States.

Reacting to the defeat of much of his New Deal legislation, President Roosevelt devised a plan to reorganize the court. In 1937 Roosevelt proposed to "pack" the Supreme

Court by appointing a new (and presumably liberal) justice to offset each sitting justice over the age of 70 who refused to retire; Hughes played a leading role in defeating the plan. Hughes successfully persuaded Justice Owen Roberts to switch his vote in the case of *West Coast Hotel Co.* v. *Parrish* (1937), which upheld Washington state's minimum wage law and also implied that the remainder of New Deal legislation would be considered constitutional, and in a letter to the Senate Judiciary Committee, Hughes attacked Roosevelt's plan to reorganize the judiciary. On April 12, 1937, Hughes delivered the opinion in *National Labor Relations Board* v. *Jones & Laughlin Steel Corporation*, which sustained the right of collective bargaining under the National Labor Relations Act of 1935 (the Wagner Act), and a few weeks later the court upheld various provisions of the Social Security Act. It was widely believed that these pro–New Deal decisions dampened the political pressure to alter the composition of the judiciary and thus contributed to the defeat of the court-packing plan.

Hughes retired from the Supreme Court in 1941 at age 79. He was the author of numerous books, including *Foreign Relations* (1924), *The Pathway of Peace* (1925), *The Supreme Court of the United States* (1928), and *Pan-American Peace Plans* (1929).

Harlan Fiske Stone

(b. Oct. 11, 1872, Chesterfield, N.H.—d. April 22, 1946, Washington, D.C.)

Harlan Fiske Stone was an associate justice of the U.S. Supreme Court (1925–41) and the 12th chief justice of the United States (1941–46). Sometimes considered a liberal and occasionally espousing libertarian ideas, he believed primarily in judicial self-restraint: the efforts of government to meet changing 20th-century social and political conditions should be restricted only on the basis of unconstitutionality rather than undesirability.

Harlan Fiske Stone, 1929. Library of Congress, Washington, D.C.

Stone graduated from Amherst College in 1894 and received his law degree in 1898 from the law school of Columbia University. He then taught at Columbia from 1899 and served as the dean of its law school from 1910, while also conducting a private law practice in New York City. Pres. Calvin Coolidge appointed him attorney general of the United States (1924), in which post he reorganized the Federal Bureau of Investigation after its reputation had been tarnished by the Teapot Dome and other scandals of Pres. Warren G. Harding's administration. Stone's effectiveness prompted Coolidge to appoint him an associate justice of the Supreme Court (1925), and Pres. Franklin D. Roosevelt promoted him to succeed Chief Justice Charles Evans Hughes (1941).

In his early years on the court, Stone was bracketed with Justices Louis Brandeis and Oliver Wendell Holmes (and later with Benjamin Nathan Cardozo, who replaced Holmes in 1932) as one of the "three great dissenters" against a conservative majority that disliked legislative regulation of business. During Roosevelt's presidency (1933–45), Stone generally affirmed the legislative reforms of the New Deal, upholding, for instance, the Social Security Act of 1935 and the enactment of a national minimum wage law in 1938. In a leading case involving federal New Deal legislation, *United States* v. *Butler*, 297 U.S. 1 (1936), he opposed the court majority's invalidation of the Agricultural Adjustment Act.

Besides advocating a new tolerance for state regulation of economic activity, Stone was instrumental in asserting the court's concern for protecting individual civil liberties from governmental coercion. He was the lone dissenter when, in *Minersville School District* v. *Gobitis*, 310 U.S. 586 (1940), the court upheld a state ruling that children who were Jehovah's Witnesses must join in saluting the American flag in public schools. This decision was overruled (1943) while Stone was chief justice. In *Girouard* v. *United States*, 328 U.S. 61, 76 (1946), the court followed Stone's dissent in a similar case, *United States* v. *Macintosh*, 283 U.S. 605 (1931), in which he had argued that religious pacifists who refused to take the statutory oath to bear arms could nonetheless be naturalized as citizens.

Stone was renowned for the judicial impartiality and objectivity that he displayed in his more than 600 opinions, many of them on important constitutional questions. He was often less successful, however, in building a consensus among his associate justices, with the result that the Supreme Court during his chief justiceship was often a bitterly divided body.

Fred Moore Vinson

(b. Jan. 22, 1890, Louisa, Ky.—d. Sept. 8, 1953, Washington, D.C.)

Fred M. Vinson was an American lawyer and the 13th chief justice of the United States. He is remembered as a vigorous supporter of a broad interpretation of federal governmental powers.

Following completion of his legal studies at Centre College in Danville, Ky., in 1911, Vinson entered private practice in Louisa and quickly assumed an active role in local political affairs. In 1923 he was appointed to fill a vacancy in the U.S. House of Representatives. The following year he was elected to the seat as a Democrat and, except for one two-year period, served as a member of Congress until 1938.

As a congressman Vinson was recognized as an outstanding expert in tax and fiscal policy. From 1938 to 1943 he served as associate justice of the U.S. Court of Appeals for the District of Columbia. Between 1943 and 1945 he held a succession of high executive posts in emergency agencies of World War II, and in 1945 he became secretary of the Treasury in the cabinet of Pres. Harry S. Truman. In this office he helped establish the International Bank for Reconstruction and Development and the International Monetary fund.

Upon appointment by President Truman, Vinson became chief justice of the U.S. Supreme Court on June 24, 1946. It is generally believed that his tact reduced personal animosities that had arisen on the court. As a judge his interpretation of the powers of the federal government often led him to reject claims of individual right asserted in opposition to the exercise of governmental authority. Perhaps his best-known opinions, however, are those upholding the rights of

Fred M. Vinson. Courtesy of the Library of Congress, Washington, D.C.

members of racial minorities under the equal-protection clause of the Fourteenth Amendment to the Constitution. He spoke for the court in refusing to permit a state court to enforce a private agreement ("restrictive covenant") to sell real property to white persons only (*Shelley* v. *Kraemer*, 1948). His opinion for the court in 1947 upheld the power of the federal courts to enjoin a strike in coal mines then under control of the federal government. He strongly dissented from the court's opinion holding unconstitutional the president's seizure of the strike-threatened steel industry during the Korean War (*Youngstown Sheet & Tube Co.* v. *Sawyer*, 1952).

Earl Warren

(b. March 19, 1891, Los Angeles, Calif.—d. July 9, 1974, Washington, D.C.)

Earl Warren was an American jurist and the 14th chief justice of the United States (1953–69). He presided over the Supreme Court during a period of sweeping changes in U.S. constitutional law, especially in the areas of race relations, criminal procedure, and legislative apportionment.

Earl Warren, 1953. UPI—EB Inc.

Warren was the son of Erik Methias Warren, a Norwegian immigrant who worked as a railroad repairman, and Christine Hernlund Warren, who emigrated with her parents from Sweden when she was a child. His father was blacklisted for a time following the Pullman Strike (1894), and Earl also worked for the railroad during his youth; his experience soured his view toward the railway, and in his memoirs he noted that his progressive political and legal attitudes resulted from his exposure to the exploitive and corrupt conduct of the railroad companies.

Warren attended the University of California, Berkeley, where he received bachelor's (1912) and law (1914) degrees. His political appetite was whetted by his work on the successful campaign of Progressive Party gubernatorial candidate Hiram Johnson. After graduation he was admitted to the bar and spent three years in private practice. In 1917 he enlisted in the U.S. Army, serving stateside during World War I and rising to the rank of first lieutenant before his discharge in 1918. Thereafter he briefly worked with the California State Assembly before becoming deputy city attorney for Oakland; in 1920 he took up the post of deputy district attorney for Alameda county. In 1925–26 he served out the remaining year of the district attorney's term of office, and in 1926 he won a full term as Alameda county district attorney.

As district attorney until 1939, Warren distinguished himself for both his honesty and hard work and for fighting corruption (e.g., he successfully prosecuted the county sheriff and several of his deputies). He also earned support within the Republican Party for prosecuting radicals under the state syndicalism laws during the 1920s and for securing the convictions of labour-union leftists in the 1930s. Enjoying an excellent reputation throughout the state and country, Warren was elected state attorney general in 1938. He was easily elected governor in 1942 and twice won reelection (1946, 1950), becoming the first California governor to win three successive terms (in 1946 he won both the Democratic and Republican party primaries for governor). As governor, he supported the controversial policy of interning Japanese Americans during World War II and progressive policies on issues such as education, health care, and prison reform.

He was nominated as the Republican candidate for vice president of the United States in 1948, losing on a ticket with Thomas Dewey (it was his only defeat in an election). Despite the 1948 loss, his national reputation continued to grow, and he gained a strong following as a potential presidential candidate in 1952. As the campaign drew near, divisions within the Republican Party began to emerge. His moderate position in the campaign against communism (led in California by fellow Republican Richard M. Nixon)—e.g., he opposed loyalty oaths for professors at the University of California—and his less-than-committed primary campaign left Warren a distant third, behind Robert A. Taft and Gen. Dwight D. Eisenhower, by the time of the Republican National Convention. Nevertheless, Warren hoped to secure the Republican nomination as a compromise candidate. However, a pair of strategic moves—one by Nixon to secretly campaign for Eisenhower despite his pledge of support for Warren, and one by Warren to support the Fair Play Act that effectively assured delegate support for Eisenhower for president—ultimately sank his nomination, and he campaigned vigorously for Eisenhower in the general election. In gratitude for his loyalty, Eisenhower considered Warren for several cabinet offices and later promised Warren the first vacant seat on the court. In July 1953 Eisenhower offered Warren the post of solicitor general, but when Chief Justice Fred Vinson died suddenly on Sept. 8, 1953, Eisenhower, honouring his commitment, appointed Warren interim chief justice; on March 1, 1954, Warren's appointment was confirmed by the U.S. Senate.

In his first term on the bench, he spoke for a unanimous court in the leading school desegregation case,

Brown v. *Board of Education of Topeka* (1954). Rejecting the doctrine that had prevailed since *Plessy* v. *Ferguson* in 1896, Warren, speaking for the court, stated that "separate educational facilities are inherently unequal," and the court subsequently called for the desegregation of public schools with "all deliberate speed." In *Watkins* v. *United States* (1957), Warren led the court in upholding the right of a witness to refuse to testify before a congressional committee, and, in other opinions concerning federal and state loyalty and security investigations, he likewise took a position discounting the fear of communist subversion that was prevalent in the United States during the 1950s.

In *Reynolds* v. *Sims* (1964), using the Supreme Court's precedent set in *Baker* v. *Carr* (1962), Warren held that representation in state legislatures must be apportioned equally on the basis of population rather than geographical areas, remarking that "legislators represent people, not acres or trees." In *Miranda* v. *Arizona* (1966)—a landmark decision of the Warren court's rulings on criminal justice—he ruled that the police, before questioning a criminal suspect, must inform him of his rights to remain silent and to have counsel present (appointed for him if he is indigent) and that a confession obtained in defiance of these requirements is inadmissible in court.

After the assassination of Pres. John F. Kennedy on Nov. 22, 1963, Pres. Lyndon B. Johnson appointed Warren to chair a commission established to investigate the killing as well as the murder of the presumed assassin, Lee Harvey Oswald. The report of the Warren Commission was submitted in September 1964 and was published later that year. Partly because of his bureaucratic naiveté and partly because of his interest in conducting a quick investigation that would allow the country—and the Kennedy family—to move beyond the tragedy, the report proved remarkably uncritical in accepting government information (particularly information provided by the Federal Bureau of Investigation and the Central Intelligence Agency). For example, Warren rushed the commission's staff, refused to interview Kennedy's widow, and kept the autopsy photos under seal. Ultimately, the report did not silence those who presumed there had been a wide conspiracy to assassinate the president.

Convinced that Nixon (whom by this time Warren detested) would win the presidency in 1968 and wanting Johnson to name his replacement, Warren notified Johnson that he would resign at the president's pleasure. Johnson subsequently attempted to elevate Justice Abe Fortas as Warren's successor (and to name Homer Thornberry to take Fortas's seat as associate justice), but, in the face of a conservative filibuster, Fortas's nomination was withdrawn; Nixon subsequently appointed Warren Burger chief justice, and Warren officially retired on June 23, 1969.

In retirement he lectured and wrote *The Memoirs of Chief Justice Earl Warren*, which was published posthumously in 1977. He was also the author of *A Republic, If You Can Keep It* (1972). In 1974 Warren suffered three heart attacks, and on the day of his death he prodded the Supreme Court to order the release to the U.S. Congress of the secret Watergate tapes (which would hasten Nixon's resignation from the presidency).

Despite the criticisms leveled at the report of the Warren Commission, Warren's reputation as a leader—ideologically, politically, and jurisprudentially—of the court is firmly established, and he stands out as one of the most influential chief justices in U.S. history. A common denominator in Warren's decisions—and indeed the legacy of what has come to be known as the Warren court—was a profound sensitivity to the impact of judicial decisions on society at large. Viewing the court as much more than an agency that merely interprets law, Warren used the court as a vessel for social change, especially in the field of civil liberties and civil rights. Commonly regarded as a liberal judicial activist, Warren interpreted the constitution in an open-ended manner, reading its provisions as potential solutions to contemporary social problems.

WARREN EARL BURGER

(b. Sept. 17, 1907, St. Paul, Minn.—d. June 25, 1995, Washington, D.C.)

Warren Burger was the 15th chief justice of the United States (1969–86).

After graduating with honours from St. Paul (now William Mitchell) College of Law in 1931, Burger joined a prominent St. Paul law firm and gradually became active in Republican Party politics. In 1953 he was appointed an assistant U.S. attorney general, and in 1955 he was nominated by Pres. Dwight D. Eisenhower to the U.S. Court of Appeals for the District of Columbia. Burger's generally conservative approach during his 13-year service (1956–69) on the nation's second highest court commended him to Pres. Richard M. Nixon, who in 1969 named Burger to succeed Earl Warren as chief justice of the Supreme Court. He was quickly confirmed and in June 1969 was sworn in as the nation's chief justice.

Contrary to some popular expectations, Burger and his three fellow Nixon-appointed justices did not try to reverse the tide of activist decision making on civil rights issues and criminal law that was the Warren court's chief legacy. The court upheld the 1966 *Miranda* decision, which required that a criminal suspect under arrest be informed of his rights, and the court also upheld busing as a

Warren E. Burger, 1976. Library of Congress, Washington, D.C. (neg. no. LC-USZC6-23)

permissible means of racially desegregating public schools and the use of racial quotas in the distribution of federal grants and contracts to minorities. Under Burger's leadership the court did dilute several minor Warren-era decisions protecting the rights of criminal defendants, but the core of the Warren court's legal precedents in this and other fields survived almost untouched. Burger voted with the majority in the court's landmark 1973 decision (*Roe v. Wade*) that established women's constitutional right to have abortions.

Burger himself took a pragmatic and accommodating stance toward controversial legal issues, and his opinions were not particularly noted either for their intellectual consistency or for their comprehensive and systematic application of legal principles. He instead became deeply involved in the administrative functions of his office, and he worked to improve the efficiency of the entire judicial system.

Burger retired from the Supreme Court in 1986 to devote himself full-time to the chairmanship of the commission planning the bicentennial celebration of the U.S. Constitution (1987). He was awarded the Presidential Medal of Freedom in 1988.

William Rehnquist

(b. Oct. 1, 1924, Milwaukee, Wis.—d. Sept. 3, 2005, Arlington, Va.)

William Hubbs Rehnquist was the 16th chief justice of the United States (1986–2005).

Rehnquist served in the U.S. Army Air Forces during World War II. After the war, he attended Stanford University, where he was awarded bachelor's (1948), master's (1948), and law (1952) degrees, finishing first in his law school class. He also received a master's degree in political science from Harvard University in 1949. Rehnquist clerked for Supreme Court Justice Robert H. Jackson in 1952–53, when the court was hearing cases on the constitutionality of racial segregation in public schools. During this period, Rehnquist authored a memorandum for Jackson in which he argued that the segregationist legal doctrine of "separate but equal" should be upheld. In later years, critics of Rehnquist used this document—along with charges that, as a Republican Party election volunteer in the 1960s, he aggressively attempted to enforce Arizona's literacy-test laws, which effectively denied African Americans and Hispanics the right to vote—in unsuccessful attempts to

William Rehnquist, 1976. Library of Congress, Washington, D.C. (neg. no. LC-USZC6-28)

defeat his nomination to the Supreme Court and his elevation to chief justice.

From 1953 to 1969, Rehnquist practiced law in Phoenix, Arizona. In 1969 Pres. Richard M. Nixon appointed him assistant attorney general of the Office of Legal Counsel for the Department of Justice, a post in which he distinguished himself as a staunch advocate of greatly enlarged police powers and as an opponent of civil rights legislation.

In October 1971 Nixon nominated Rehnquist to fill the vacancy on the U.S. Supreme Court left by the death of Justice Hugo Black. Given his legal and political conservatism, Rehnquist was a logical choice for Nixon, who wished to use the appointment as a way of curtailing the perceived influence of liberal jurisprudence on social policy. After extended and often heated Senate committee hearings, Rehnquist was finally confirmed by the Senate by a vote of 68–26 in December 1971. (In contrast, Nixon's October 1971 appointment of Lewis F. Powell, Jr., to another court vacancy won near-unanimous confirmation.) Rehnquist took his seat on the court in January 1972.

Rehnquist's reputation as a justice was based on his encyclopaedic knowledge of constitutional law, his conservative voting record, and his leadership of the court as it moved from generally liberal to mostly conservative. During the 1970s and into the '80s, the vigorous and articulate Rehnquist formed the anchor of the court's conservative minority bloc. His polished legal opinions and consistently conservative stance on almost all legal issues prompted Pres. Ronald Reagan in June 1986 to nominate him to replace Warren E. Burger as chief justice. In much the same way that he appealed to Nixon's desire for a "cleaner and safer" America, Rehnquist suited Reagan's positions on abortion rights and religious liberty, among other issues. An opponent of legalized abortion and an establishment-clause accommodationist (i.e., he favoured extending religion farther into the public sphere), Rehnquist—like other Reagan appointees—shared the president's vision that the court's interpretation of the Constitution and individual laws should be limited to reflect the original intent of the framers and the letter of legislative statutes, respectively. Once again, Rehnquist endured a contentious confirmation hearing, but he was approved by the Senate 65–33.

As chief justice, Rehnquist dramatically reduced the court's caseload and improved its efficiency. With the support of other Reagan appointees (Sandra Day O'Connor, Antonin Scalia, and, later, Anthony Kennedy), the court curbed the ability of Congress to expand federal authority and curtailed affirmative action. Federal laws regulating conduct as disparate as religious expression (under the Religious Freedom Restoration Act), intrastate commerce, and criminal procedure were invalidated in deference to states' rights. In 2003, however, Rehnquist found himself in the minority in cases in which a majority of the court struck down state sodomy laws and upheld affirmative action policies. Although many conservatives had hoped that Rehnquist would lead the court in a reversal of *Roe* v. *Wade* (1973), the ruling that established the legal right to abortion, the decision of three Republican appointees in *Planned Parenthood of Southeastern Pennsylvania* v. *Casey* (1992) permitted greater legal restrictions on abortion but also reaffirmed the right found in *Roe*.

In his essay "The Notion of a Living Constitution" (1976), Rehnquist articulated the role of the court in a democratic society, concluding that judicial restraint and deference to lawmaking majorities are essential elements of a responsible judicial system. The liberal concept of a living constitution, he argued, constitutes "an end run around popular government" that is "corrosive of the fundamental values of our democratic society."

NOTABLE PAST JUSTICES AND JURISTS

SAMUEL CHASE

(b. April 17, 1741, Princess Anne, Md.—d. June 19, 1811, Washington, D.C.)

Samuel Chase was an associate justice of the U.S. Supreme Court from 1796 to 1811. His acquittal in an impeachment trial (1805) inspired by Pres. Thomas Jefferson for political reasons strengthened the independence of the judiciary.

Samuel Chase, portrait by an unknown artist. Library of Congress, Washington, D.C.

A member of the Maryland assembly (1764–84) and the Continental Congress (1774–78, 1784–85) and a signer of the Declaration of Independence, Chase served as chief judge of the Maryland General Court from 1791 to 1796, when Pres. George Washington appointed him to the U.S. Supreme Court. In *Ware* v. *Hylton* (1796), an important early test of nationalism, he upheld the primacy of U.S. treaties over state statutes. In *Calder* v. *Bull* (1798), he asserted that legislative power over liberty and property is limited by "certain vital principles in our free Republican governments"; later courts read these principles into the "due process of law" clauses of the Fifth and Fourteenth amendments to the Constitution.

During the struggle between the Federalist and Jeffersonian Republican parties, Chase, a Federalist, conducted his circuit court in a partisan manner. The House of Representatives, encouraged by Jefferson, charged Chase with improper actions in treason and sedition trials and with a political address to a grand jury. In March 1805 the Senate, acting as trial court, found him not guilty. His acquittal, by establishing the principle that federal judges could be removed only for indictable criminal acts, clarified the constitutional provision (Article III, section 1) that judges shall hold office during good behaviour. Some scholars believe that if Chase had been found guilty, the Jefferson administration would have proceeded against other Federalist justices, particularly Chief Justice John Marshall, a leading opponent of Jefferson.

William Johnson

(b. Dec. 27, 1771, Charleston, S.C.—d. Aug. 4, 1834, Brooklyn, N.Y.)

William Johnson was an associate justice of the U.S. Supreme Court from 1804 to 1834. He established the practice of rendering individual opinions—concurring or dissenting—in addition to the majority opinion of the court. A deeply sensitive man and a learned, courageous jurist, he set himself against the dominance exercised over the court by Chief Justice John Marshall.

After serving in the South Carolina House of Representatives (1794–99; speaker, 1798–99), Johnson was elected by the legislature to the Court of Common Pleas, at that time the highest tribunal in the state. During his tenure as a state judge he was active in organizing at Columbia a college that later became the University of South Carolina.

Appointed by Pres. Thomas Jefferson in March 1804, Johnson was the first Democratic-Republican justice of the U.S. Supreme Court. In attempting to secure the court's position as the interpreter of the law and the Constitution (largely according to Federalist Party principles), Chief Justice Marshall discouraged the writing of seriatim (separate) opinions, delivered the opinion of the court in most major cases, and strove for unanimity among his colleagues. Johnson, however, often expressed independent views; he had been accustomed to preparing seriatim opinions in the state court, and in this predisposition he was supported by Jefferson, a political opponent of Marshall.

Although Jefferson and Johnson remained friends until the former's death in 1826, Johnson did not always sustain Jeffersonian policy. In *Gilchrist* v. *Collector of Charleston* (1808), Johnson, while holding federal circuit court, allowed clearance from the port of Charleston to a ship detained under Jefferson's Embargo Act of 1807, a measure intended to preserve U.S. neutrality in the Napoleonic Wars. In Supreme Court cases Johnson usually agreed with Marshall's insistence on broad federal power unhampered by state action. More than his fellow justices, however, Johnson favoured cooperation rather than antagonism between federal and state governments and economic regulation in the public interest. Concurring with Marshall's opinion in *Gibbons* v. *Ogden* (1824), he defended the regulatory power of Congress over interstate and foreign commerce; over one of Marshall's few dissents, he upheld, in *Ogden* v. *Saunders* (1827), state power to alleviate economic distress. Late in his life Johnson angered many in his state by his circuit court decision in *Holmes* v.

United States (1832), rejecting state nullification of federal statutes.

Joseph Story

(b. Sept. 18, 1779, Marblehead, Mass.—d. Sept. 10, 1845, Cambridge, Mass.)

Joseph Story was an associate justice of the United States Supreme Court from 1811 to 1845. He joined Chief Justice John Marshall in giving juristic support to the development of American nationalism. While also teaching law at Harvard (1829–45), he delivered lectures that he elaborated into a monumental series of nine legal commentaries, some of which had international influence.

After graduation from Harvard, Story practiced law at Salem, Mass. (1801–11), became prominent in the Jeffersonian Republican (afterward called the Democratic) Party, was elected to the state legislature (1805), served part of a term in the U.S. House of Representatives (1808–09), returned to the Massachusetts House of Representatives (1810), and was chosen its speaker (1811).

In November 1811 Pres. James Madison appointed Story, at the age of only 32 and without judicial experience, to the Supreme Court. The president did so despite the opposition of Thomas Jefferson, who believed Story had contributed to the failure of the foreign trade embargo enacted during Jefferson's presidency. Although Madison thought Story would contest the Federalist Party nationalism of Chief Justice Marshall, the new justice soon joined Marshall in construing the Constitution broadly in favour of expanding federal power. His opinion for the court in *Martin* v. *Hunter's Lessee* (1816) established the appellate authority of the Supreme Court over the highest state courts in all civil cases involving the federal Constitution, statutes, and treaties. This decision was called by Charles Warren, historian of the Supreme Court, "the keystone of the whole arch of Federal judicial power."

From the death of Marshall (July 6, 1835) until the confirmation of Roger Brooke Taney as his successor (March 16, 1836), Story presided over the court. In *Prigg* v. *Pennsylvania*, 16 Peters 539 (1842), Story, who opposed slavery, upheld the federal Fugitive Slave Act of 1793 in order to strike down state statutes concerning the recapture of escaped slaves. In *Swift* v. *Tyson*, 16 Peters 1 (1842; overruled 1938), he, in effect, created a "federal common law" for commercial cases by holding that federal trial courts, taking jurisdiction when the parties were citizens of different states, need not follow decisions by the courts of the state in which the cause of action arose.

Joseph Story, photograph by Mathew Brady. Courtesy of the Library of Congress, Washington, D.C.

In 1829 Story accepted the first Dane professorship of law, founded specifically for him at Harvard Law School by a writer on law, Nathan Dane. The endowment paid for the publication of Story's commentaries: *Bailments (1832), On the Constitution*, 3 vol. (1833),

The Conflict of Laws (1834), Equity Jurisprudence, 2 vol. (1836), *Equity Pleadings* (1838), *Agency* (1839), *Partnership* (1841), *Bills of Exchange* (1843), and *Promissory Notes* (1845). His works on equity made him, along with Chancellor James Kent of New York, a founder of equity jurisprudence in the United States. The commentary on conflicts affected numerous statutes and treaties of Latin American nations. Alexis de Tocqueville drew heavily on Story's constitutional commentary.

John McLean

(b. March 11, 1785, Morris County, N.J.—d. April 4, 1861, Cincinnati, Ohio)

John McLean was a cabinet member and an associate justice of the U.S. Supreme Court from 1829 to 1861. His most famous opinion was his dissent in the *Dred Scott* decision (1857). He was also perhaps the most indefatigable seeker of the presidency in U.S. history; although he was never nominated, he made himself "available" in all eight campaigns from 1832 through 1860.

After two terms in the U.S. House of Representatives (1812–16), McLean was appointed a judge in the Supreme Court of Ohio, a position he resigned in 1822 to become commissioner of the General Land Office under Pres. James Monroe. In 1823 he was named postmaster general and became noted for his efficiency and nonpartisanship in that office. After Pres. Andrew Jackson took office, McLean resigned in protest over Jackson's open advocacy of the spoils system of political patronage, which undermined McLean's recent reforms. Jackson thereupon appointed him an associate justice of the U.S. Supreme Court.

In *Dred Scott* v. *Sandford* (1857), McLean insisted, in a minority opinion, that a slave became free when his owner took him into a state where slavery was not legally established. In McLean's view, an African American was a citizen and thus was able to sue, in a case involving diversity of state citizenship, in a federal court. His position was reflected in the Fourteenth Amendment to the U.S. Constitution.

Samuel Miller

(b. April 5, 1816, Richmond, Ky.—d. Oct. 13, 1890, Washington, D.C.)

Samuel Freeman Miller was an associate justice of the U.S. Supreme Court from 1862 to 1890. He was a leading opponent of efforts to use the Fourteenth Amendment of the Constitution to protect business against government regulation. He was spokesman for the court in its first attempt to construe the amendment, passed after the American Civil War largely to assure the rights of the newly freed slaves. He was in the majority then, but his view that the amendment did not bar legislative restraints on industry ceased to prevail by the 1890s and did not again predominate until the late 1930s.

A practicing physician for 12 years, Miller also read law and was admitted to the bar in 1847. His opposition to slavery caused him to move in 1850 from the slave state of Kentucky to the free state of Iowa, where he became a prominent lawyer and a Republican Party leader. Appointed to the Supreme Court by Pres. Abraham Lincoln on July 16, 1862, Miller was the first justice from any state west of the Mississippi River.

During the Civil War, Miller supported military trials of dissident civilians and the Union blockade of the Confederacy. Dissenting from the court, he also approved the federal and state loyalty oaths required of lawyers, teachers, and clergymen immediately after the war. His dissenting opinion in favour of "greenbacks" as war-emergency legal tender (*Hepburn* v. *Griswold*, 1870) became the majority's stand when the court reversed itself the next year and led to the permanent legitimation of paper money in the United States.

The court's first opportunity to construe the Fourteenth Amendment was given by the Slaughterhouse Cases (1873). The amendment, which was supposed to confer civil rights on African Americans, was invoked by the challengers to support the proposition that the right to run a business without state-government interference was one of the protected "privileges and immunities" of citizenship. Concluding that there was no such federal right, Miller strictly limited the amendment's guarantees of "due process of law" and "equal protection of the laws," as well as "privileges and immunities of citizens." While Miller's view prevailed, business corporations were unable to shield themselves from legislative regulation by claiming to be among the "persons" or "citizens" whose rights the framers of the Fourteenth Amendment intended to safeguard. (In the 1890s, however, the court came to accept Justice Stephen J. Field's contrary conception of the amendment as an aid to big business.)

By declaring most civil rights to be aspects of state rather than of federal citizenship, Miller unwittingly deprived the federal government of jurisdiction over many problems of the political and social equality of African Americans. In *Ex Parte Yarbrough* (1884), however, he upheld federal protection, against repression by private persons, of African Americans' right to vote in congressional elections. Another libertarian opinion by Miller, *Kilbourn* v. *Thompson* (1881), checked irresponsible investigation by congressional committees.

Stephen Johnson Field

(b. Nov. 4, 1816, Haddam, Conn.—d. April 9, 1899, Washington, D.C.)

Stephen Field was an associate justice of the U.S. Supreme Court from 1863 to 1897. He was the chief architect of the constitutional approach that largely exempted the rapidly expanding industry of the United States from governmental regulation after the Civil War. He found the judicial instrument for the protection of private enterprise principally in the Fourteenth Amendment, which had been passed as a civil rights measure. In his interpretation, the privileges and immunities of citizens secured by the amendment included the right to run a business without government interference, a view that prevailed in the court from the 1890s until the 1930s.

A graduate of Williams College, Williamstown, Mass. (1837), Field practiced law in New York City with one of his brothers, the legal reformer David Dudley Field. In 1849 he went to California, where he bought land in the Sacramento River gold-mining area, organized a town government, and became a state legislator and (in 1857) a state supreme court justice. Appointed by Pres. Abraham Lincoln, Field sat on the U.S. Supreme Court from March 10, 1863, until Dec. 1, 1897, the second longest service in the court's history (after that of Justice William O. Douglas).

Field spoke for the court when it invalidated federal and state loyalty oaths required after the Civil War. His opposition to interference with private enterprise came to the fore in the Slaughterhouse Cases (1873), in which a state law granting a monopoly to a single livestock-butchering business was challenged by rival entrepreneurs as an infringement of their rights under the Fourteenth Amendment. Field dissented against the majority decision upholding the state law. The court eventually adopted his interpretation of the amendment's "due-process" clause; corporations were regarded as persons whose liberty or property was not to be taken by the federal government (Fifth Amendment) or by the states (Fourteenth Amendment) without due process of law, the standard of which came to be so rigorous as to exclude governmental control. In joining the court majority that declared unconstitutional the federal income tax law of 1894, Field expressed fear of "a war of the poor against the rich."

In 1880 and 1884 Field was a serious contender for the Democratic presidential nomination. His second candidacy was frustrated by party leaders in his own state because of his courageous upholding of the rights of California's Chinese minority.

Oliver Wendell Holmes, Jr.

byname The Great Dissenter (b. March 8, 1841, Boston, Mass.—d. March 6, 1935, Washington, D.C.)

Oliver Wendell Holmes, Jr., was an associate justice of the United States Supreme Court from 1902 to 1932, a U.S. legal historian, and a philosopher who advocated judicial restraint. He stated the concept of "clear and present danger" as the only basis for limiting free speech.

Oliver Wendell Holmes, Jr., was the first child of the celebrated writer and physician Oliver Wendell Holmes. The family background on both sides represented the New England "aristocracy" of character and accomplishment. His father was descended from the Puritan poet Anne Bradstreet; he married Amelia Lee Jackson, whose father, Charles, was a justice of the Supreme Judicial Court of the State of Massachusetts, a bench on which Oliver Wendell Holmes, Jr., was to sit for 20 years. He was proud

Oliver Wendell Holmes, Jr. Encyclopædia Britannica, Inc.

of this heritage and spoke of it often. It helped shape his mind and character.

Young Holmes went to a private school and then to Harvard College. He was graduated in the class of 1861 and like his father before him was class poet. At the outbreak of the U.S. Civil War he enlisted as a private in the 4th Battalion of Infantry and began training at Boston's Fort Independence, not expecting to finish the academic year or take his degree. The battalion was not called up, and after graduation the young man applied for and received, in July, a commission as first lieutenant in the 20th Massachusetts Regiment of Volunteers. He was 20 years old at that time.

His letters and diary give vivid pictures of his war experiences. He was seriously wounded three times, at the battles of Ball's Bluff, Antietam, and Chancellorsville. He left the army after three years, having been commissioned lieutenant colonel although mustered out with the rank of captain. Holmes described war as "an organized bore." He said, "I trust I did my duty as a soldier respectably, but I was not born for it and did nothing remarkable in that way." In a Memorial Day address to fellow veterans, in 1884, he attributed a certain value to the war experience:

"Through our great good fortune, in our youth our hearts were touched with fire. It was given to us to learn at the outset that life is a profound and passionate thing." This is an aspect of his conviction that ". . . it is required of a man that he should share the passion and action of his time at peril of being judged never to have lived."

In the autumn of 1864 he entered Harvard Law School, ironically without any clear sense of vocation. He had even contemplated medicine, to which his father objected. On different occasions, he said that his "Governor" "put on the screws to have me go to the Law School" or "kicked" him into it. There is a story that, when young Holmes announced to his father the decision to enter the law school, the doctor said, "What's the use of that, Wendell? A lawyer can't be a great man." There was not a deep affinity between father and son. The little doctor's puns and quips, his easy display of emotion, and a somewhat patronizing attitude chafed the tall, less talkative, inherently shy law student. The philosopher William James, perhaps the closest friend of Holmes in the immediate postwar years, once remarked that "no love is lost" between father and son.

Holmes experienced a certain restlessness in law school, finding the tradition of the law as presented in an uninspired curriculum to be stagnant and narrowly precedent-centred. The science, philosophy, or history of law were slighted, and these, rather than what he later called "the small change of legal thought," were what captured Holmes's mind and drew him into the depths of a profession toward which at first he had not felt a powerful incentive.

After finishing law school in 1866 he made the conventional "pilgrimage" abroad, visiting England, France, and Switzerland and meeting a variety of distinguished men.

He was admitted to the bar in 1867 and for 15 years practiced law as a member of several firms. From 1870–73 he was an editor of the *American Law Review*. He edited the 12th edition of the classic survey of early American law, Chancellor James Kent's (1763–1847) *Commentaries on American Law* (1873). He also lectured at Harvard on law.

During this busy time he was engaged in courtship. Always something of a ladies' man, he had maintained a long friendship with Fanny Bowditch Dixwell, daughter of his onetime schoolmaster. She had waited patiently through wartime, his law studies, travel, and apprenticeship. Holmes and Dixwell were married at last on June 17, 1872. The marriage, happy and long lasting, was childless.

In 1880–81 Holmes was invited to lecture on the common law at the Lowell Institute in Boston, and from these addresses developed his book *The Common Law* (1881). Here the genius of Holmes was first clearly revealed and the consistent direction of his thought made evident. A fresh voice was speaking in his words:

> *The life of the law has not been logic: it has been experience. The felt necessities of the time, the prevalent moral and political theories, intuitions of public policy, avowed or unconscious, even the prejudices which judges share with their fellow-men, have had a good deal more to do than the syllogism in determining the rules by which men should be governed. The law embodies the story of a nation's development through many centuries, and it cannot be dealt with as if it contained only the axioms and corollaries of a book of mathematics. In order to know what it is, we must know what it has been, and what it tends to become. We must alternately consult history and existing theories of legislation. But the most difficult labor will be to understand the combination of the two into new products at every stage. The substance of the law at any given time pretty nearly corresponds, so far as it goes, with what is then*

understood to be convenient; but its form and machinery, and the degree to which it is able to work out desired results, depend very much upon its past.

In January 1882 Holmes was made Weld professor of law, a chair established for him at Harvard Law School. In December of the same year he accepted appointment to the Supreme Judicial Court of the State of Massachusetts, knowing the judgeship was his destiny and the function through which he could most influence the development of law. He was to sit on that bench for 20 years, becoming its chief justice in 1899. In 1902 Pres. Theodore Roosevelt appointed him associate justice of the United States Supreme Court. He sat on that court to a more advanced age than did any other man, retiring on Jan. 12, 1932, soon before his 91st birthday.

Fanny Holmes, devoted, witty, wise, tactful, and perceptive, died on April 30, 1929. Holmes wrote to his intimate friend, the English jurist Sir Frederick Pollock, "For sixty years she made life poetry for me and at 88 one must be ready for the end. I shall keep at work and interested while it lasts—though not caring very much for how long." He died two days before his 94th birthday.

In that long span of years on the Supreme Court he became acknowledged as one of the most notable jurists of the age—in the opinion of many the foremost. Often he has been called The Great Dissenter because of the brilliance of his dissenting opinions, but the phrase gives a falsely negative emphasis, and his penetration and originality are seen as fully in the opinions in which he expressed or concurred in the majority view of the court as in those in which he was in dissent.

Holmes believed that the making of laws is the business of legislative bodies, not of courts, and that within constitutional bounds the people have a right to whatever laws they choose to make, good or bad, through their elected representatives. He stated the concept of "clear and present danger" as the only basis for curtailing the right of freedom of speech, illustrating it with the homely example: "The most stringent protection of free speech would not protect a man in falsely shouting fire in a theatre and causing a panic."

He wrote that "the best test of truth is the power of the thought to get itself accepted in the competition of the market. . . . That at any rate is the theory of our Constitution." Again: "If there is any principle of the Constitution that more imperatively calls for attachment than any other it is the principle of free thought—not free thought for those who agree with us but freedom for the thought that we hate."

A man austerely dedicated to his work, he also enjoyed the earthy and the droll. He loved Rabelais. Sometimes in Washington he attended burlesque shows and was said to have remarked, "I thank God I am a man of low tastes." The newly inaugurated Pres. Franklin D. Roosevelt called upon the retired justice and found him reading Plato. "Why do you read Plato, Mr. Justice?" "To improve my mind, Mr. President," replied the 92-year-old man.

Holmes won the love and admiration of generations of lawyers and judges in his long career. When he resigned from the Supreme Court, his "brethren," as he always addressed his fellow justices, wrote him a letter signed by all, saying in part: "Your profound learning and philosophic outlook have found expression in opinions which have become classic, enriching the literature of the law as well as its substance. . . . While we are losing the privilege of daily companionship, the most precious memories of your unfailing kindliness and generous nature abide with us, and these memories will ever be one of the choicest traditions of the Court."

Louis Brandeis

(b. Nov. 13, 1856, Louisville, Ky.—d. Oct. 5, 1941, Washington, D.C.)

Louis Brandeis. Library of Congress, Washington, D.C.

Louis Dembitz Brandeis was an associate justice of the U.S. Supreme Court from 1916 to 1939. He was the first Jew to sit on the high court.

Brandeis's parents, members of cultivated Bohemian Jewish families, had emigrated from Prague to the United States in 1849. Brandeis attended the public schools of Louisville and the Annen Realschule in Dresden, Ger., before entering the Harvard Law School, from which he graduated at the head of his class in 1877. After less than a year of practice in St. Louis, Mo., he returned to Boston, where he maintained an active and prosperous practice until his appointment to the Supreme Court of the United States in 1916.

At the bar Brandeis came to be known as the people's attorney, by virtue of his representation of interests that had not commonly enjoyed such formidable advocacy. When the affairs of the Equitable Life Assurance Society of New York precipitated widespread alarm in 1905, Brandeis became unpaid counsel for the New England Policy-Holders' Protective Committee. Eventually, to remedy abuses by life-insurance firms, Brandeis devised a system, used in Massachusetts (from 1907), New York, and Connecticut, whereby life insurance was offered over the counter by savings banks at rates within the means of workingmen. From 1907–14 he defended, against charges of unconstitutionality, statutes of various states prescribing maximum hours of labour and minimum wages. At that time he devised what is still known to lawyers as the Brandeis brief, in which economic and sociological data, historical experience, and expert opinions are marshaled to support the legal propositions. His most notable book, a volume of essays, *Other People's Money, and How the Bankers Use It* (1914), dealt with the control exercised by investment bankers over American industry. His work attacking monopolies and interlocking directorates influenced the passage in 1914 of the Clayton Anti-Trust Act and the Federal Trade Commission Act, which strengthened the government's antitrust power. Brandeis' support of Pres. Woodrow Wilson's theory of enforced competition among businesses was repaid on Jan. 28, 1916, when the president appointed him to the Supreme Court. Over bitter opposition by numerous business interests and anti-Semites, the nomination was confirmed by the U.S. Senate, and Brandeis took office on June 5.

In his major judicial opinions, Brandeis mistrusted both the unlimited exercise of governmental power in the name of the people and a conception of individual liberty resulting in the agreement of a few persons to monopolize an economic activity affecting everyone. He believed that, to preserve federalism, state legislatures must be able to make laws suited to varied and changing needs, but he wished to restrict them when they interfered with the freedom to express ideas. In the case of (Charlotte) Anita Whitney (*Whitney* v. *California*, 1927), a communist who had been convicted under a state criminal-syndicalism statute, he delivered a concurring opinion urging that penalties on speech be applied only if they met the "clear and present danger" (of inciting to admittedly illegal acts) test formulated earlier by Justice Oliver Wendell Holmes, Jr. Observing the procedural limits on the court, however, he voted to affirm the conviction because Whitney's lawyer had not properly raised the constitutional free speech issue in the trial court. Previously he had dissented when the Supreme Court upheld convictions under the Espionage Act of 1917 for publishing criticisms of the U.S. entry into World War I.

On most important issues Brandeis was aligned, often in the minority, with his colleague Oliver Wendell Holmes, Jr. During the period of the New Deal, however, many of the dissenting positions of Holmes and Brandeis came to be accepted by the court. While Brandeis supported the constitutional validity of most New Deal legislation, he did not do so indiscriminately; he joined, for example, in the court's decision holding the National Industrial Recovery Act of 1933 to be unconstitutional. He retired on Feb. 13, 1939.

From 1912 Brandeis was an enthusiastic supporter of Zionism, the only cause with which he was publicly identified. Brandeis University, opened in 1948 in Waltham, Mass., was named for him.

John Hessin Clarke

(b. Sept. 18, 1857, New Lisbon, Ohio—d. March 22, 1945, San Diego, Calif.)

John Clarke was an associate justice of the U.S. Supreme Court from 1916 to 1922.

Clarke was the son of John Clarke, a lawyer, and Melissa Hessin Clarke. He attended Western Reserve College (now Case Western University) in Cleveland, Ohio, where he graduated in 1877. After studying law under his father,

Clarke opened a law practice in 1880 in Youngstown, Ohio, where he also bought an interest in the *Youngstown Vindicator* and helped to make it an influential liberal newspaper. He gained a reputation in railroad law and was active in local Democratic Party politics. A delegate to the Democratic National Convention in 1896, Clarke briefly broke with the party over the issue of free silver and became chairman of the Ohio State Democratic Sound Money Convention and a delegate to the national convention of the Gold Democratic Party, a splinter group of Democrats. On his return to the party fold, Clarke become an active supporter of Tom L. Johnson (1901–09), the reform mayor of Cleveland, and Newton Baker, Johnson's successor. After an unsuccessful bid for the U.S. Senate in 1903, he was appointed a federal district judge in 1914. Two years later Pres. Woodrow Wilson nominated Clarke to serve on the U.S. Supreme Court, and he was confirmed by voice vote by the Senate on July 24, 1916.

Clarke generally favoured the extension of government regulatory powers over the economy, and his opinions were used later as precedents in some of the antitrust decisions backing the New Deal policies of Pres. Franklin D. Roosevelt. His position on civil liberties was ambivalent, however, and he relied on a very narrow construction of First Amendment rights in his decisions concerning the suppression of free speech during the Red Scare of 1919–20. After the death of his two sisters, with whom he had lived in Youngstown, Clarke resigned from the court in 1922. In his brief tenure on the court, he wrote 129 opinions and earned the respect of his fellow justices. Afterward he headed a campaign favouring U. S. participation in the League of Nations. He then retired from public life, emerging briefly in a national radio address in 1937 to support Roosevelt's court-reorganization ("court-packing") plan.

Owen Josephus Roberts

(b. May 2, 1875, Germantown, Pa.—d. May 17, 1955, Chester Springs, Pa.)

Owen Roberts was an associate justice of the U.S. Supreme Court from 1930 to 1945.

Roberts was the son of Josephus R. Roberts, a hardware merchant, and Emma Lafferty Roberts. He graduated Phi Beta Kappa in 1895 from the University of Pennsylvania and then entered the university's law school, where he served as associate editor of the *American Law Register* (now *University of Pennsylvania Law Record*) and graduated with highest honours in 1898. Upon his graduation, he continued his association with the University of Pennsylvania for the next two decades, teaching contracts and property law, and he also engaged in private legal practice.

Roberts served briefly as assistant district attorney (1903–06) for Philadelphia county before returning to private legal practice. In 1918 he was appointed special deputy U.S. attorney to prosecute violations of the Espionage Act of 1917. Excelling in this position, Roberts drew the attention of Pres. Calvin Coolidge, who in 1924 named him one of the two attorneys to prosecute parties named in the Teapot Dome Scandal that tarnished the administration of Pres. Warren G. Harding. After a methodical investigation, former Interior Secretary Albert Bacon Fall was convicted of taking bribes in 1929. The following year, Pres. Herbert Hoover had the opportunity to fill a pair of Supreme Court vacancies caused by the unexpected deaths of Chief Justice William Howard Taft and Justice Edward T. Sanford. While Charles Evans Hughes won confirmation to the position of chief justice, Hoover's appointment of John J. Parker met with stiff opposition and was rejected by the Senate 41–39. Hoover subsequently nominated Roberts, who won unanimous confirmation from the Senate on May 20, 1930.

By the time Roberts joined the Supreme Court, the conservative majority that had been dominant in the 1920s had diminished, and the institution was clearly divided along ideological lines. With four reliable conservatives (George Sutherland, Pierce Butler, James McReynolds, and Willis Van Devanter) holding only a slight numerical advantage over the more liberal bloc (Louis Brandeis, Oliver Wendell Holmes, Jr., and Harlan Fiske Stone), Hughes and Roberts entered the court as potential swing votes. As their service on the bench would reveal, Hughes and Roberts did often vote in similar fashion, leading some to regard their seemingly inevitable coupling—and ability to tilt decisions in a liberal or conservative direction—as the "Hughberts" vote. Often characterized as "unreliable members of the so-called liberal majority," Roberts and Hughes cast the deciding vote on several New Deal programs of the Franklin D. Roosevelt administration, upholding some and striking down others.

Roberts, a social liberal, made some of his most important contributions to the court in the area of civil liberties. A supporter of the doctrine of selective incorporation, Roberts voted to extend the authority of the Fourteenth Amendment, through its due-process clause, to the states in order to protect individual rights from being infringed by both the federal and state governments. This tendency was most apparent in *Stromberg* v. *California* and *Near* v. *Minnesota* (both 1931), in which the court invalidated state-led attempts to restrict the First Amendment rights of speech and the press. In perhaps the most famous decision that he wrote, *Herndon* v. *Lowry* (1937), Roberts set aside the conviction of an African American communist organizer convicted under a law that provided no clear standard of guilt. In the area of economic and commerce law, Roberts's opinion in *Nebbia* v. *New York* (1934) upheld the price-setting activities of the New York State Milk Control Board and provided a legal foundation for government regulation of business "affected with a public interest." This liberal orientation was also apparent in Roberts's decisions to uphold the National Labor Relations Act of 1935 (commonly known as the Wagner Act), the Social Security Act of 1935, and the Fair Labor Standards Act of 1938. However, in a series of cases involving prized elements of the New Deal, Roberts sided with the economic conservatives in declaring unconstitutional the Railroad Retirement Act, the National Industrial Recovery Act, the Agricultural Adjustment Act, and the Bituminous Coal Conservation Act.

Despite his role in the New Deal cases, however, Roberts is best remembered for his role as the famous "switch in time that saved nine." In a move assumed to have been politically motivated, Chief Justice Hughes is widely believed to have persuaded Roberts to change his vote in the case of *West Coast Hotel Co.* v. *Parrish* (1937), in which the court upheld Washington state's minimum wage law. The ruling also signaled that the remainder of the New Deal legislation would be declared constitutional and helped to undermine the momentum behind Roosevelt's court-reorganization ("court-packing") plan.

Roberts's tenure on the court also included a stint overseeing commissions that investigated the attack on Pearl Harbor in 1941 and the theft of art objects by the Germans during World War II. Roberts retired from the Supreme Court on July 31, 1945, after which he served as dean of the University of Pennsylvania Law School and as chair of the Security Board of the Atomic Energy Commission and the Fund for the Advancement of Education. His 1951 Oliver Wendell Holmes lectures for

Harvard University were published that same year under the title *The Court and the Constitution*.

Benjamin Cardozo

(b. May 24, 1870, New York, N.Y.—d. July 9, 1938, Port Chester, N.Y.)

Benjamin Nathan Cardozo was an associate justice of the U.S. Supreme Court from 1932 to 1938. He was a creative common-law judge and legal essayist who influenced a trend in American appellate judging toward greater involvement with public policy and a consequent modernization of legal principles. Generally a liberal, he was less concerned with ideology than with the nature of the judicial process; largely for this reason, his importance—while universally conceded—is difficult to fix precisely. Although esteemed for his service on the Supreme Court, he was probably more significant for his work on the highest state tribunal in New York, the Court of Appeals (1914–32; chief judge from 1926).

A member of a distinguished Sephardic Jewish family, Cardozo enjoyed an unblemished personal reputation, although his father, Albert Jacob Cardozo, a New York Supreme Court justice with Tammany Hall connections, had resigned in 1872 under threat of impeachment. Admitted to the New York bar in 1891, Benjamin Cardozo was highly successful as a courtroom lawyer despite his mild, reserved manner. Elected to the state Supreme Court as a reform candidate in 1913, he was quickly promoted to the Court of Appeals. During his tenure, the quality of this appellate bench was thought by many to exceed that of the Supreme Court. In *MacPherson* v. *Buick Motor Company* (1916), Cardozo announced a doctrine that was later adopted elsewhere in the United States and Great

Britain: an implied warranty of safety exists between a manufacturer and a private purchaser, despite intermediate ownership of the product by a retail dealer. His decision in *Palsgraf* v. *Long Island Railroad Co.* (1928) helped to redefine the concept of negligence in American tort law.

After the resignation of Justice Oliver Wendell Holmes, Jr., in 1932, Pres. Herbert Hoover appointed Cardozo to the United States Supreme Court. In the New Deal period under Pres. Franklin D. Roosevelt, Cardozo usually sided with the liberally inclined Justices Louis D. Brandeis and Harlan Fiske Stone. He wrote a majority opinion for *Helvering* v. *Davis*, 301 U.S. 619, and other Social Security cases (1937), upholding the federal Social Security program on the basis of the general welfare provision of the United States Constitution (Article I, section 8). In *Palko* v. *Connecticut*, 302 U.S. 319 (1937), a criminal case involving a claim of double jeopardy, he held that the Fourteenth Amendment to the Constitution imposed on the states only those provisions of the Bill of Rights (the first 10 amendments) that were "of the very essence of a scheme of ordered liberty." Although it offered a minimum of guidance and may have encouraged much more constitutional litigation than would a specific standard, this test was retained by the court through the 1960s. In 1969, however, the Supreme Court reversed the *Palko* ruling, holding in *Benton* v. *Maryland* that the rule against double jeopardy was so fundamental to justice as to be a requirement of due process of law.

Aside from his published opinions, Cardozo is noted for his jurisprudential work, especially *The Nature of the Judicial Process* (1921), based on lectures he delivered at Yale University. He was also among the early leaders of the American Law Institute, which was created to "promote the clarification and simplification of the law and its better adaptation to social needs, to secure the better administration of justice, and to encourage and carry on scholarly and scientific legal work."

Learned Hand

(b. Jan. 27, 1872, Albany, N.Y.—d. Aug. 18, 1961, New York City)

Learned Hand was an American jurist whose tough and sometimes profound mind, philosophical skepticism, and faith in the United States were employed throughout a record tenure as a federal judge (52 years, from April 10, 1909, until his death). Although he was never a justice of the Supreme Court, he is generally considered to have been a greater judge than all but a few of those who have sat on the highest U.S. court.

At Harvard University, Hand studied philosophy (under William James, Josiah Royce, and George Santayana) and law, and thereafter he practiced law in Albany and New York City. In 1909 he was appointed a federal district judge in New York, and in 1924 he was elevated to the United States Court of Appeals for the second circuit (New York, Connecticut, and Vermont), one of his colleagues being his cousin Augustus Noble Hand. From 1939 he served as chief judge. He sat in many cases after his official retirement in 1951.

Learned Hand. Library of Congress, Washington, D.C. (Digital File Number: ggbain-01256)

Because several Supreme Court justices disqualified themselves, Hand's court rendered the final decision (1945) in a major antitrust suit against the Aluminum Company of America (usually called the Alcoa case). After a trial lasting four years, Hand wrote for the court an opinion rejecting the "rule of reason" that the Supreme Court had applied in antitrust cases since 1911. He ruled that evidence of greed or lust for power was inessential; monopoly itself was unlawful, even though it might result from otherwise unobjectionable business practices. In his view, "Congress did not condone 'good trusts' and condemn 'bad ones'; it forbade all."

In 1950 Hand sustained the conviction of 11 American Communist Party leaders on Smith Act charges of conspiracy to teach and advocate the overthrow of the government. His reasoning was adopted by Chief Justice Fred M. Vinson when the Supreme Court also upheld the convictions (*Dennis* v. *United States*, 1951). In a later case (*Yates* v. *United States*, 1957), the Supreme Court under Chief Justice Earl Warren considerably restricted the applicability of the Smith Act.

A collection of Hand's papers and speeches was edited as *The Spirit of Liberty* (1952; 3rd ed., 1960) by Irving Dilliard. Hershel Shanks selected and annotated 43 opinions by Hand for *The Art and Craft of Judging* (1968).

Hugo La Fayette Black

(b. Feb. 27, 1886, Harlan, Ala.—d. Sept. 25, 1971, Bethesda, Md.)

Hugo Black was an associate justice of the Supreme Court of the United States from 1937 to 1971. Black's legacy as a Supreme Court justice derives from his support of the doctrine of selective incorporation, according to which the Fourteenth Amendment to the Constitution of the

Hugo Black. Library of Congress, Washington, D.C. (neg. no. LC-USZ62-52112)

United States makes the Bill of Rights—originally adopted to limit the power of the national government—equally restrictive on the power of the states to curtail individual freedom.

Hugo Black was the youngest of eight children of William La Fayette Black, a poor farmer, and Martha Toland Black. He enrolled in Birmingham (Alabama) Medical School in 1903 but transferred after one year to study law at the University of Alabama in Tuscaloosa. After graduating and passing the bar in 1906, Black practiced law in Birmingham. Appointed a part-time police-court judge in 1911, he fought against the unfair treatment of African Americans and the poor by the local criminal-justice system; as a lawyer, he also represented striking miners and other industrial labourers. His popularity encouraged him to seek political office, and in 1914 he was elected prosecuting attorney for Jefferson county.

After serving in the U.S. Army (1917–19) during World War I, Black resumed the practice of law in Birmingham. His successful defense of a Protestant minister accused of killing a Roman Catholic priest drew the favourable attention of the Ku Klux Klan (KKK), and in 1923 Black joined the organization. Although he openly opposed the

Klan's activities, he understood that its support was a prerequisite for political success in the Deep South. Therefore, even after his resignation from the KKK in 1925, he maintained good relations with its leaders.

Elected to the U.S. Senate as a Democrat in 1926, Black won considerable acclaim for his investigation of utility lobbyists but was criticized for his opposition to the Wagner-Costigan anti-lynching bill, which he believed would offend white Southerners. In 1932 he supported the presidential campaign of Franklin D. Roosevelt, who easily defeated Pres. Herbert Hoover; that year Black also won reelection to the Senate. Black was a strong supporter of Roosevelt's New Deal legislation and court-reorganization ("court-packing") plan. He also sponsored what would become in 1938 the Fair Labor Standards Act, the first federal law to regulate wages and hours. Grateful for Black's support, Roosevelt nominated him to the Supreme Court in August 1937.

Because of his controversial career in the Senate and consistent support of Roosevelt's policies, Black's nomination drew strong opposition. During the Senate hearings, his KKK membership was not a highly contentious issue, though the NAACP demanded answers about Black's membership in the KKK and the African American physicians of the National Medical Association opposed his nomination. The dominant issue during the Senate hearings was whether Black was eligible to serve on the court, because Congress had passed legislation increasing the benefits for Supreme Court retirees, and federal law prohibited a member of Congress from being appointed to a position affected by such legislation during the term in which the legislation was passed. Nevertheless, Black was confirmed by the Senate 63–16. After Black's confirmation but before he sat on the bench, however, solid evidence of his membership in the KKK was made public, causing even

Roosevelt to demand an explanation. In an unprecedented move, Black participated in a radio address and admitted to Klan membership, though he claimed that he never participated in any of its activities. Public opinion had turned against Black, however; on his first day on the court in October 1937 he entered through the court's basement, and hundreds of protesters wore black armbands to express their dissatisfaction.

In the early part of his tenure, Black acted with a growing court majority in its reversal of previous vetoes of New Deal legislation. Black combined this tolerance for increased federal powers of economic regulation with an activist stance on civil liberties. He advocated a literal interpretation of the Bill of Rights, developing a virtually absolutist position on First Amendment rights. During the 1940s and '50s he frequently dissented from the court's majority in free speech cases, denouncing governmental restrictions on core liberties as unconstitutional.

During the 1960s Black held a prominent position among the liberal majority on the court who struck down mandatory school prayer and who guaranteed the availability of legal counsel to suspected criminals. He was, however, torn on issues involving civil disobedience and privacy rights. Although protests were not necessarily viewed as on a par with plain speech, he nevertheless supported the right of the *New York Times* to publish the so-called Pentagon Papers in 1971 in the face of government attempts to restrict their publication. True to the literal foundation of his liberal jurisprudence, he dissented from the majority opinion in *Griswold* v. *Connecticut* (1965), which established a constitutional right to privacy. Although he claimed that Connecticut's law, which prohibited using or aiding in the use of any contraceptive device, was "offensive," he nonetheless argued it was constitutional because he was unable to locate any explicit privacy right within the Constitution.

Black resigned from the Supreme Court on Sept. 17, 1971, and died just one week later. He was buried at Arlington National Cemetery.

Felix Frankfurter

(b. Nov. 15, 1882, Vienna, Austria-Hungary—d. Feb. 22, 1965, Washington, D.C.)

Felix Frankfurter was an associate justice of the United States Supreme Court from 1939 to 1962 and a noted scholar and teacher of law. He was in his time the high court's leading exponent of the doctrine of judicial self-restraint. He held that judges should adhere closely to precedent, disregarding their own opinions, and decide only "whether legislators could in reason have enacted such a law."

Felix Frankfurter. Library of Congress, Washington, D.C.

Frankfurter was the son of a Jewish merchant who left Vienna for New York in 1893. Young Frankfurter was educated at the City College of New York and at the Harvard Law School, where he later taught (1914–39). He served as assistant to Henry L. Stimson when Stimson was U.S. attorney for the Southern District of New York (1906–09) and secretary of war under Pres. William Howard Taft

(1911–13). Frankfurter's influence on Pres. Franklin D. Roosevelt was largely responsible for Stimson's return (1940) as head of the War Department during World War II.

Frankfurter was a legal adviser to Pres. Woodrow Wilson at the Paris Peace Conference (1919). During the immediate postwar period he was one of the most active American Zionists, and he helped to found the American Civil Liberties Union (1920). He delivered blistering attacks on the conviction of Nicola Sacco and Bartolomeo Vanzetti—in which he was encouraged by U.S. Supreme Court Justice Louis Brandeis under a secret arrangement that was not revealed until 1982, when their correspondence was published. Brandeis, from his appointment in 1916 until 1939, when Frankfurter himself joined the court, corresponded frequently with Frankfurter, sending him a yearly stipend for legislative research and for such politico-social actions as the defense of Sacco and Vanzetti.

When Franklin D. Roosevelt became president (1933), Frankfurter, who had advised him during his term as governor of New York, advised him on New Deal legislation and other matters. He was appointed by Roosevelt to the Supreme Court on Jan. 5, 1939. Concerned more with the integrity of government than with the victims of legal injustice, Frankfurter evinced toward federal and state legislative action a hands-off attitude similar to that of his friend Justice Oliver Wendell Holmes, Jr. His insistence on freedom of expression was partly offset by his disinclination to uphold the civil liberties of political radicals, especially members of the U.S. Communist Party during the "witch hunt" of the 1950s. In *Sweezy* v. *New Hampshire* (1957), however, he upheld a claim of academic freedom by a socialist college professor subjected to a state investigation.

Frankfurter's belief that decent government depends in part on procedural safeguards for criminal suspects occasionally conflicted with his policy that the Supreme Court should defer to other branches of the federal government and to the states. In the criminal case of *Wolf* v. *Colorado* (1949), for example, he spoke for the court in condemning illegal seizure of evidence by state officials, but he ruled that the "due process of law" clause of the 14th Amendment to the U.S. Constitution did not require a state court to exclude evidence unlawfully obtained. (The Supreme Court repudiated this theory in 1961.) In his last major opinion, a 64-page dissent in *Baker* v. *Carr* (1962; the first of a series of legislative reapportionment cases in the 1960s), he unsuccessfully asserted that inequitable representation in legislatures is a "political controversy" not subject to the federal judicial power.

Frankfurter retired in 1962. In July 1963 Pres. John F. Kennedy awarded him the Medal of Freedom. Among his books are *The Business of the Supreme Court* (1927; with James Landis); *Mr. Justice Holmes and the Supreme Court* (1938); *The Case of Sacco and Vanzetti* (2nd ed., 1954); and *Felix Frankfurter Reminisces* (1960).

WILLIAM O. DOUGLAS

(b. Oct. 16, 1898, Maine, Minn.—d. Jan. 19, 1980, Washington, D.C.)

William Orville Douglas was a public official, a legal educator, and an associate justice of the U.S. Supreme Court from 1939 to 1975. He was best known for his consistent and outspoken defense of civil liberties. His 36 ½ years of service on the Court constituted the longest tenure in U.S. history.

William O. Douglas. Library of Congress, Washington, D.C. (neg. no. LC-USZ62-44543)

The son of a Presbyterian minister, Douglas moved with his family first to California and then to Washington. His father died when William was a small child, and his mother then settled the family in Yakima, Wash. Although Douglas contracted polio as a youth, he escaped permanent paralysis and developed what would become a lifelong love of the outdoors through his self-imposed regimen of exercise during recovery.

After graduating from Whitman College (Walla Walla, Wash.) in 1920, Douglas briefly taught school. Resolving to enter law school, he worked his way across the country in 1922 and enrolled at Columbia University Law School, where he later edited the law review.

In 1925, Douglas was graduated second in his class from Columbia and shortly thereafter joined a Wall Street law firm to learn the intricacies of financial and corporate law. He left the firm one year later to teach law at Columbia, and a year after that he joined the law faculty at Yale, where he taught until 1936.

In 1934, after having worked with the Department of Commerce on bankruptcy studies, Douglas directed a study for the Securities and Exchange Commission (SEC) on the reorganization of bankrupt corporations. He became a member of the SEC in 1936, and in 1937 he was appointed chairman of the commission. In this capacity he engineered the reorganization of the nation's stock exchanges, instituted measures for the protection of small investors, and began government regulation of the sale of securities.

During his tenure with the SEC, Douglas became a friend and adviser of Pres. Franklin Roosevelt. When Justice Louis Brandeis retired from the Supreme Court in February 1939, Roosevelt nominated Douglas to fill the vacancy. Following his confirmation by the Senate, Douglas took his seat on April 17, 1939, becoming at 40 years of age the second youngest Supreme Court justice in U.S. history.

Although responsible for writing many of the opinions in complicated financial cases, Douglas became most famous for his pronouncements on civil liberties. Like his fellow justice and close friend Hugo Black, Douglas was an absolutist on the guarantees of freedom in the Bill of Rights. He rejected government limitations on free speech, and he was an outspoken defender of an unfettered press. His total opposition to any form of censorship made him a frequent target for criticism from political conservatives and religious fundamentalists.

Douglas also strove to ensure the protection of the constitutional rights of the criminally suspect, and he took a leading part in the Court's decisions that curbed coerced confessions, buttressed the accused's right against self-incrimination, and strengthened prohibitions against illegal searches.

Felled by a stroke on Dec. 31, 1974, Douglas struggled to overcome its debilitating effects and returned briefly to the bench before retiring on Nov. 12, 1975. Throughout his judicial career Douglas remained a prolific writer, especially on conservation, history, politics, and foreign relations; his books include *Of Men and Mountains* (1950) and *A Wilderness Bill of Rights* (1965).

John Marshall Harlan

(b. May 20, 1899, Chicago, Ill.—d. Dec. 29, 1971, Washington, D.C.)

John Marshall Harlan was an associate justice of the U.S. Supreme Court from 1955 to 1971.

He was the grandson of John Marshall Harlan, who sat on the Supreme Court from 1877 to 1911. The younger John Marshall graduated from Princeton University in 1920, took his master's degree from the University of Oxford in 1923, and received his law degree from the New York Law School in 1924, being admitted to the bar the following year. He then practiced law and held several public posts, served in the Army Air Forces during World War II, and resumed his prestigious law practice after the war. In 1954 he was appointed judge of the U.S. Court of Appeals by Pres. Dwight D. Eisenhower, and a few months later Eisenhower appointed him to the Supreme Court.

Harlan proved to be a conscientious and firmly independent member of the Court who was noted for his lucid, closely reasoned opinions. He believed in maintaining a strict dividing line between federal and state authority and opposed the tendency of the Court under Chief Justice Earl Warren to intrude into what Harlan considered matters not under its strictly constitutional purview. This stance earned him the reputation of a conservative, despite the moderate cast of some of his opinions.

William Brennan, Jr.

(b. April 25, 1906, Newark, N.J.—d. July 24, 1997, Arlington, Va.)

William Joseph Brennan, Jr., was an associate justice of the Supreme Court of the United States from 1956 to 1990.

Brennan was the son of William Joseph Brennan, an Irish immigrant who was a brewery worker and union

William Brennan, Jr., 1976. Library of Congress, Washington, D.C. (neg. no. LC-USZC6-25)

organizer, and Agnes McDermott Brennan. He graduated from the University of Pennsylvania in 1928 and then studied law under Felix Frankfurter at Harvard University, where he received a law degree in 1931. After graduation, he joined a Newark, N.J., law firm and specialized in labour law. His practice was interrupted by service in the U.S. Army during World War II, in which he rose to the rank of colonel, but after the war he returned to Newark to practice law. In 1949 Brennan was appointed to the newly created New Jersey Superior Court by Gov. Alfred E. Driscoll, and the following year he was named to the appellate division. In 1952 he was elevated to the state Supreme Court. Brennan's service on the state bench was marked by his administrative skill in speeding litigation and clearing a calendar severely in arrears. Despite being a Democrat, Brennan was appointed to the U.S. Supreme Court by Republican Pres. Dwight D. Eisenhower in October 1956. A recess appointment, he was formally nominated to the Supreme Court in January 1957 and was confirmed by the U.S. Senate by voice vote on March 19.

A liberal constructionist and articulate defender of the Bill of Rights, Brennan was nonetheless able to secure general consensus among several of the justices by tailoring constitutional issues to precise questions and, when possible, to specific elements of constitutional text. Despite these efforts, he is regarded as a leading liberal and broad-themed interpretivist—a justice unusually willing to acknowledge that "we current justices read the Constitution in the only way that we can: as 20th-century Americans." He is perhaps best remembered for his role in a series of obscenity cases, beginning with *Roth* v. *United States* (1957), many of which broadened the protection accorded to publishers but which also showed an attempt to balance individual freedoms with the interests of the community. In *New York Times Co.* v. *Sullivan* (1964), Brennan created the "right to be wrong"—the speech and press rule stipulating that even false statements about public officials should be entitled to protection under the First and Fourteenth amendments of the Constitution of the United States unless "actual malice" could be demonstrated.

Brennan was a strong believer in the importance of an independent judiciary and of the impact of procedure upon substantive rights. These concerns informed his opinions in the loyalty oath cases; in his dissent in *State* v. *Tune* (1953), in which the defendant was denied a copy of the confession; and in *Jencks* v. *United States* (1957), in which Brennan gave the court's opinion, establishing a defendant's right to examine the reports of government witnesses. In his dissents in *Ker* v. *California* and *Lopez* v. *United States* (both 1963), Brennan argued for the right to privacy as implicit in the Fourth Amendment (which prohibits unlawful search and seizure). His decision for the court in *Baker* v. *Carr* (1962), which established the principle of "one person, one vote," provided the grounds for national legislative redistricting.

After suffering a stroke, Brennan retired from the court in 1990. In 1993 he received the Presidential Medal of Freedom, the country's highest civilian honour. In more than three decades on the Supreme Court, Brennan wrote more than 1,300 opinions, including 461 majority opinions. Many Supreme Court analysts consider Brennan's decisions among the most influential in the modern history of the Supreme Court. In addition to working for the redefinition of obscenity and libel, expansion of individual rights, and reapportionment of political boundaries, he opposed capital punishment and supported abortion rights, affirmative action, and school desegregation.

Brennan was buried in Arlington National Cemetery, where he rests next to his first and second wives (respectively, Marjorie Leonard Brennan [died 1982] and Mary Fowler Brennan [died 2000]).

Thurgood Marshall

(b. July 2, 1908, Baltimore, Md.—d. Jan. 24, 1993, Bethesda, Md.)

Thurgood (born Thoroughgood) Marshall was a lawyer, a civil rights activist, and an associate justice of the Supreme Court of the United States from 1967 to 1991. He was the first African American member of the Supreme Court. As an attorney, he successfully argued before the U.S. Supreme Court the case of *Brown* v. *Board of Education of Topeka* (1954).

Marshall was the son of William Canfield Marshall, a railroad porter and a steward at an all-white country club, and Norma Williams Marshall, an elementary school teacher. He graduated with honours from Lincoln University (Pennsylvania) in 1930. After being rejected by the University of Maryland Law School because he was not white, Marshall attended Howard University Law School; he received his degree in 1933, ranking first in his class. At Howard he was the protégé of Charles Hamilton Houston, who encouraged Marshall and other law students to view the law as a vehicle for social change.

Upon his graduation from Howard, Marshall began the private practice of law in Baltimore. Among his first legal victories was *Murray* v. *Pearson* (1935), in which Marshall successfully sued the University of Maryland for denying an African American applicant admission to its law school simply on the basis of race. In 1936 Marshall became a staff lawyer under Houston for the NAACP; in 1938 he became the lead chair in the legal office of the NAACP, and two years later he was named chief of the NAACP Legal Defense and Educational Fund.

Throughout the 1940s and '50s Marshall distinguished himself as one of the country's top lawyers, winning 29 of the 32 cases that he argued before the U.S. Supreme Court. Among them were cases in which the court declared unconstitutional a Southern state's exclusion of African American voters from primary elections (*Smith* v. *Allwright* [1944]), state judicial enforcement of racial "restrictive covenants" in housing (*Shelley* v. *Kraemer* [1948]), and "separate but equal" facilities for African American professionals and graduate students in state universities (*Sweatt* v. *Painter* and *McLaurin* v. *Oklahoma State Regents* [both 1950]). Without a doubt, however, it was his victory before the Supreme Court in *Brown* v. *Board of Education of Topeka* that established his reputation as a formidable and creative legal opponent and an advocate of social change. Indeed, students of constitutional law still examine the oral arguments of the case and the ultimate decision of the court from both a legal and a political perspective; legally, Marshall argued that segregation in public education produced unequal schools for African Americans and whites (a key element in the strategy to have the court overrule *Plessy* v. *Ferguson* [1896]), but it was Marshall's reliance on psychological, sociological, and historical data that presumably sensitized the court to the deleterious effects of institutionalized segregation on the self-image, social worth, and social progress of African American children.

Thurgood Marshall. Library of Congress, Washington, D.C. (neg. no. LC-USZC6-26)

In September 1961 Marshall was nominated to the U.S. Court of Appeals for the Second Circuit by Pres. John F. Kennedy, but opposition from Southern senators delayed his confirmation for several months. Pres. Lyndon B. Johnson named Marshall U.S. solicitor general in July 1965 and nominated him to the Supreme Court on June 13, 1967; Marshall's appointment to the Supreme Court was confirmed (69–11) by the U.S. Senate on Aug. 30, 1967.

During Marshall's tenure on the Supreme Court, he was a steadfast liberal, stressing the need for equitable and just treatment of the country's minorities by the state and federal governments. A pragmatic judicial activist, he was committed to making the U.S. Constitution work; most illustrative of his approach was his attempt to fashion a "sliding scale" interpretation of the Fourteenth Amendment's equal-protection clause that would weigh the objectives of the government against the nature and interests of the groups affected by the law. Marshall's sliding scale was never adopted by the Supreme Court, though in several major civil rights cases of the 1970s the court echoed Marshall's views. He was also adamantly opposed to capital punishment and generally favoured the rights of the national government over the rights of the states.

Marshall served on the Supreme Court as it underwent a period of major ideological change. In his early years on the bench, he fit comfortably among a liberal majority under the leadership of Chief Justice Earl Warren. As the years passed, however, many of his closest allies, including Warren, either retired or died in office, creating opportunities for Republican presidents to swing the pendulum of activism in a conservative direction. By the time he retired in 1991, he was known as "the Great Dissenter," one of the last remaining liberal members of a Supreme Court dominated by a conservative majority.

Harry Blackmun

(b. Nov. 12, 1908, Nashville, Ill.—d. March 4, 1999, Arlington, Va.)

Harry Andrew Blackmun was an associate justice of the United States Supreme Court from 1970 to 1994.

Blackmun graduated in mathematics from Harvard University in 1929 and received his law degree from that institution in 1932. He joined a Minneapolis, Minn., law firm in 1934, and while advancing to general partner in the firm he also taught at the St. Paul College of Law (1935–41). In 1950 he became resident counsel for the Mayo Clinic in Rochester, Minn., and held this post until 1959, when he was appointed a judge of the U.S. Court of Appeals by Pres. Dwight D. Eisenhower.

In 1970, after two of his previous nominees had been rejected by the Senate as unqualified, Pres. Richard M. Nixon named Blackmun to the Supreme Court. Blackmun was unanimously confirmed by the Senate and took his seat in June 1970. On the court he joined his close friend from childhood, Chief Justice Warren E. Burger. He was expected to vote as a conservative constitutionalist, and for the first few years of his judgeship he did just that, voting in line with court conservatives.

In 1973, however, he wrote the court's majority decision in *Roe* v. *Wade*, the landmark case in which a woman's right to terminate a pregnancy was guaranteed under the constitutional right to privacy. While the decision cannot be construed as legally conservative, in that the case made law in an area (abortion rights) in which the Supreme Court had rarely before issued an opinion, it can be seen as politically conservative, in that it followed from Blackmun's deeply held belief in a citizen's right to privacy without governmental interference. Although there were six justices who joined with Blackmun in the majority opinion of *Roe* v. *Wade*, Blackmun was linked with and characterized by that decision for the rest of his career.

At times, Blackmun's dissenting opinions became just as important to the legal debate on individual liberty as were his concurring opinions. For instance, on the issue of gay rights Blackmun wrote an eloquent dissent from the majority decision in *Bowers* v. *Hardwick* in 1986, in which the court decided 5–4 to reject a right-to-privacy claim made by a gay man convicted under a state sodomy law. Blackmun's dissent eventually framed the legal debate around this issue. Blackmun frequently argued that U.S. citizens have a fundamental right "to be left alone" by their government, and while Blackmun's opinions rarely expanded the legal rights of those accused of criminal acts, they did provide an increased right to privacy on the part of ordinary citizens. Blackmun was also a staunch supporter of the First Amendment, of the strong separation of church and state, and of affirmative action. At the end of his legal career, Blackmun shifted his opinion on the constitutionality of the death penalty because of his growing belief that the death penalty was applied in an inherently random and arbitrary fashion. He retired from the bench in 1994.

Lewis Powell, Jr.

(b. Sept. 19, 1907, Suffolk, Va.—d. Aug. 25, 1998, Richmond, Va.)

Lewis Franklin Powell, Jr., was an associate justice of the U.S. Supreme Court from 1972 to 1987.

Powell was the eldest child of Louis Powell, a businessman, and Mary Gwaltney Powell. Educated at McGuire's University School, a private academy that prepared students for admission to the University of Virginia, Powell instead attended Washington and Lee University in Lexington, Va., where he was elected student body president and received bachelor's (1929) and law (1931) degrees. He then earned a master's degree in law from the Harvard Law School in 1932 and joined a Richmond law firm that same year. In 1935 he moved to a more prestigious Richmond law firm, where he was made a partner in 1938.

Powell volunteered for the U.S. Army Air Force during World War II, serving in both combat and intelligence positions. After the war he renewed his law practice and served in several civic posts. As chairman of the public school board in Richmond (1952–61), he began the process of integrating the schools—emerging as a conservative opponent of politicians who endorsed "massive resistance" to avoid integration—while other school districts in Virginia were experiencing bitter disputes. He also served on the state board of education (1961–69), including a term as president in 1968–69, and as president of the American Bar Association from 1964 to 1965.

Widely respected in legal circles, the thoughtful, pragmatic, and conciliatory Powell was nominated in October 1971 by Pres. Richard M. Nixon to fill the seat on the

Supreme Court being vacated by Justice Hugo L. Black. He was easily confirmed (89–1) by the Senate on Dec. 6, 1971, and he took his seat on the court in January 1972. Powell was one of the more conservative members of the court during the 1970s and early '80s, but he came to occupy a key centrist position as Pres. Ronald Reagan's appointments shifted the court's composition in a conservative direction. Powell took a moderate-to-liberal stance on such issues as legalized abortion (e.g., he supported abortion rights in *Roe* v. *Wade* [1973] but also later endorsed a Missouri law that required minors to receive parental consent when seeking an abortion and ruled that states did not have to fund abortions for poor women), separation of church and state, and civil rights questions, but he was basically a conservative on matters of crime and law enforcement. He also voted with the majority in *Bowers* v. *Hardwick* (1986) to uphold Georgia's prohibition against sodomy (though he wrote that severe punishment might violate the Eighth Amendment's cruel and unusual punishment clause). Among his most well-known decisions was *Regents of the University of California* v. *Bakke* (1978), in which Powell led the court in ruling that affirmative action was constitutional as a mechanism to achieve diversity, though the court rejected the use of strict numerical quotas as a means to that end.

Owing to uncertain health, Powell retired in 1987. Until 1996 Powell sat as a judge on the U.S. Court of Appeals for the Fourth Circuit in Richmond.

Sandra Day O'Connor

(b. March 26, 1930, El Paso, Texas)

Sandra Day O'Connor (née Sandra Day) was an associate justice of the Supreme Court of the United States from 1981 to 2006. She was the first woman to serve on the

Supreme Court. A moderate conservative, she was known for her dispassionate and meticulously researched opinions.

Sandra Day grew up on a large family ranch near Duncan, Ariz. She received undergraduate (1950) and law (1952) degrees from Stanford University, where she met the future chief justice of the United States William Rehnquist. Upon her graduation she married a classmate, John Jay O'Connor III. Unable to find employment in a law firm because she was a woman—despite her academic achievements, one firm offered her a job as a secretary—she became a deputy district attorney in San Mateo county, Calif. After a brief tenure, she and her husband, a member of the U.S. Army Judge Advocate General Corps, moved to Germany, where she served as a civil attorney for the army (1954–57).

Upon her return to the United States, O'Connor pursued private practice in Maryville, Ariz., becoming an assistant attorney general for the state (1965–69). In 1969 she was elected as a Republican to the Arizona Senate (1969–74), rising to the position of majority leader—the first woman in the United States to occupy such a position. In 1974 she was elected a Superior Court judge in Maricopa county, and in 1979 she was appointed to the Arizona Court of Appeals in Phoenix. In July 1981 Pres. Ronald Reagan nominated her to fill the vacancy left on the Supreme Court by the retirement of Justice Potter Stewart. Described by Reagan as a "person for all seasons," O'Connor was confirmed unanimously by the Senate and was sworn in as the first female justice on Sept. 25, 1981.

O'Connor quickly became known for her pragmatism and was considered, with Justice Anthony Kennedy, a decisive swing vote in the Supreme Court's decisions. In such disparate fields as election law and abortion rights, she attempted to fashion workable solutions to major constitutional questions, often over the course of several cases.

In her decisions in election law she emphasized the importance of equal-protection claims (*Shaw* v. *Reno* [1993]), declared unconstitutional district boundaries that are "unexplainable on grounds other than race" (*Bush* v. *Vera* [1996]), and sided with the court's more liberal members in upholding the configuration of a congressional district in North Carolina created on the basis of variables including but not limited to race (*Easley* v. *Cromartie* [2001]).

In similar fashion, O'Connor's views on abortion rights were articulated gradually. In a series of rulings, she signaled a reluctance to support any decision that would deny women the right to choose a safe and legal abortion. By "defecting" in part from the conservative majority in *Webster* v. *Reproductive Health Services* (1989)—in which the court upheld a Missouri law that prohibited public employees from performing or assisting in abortions not necessary to save a woman's life and that required doctors to determine the viability of a fetus if it was at least 20 weeks old—she reduced the court's opinion to a plurality. Through her stewardship in *Planned Parenthood of Southeastern Pennsylvania* v. *Casey* (1992), the court refashioned its position on the right to abortion. The court's opinion, which O'Connor wrote with Justices Anthony Kennedy and David Souter, reaffirmed the constitutionally protected right to abortion established in *Roe* v. *Wade* (1973) but also lowered the standard that legal restrictions on abortion must meet in order to pass constitutional muster. After *Casey*, such laws would be considered unconstitutional only if they constituted an "undue burden" on women seeking to obtain an abortion.

David Souter

(b. Sept. 17, 1939, Melrose, Mass.)

David Hackett Souter was an associate justice of the U.S. Supreme Court from 1990 to 2009.

Souter's father was a bank manager and his mother a store clerk. He spent his early childhood in a Boston suburb before his family moved to rural East Weare, N.H., in 1950. He attended Harvard University, from which he graduated magna cum laude in 1961. He then spent two years at Magdalen College, Oxford, on a Rhodes scholarship. Upon his return to the United States in 1963, he entered Harvard Law School, receiving his law degree in 1966.

After graduation, Souter spent two years in private practice in Concord, N.H., before joining the state attorney general's office. Appointed state attorney general in 1976, he was a frequent defender of the ultraconservative policies of Gov. Meldrim Thomson, Jr. Two years later, Thomson appointed Souter associate justice of New Hampshire's Superior Court, where he served for four years. In 1983 Gov. John Sununu appointed him to the state Supreme Court. As a judge, Souter was considered tough on crime, favouring prosecutors and resisting reversals of criminal convictions.

In February 1990 Pres. George Bush nominated Souter to the U.S. Court of Appeals for the First Circuit in Boston. Confirmed by the U.S. Senate in May, Souter was nominated by Bush to the U.S. Supreme Court in July—before he had issued his first decision as a federal judge. In October he was easily confirmed (90–9). During the hearings, abortion-rights supporters unsuccessfully attempted to coax Souter to divulge his judicial position on abortion; indeed, his decision not to answer such questions was the central reason cited by those who voted against his confirmation.

Souter's judicial record in New Hampshire indicated that he would be ideologically compatible with the conservative justices appointed by Bush's predecessor, Pres. Ronald Reagan. During his early tenure on the court, however, Souter gradually emerged as a moderate liberal, routinely aligning himself with more liberal members of the court, such as Justices Ruth Bader Ginsburg and John Paul Stevens. His gravitation to the left began with his role in *Planned Parenthood of Southeastern Pennsylvania* v. *Casey* (1992). Although Souter was expected to support Justices William Rehnquist and Antonin Scalia in their effort to use the case to overturn *Roe* v. *Wade* (1973), the ruling that established the legal right to abortion, instead he joined with conservative Justices Anthony Kennedy and Sandra Day O'Connor in devising a new "undue burden" standard for determining the constitutionality of laws intended to limit abortion, the effect of which was to restrict abortion rights but not to eliminate them.

Souter also adopted left-of-centre positions in cases involving school desegregation and race-conscious electoral districting, arguing in a powerful dissent in 1995 that lower courts must be granted the latitude to correct problems emanating from constitutional violations created by public officials. In 1996 he opposed the court's decision to strike down congressional districting plans in North Carolina and Texas that were aimed at ensuring African American representation in the U.S. Congress, maintaining that in each case no harm would be—or had been—done to the white voters of the state.

By the late 1990s, Souter was recognized for his intellectual leadership among the court's moderate members and for his skill at building consensus. At the same time, he made no secret about his unhappiness with life in Washington and his desire to return to his home state of New Hampshire. On June 29, 2009, Souter retired from the Supreme Court.

Appendix: Table of Supreme Court Justices

Name	Term of Service*	Appointed by President
John Jay	1789–95	Washington
James Wilson	1789–98	Washington
John Rutledge	1790–91	Washington
William Cushing	1790–1810	Washington
John Blair	1790–96	Washington
James Iredell	1790–99	Washington
Thomas Johnson	1792–93	Washington
William Paterson	1793–1806	Washington
*John Rutledge***	1795	Washington
Samuel Chase	1796–1811	Washington
Oliver Ellsworth	1796–1800	Washington
Bushrod Washington	1799–1829	J. Adams
Alfred Moore	1800–04	J. Adams
John Marshall	1801–35	J. Adams
William Johnson	1804–34	Jefferson
Henry Brockholst Livingston	1807–23	Jefferson
Thomas Todd	1807–26	Jefferson
Gabriel Duvall	1811–35	Madison
Joseph Story	1812–45	Madison
Smith Thompson	1823–43	Monroe
Robert Trimble	1826–28	J.Q. Adams

Name	Term of Service*	Appointed by President
John McLean	1830–61	Jackson
Henry Baldwin	1830–44	Jackson
James M. Wayne	1835–67	Jackson
Roger Brooke Taney	1836–64	Jackson
Philip P. Barbour	1836–41	Jackson
John Catron	1837–65	Van Buren
John McKinley	1838–52	Van Buren
Peter V. Daniel	1842–60	Van Buren
Samuel Nelson	1845–72	Tyler
Levi Woodbury	1845–51	Polk
Robert C. Grier	1846–70	Polk
Benjamin R. Curtis	1851–57	Fillmore
John Archibald Campbell	1853–61	Pierce
Nathan Clifford	1858–81	Buchanan
Noah H. Swayne	1862–81	Lincoln
Samuel Freeman Miller	1862–90	Lincoln
David Davis	1862–77	Lincoln
Stephen Johnson Field	1863–97	Lincoln
Salmon P. Chase	1864–73	Lincoln
William Strong	1870–80	Grant
Joseph P. Bradley	1870–92	Grant
Ward Hunt	1873–82	Grant
Morrison Remick Waite	1874–88	Grant
John Marshall Harlan	1877–1911	Hayes
William B. Woods	1881–87	Hayes
Stanley Matthews	1881–89	Garfield
Horace Gray	1882–1902	Arthur
Samuel Blatchford	1882–93	Arthur
Lucius Q.C. Lamar	1888–93	Cleveland

Name	Term of Service*	Appointed by President
Melville Weston Fuller	1888–1910	Cleveland
David J. Brewer	1890–1910	B. Harrison
Henry B. Brown	1891–1906	B. Harrison
George Shiras, Jr.	1892–1903	B. Harrison
Howell E. Jackson	1893–95	B. Harrison
Edward Douglass White	1894–1910	Cleveland
Rufus Wheeler Peckham	1896–1909	Cleveland
Joseph McKenna	1898–1925	McKinley
Oliver Wendell Holmes, Jr.	1902–32	T. Roosevelt
William R. Day	1903–22	T. Roosevelt
William H. Moody	1906–10	T. Roosevelt
Horace H. Lurton	1910–14	Taft
Charles Evans Hughes	1910–16	Taft
Willis Van Devanter	1911–37	Taft
Joseph R. Lamar	1911–16	Taft
Edward Douglass White	1910–21	Taft
Mahlon Pitney	1912–22	Taft
James C. McReynolds	1914–41	Wilson
Louis Brandeis	1916–39	Wilson
John H. Clarke	1916–22	Wilson
William Howard Taft	1921–30	Harding
George Sutherland	1922–38	Harding
Pierce Butler	1923–39	Harding
Edward T. Sanford	1923–30	Harding
Harlan Fiske Stone	1925–41	Coolidge
Charles Evans Hughes	1930–41	Hoover
Owen Roberts	1930–45	Hoover
Benjamin Nathan Cardozo	1932–38	Hoover

Name	Term of Service*	Appointed by President
Hugo L. Black	1937–71	F. Roosevelt
Stanley F. Reed	1938–57	F. Roosevelt
Felix Frankfurter	1939–62	F. Roosevelt
William O. Douglas	1939–75	F. Roosevelt
Frank Murphy	1940–49	F. Roosevelt
Harlan Fiske Stone	1941–46	F. Roosevelt
James F. Byrnes	1941–42	F. Roosevelt
Robert H. Jackson	1941–54	F. Roosevelt
Wiley B. Rutledge	1943–49	F. Roosevelt
Harold H. Burton	1945–58	Truman
Fred M. Vinson	1946–53	Truman
Tom C. Clark	1949–67	Truman
Sherman Minton	1949–56	Truman
Earl Warren	1953–69	Eisenhower
John Marshall Harlan	1955–71	Eisenhower
William J. Brennan, Jr.	1956–90	Eisenhower
Charles E. Whittaker	1957–62	Eisenhower
Potter Stewart	1958–81	Eisenhower
Byron R. White	1962–93	Kennedy
Arthur J. Goldberg	1962–65	Kennedy
Abe Fortas	1965–69	L. Johnson
Thurgood Marshall	1967–91	L. Johnson
Warren E. Burger	1969–86	Nixon
Harry A. Blackmun	1970–94	Nixon
Lewis F. Powell, Jr.	1972–87	Nixon
William H. Rehnquist	1972–86	Nixon
John Paul Stevens	1975–	Ford
Sandra Day O'Connor	1981–2006	Reagan
William H. Rehnquist	1986–2005	Reagan

Name	Term of Service*	Appointed by President
Antonin Scalia	1986–	Reagan
Anthony M. Kennedy	1988–	Reagan
David H. Souter	1990–	G.H.W. Bush
Clarence Thomas	1991–	G.H.W. Bush
Ruth Bader Ginsburg	1993–	Clinton
Stephen G. Breyer	1994–	Clinton
John G. Roberts, Jr.	2005–	G.W. Bush
Samuel A. Alito	2006–	G.W. Bush
Sonia Sotomayor	2009–	Obama

* The date the justice took the judicial oath is here used as the beginning date of service, for until that oath is taken the justice is not vested with the prerogatives of the office. Justices, however, receive their commissions ("letters patent.") before taking their oaths—in some instances, in the preceding year.

** John Rutledge was acting chief justice; the U.S. Senate refused to confirm him.

Glossary

adjudication The act of a court in making a judgment or decree.
amalgam A mixture or combination.
appellate Possessing the authority to review appeals.
arbitration The process by which a disagreement is settled by a person or persons chosen by the disputing parties.
arrears The state of being behind in the fulfillment of an obligation or payment.
auspices Patronage; support; protection.
bicameral Consisting of two legislative bodies.
circumscribed Limited or confined.
coercion Intimidation or force used to gain compliance.
efficacious Effective as a means to an end; capable of having the desired result.
expatriate To withdraw oneself from residence in one's native country.
expositor A person who expounds or gives a presentation or explanation of a view.
ex post facto Having retroactive force.
factious Prone to dissension.
habeas corpus A protection against unjust imprisonment which requires a person to be brought before a judge or court for the purpose of being formally charged or released.
ideologue A strong and often blindly partisan advocate of a given ideology or theory of politics or society.

indigent Lacking necessities of life due to poverty.
injunction A judicial order to do or not do something.
intercourse Dealings or communication between individuals or groups.
jurisprudence A body or system of law; the philosophy of law.
justiciable Something that can be appropriately settled by a court.
maxim A saying.
monistic Characterized by the idea that there is one substance or explanatory principle.
ombudsman A government official who investigates other government officials when claims by private citizens are made against them.
perfunctory Superficial; performed merely in a routine manner.
plaintiff One who brings a legal action in a court.
putsch A secretly plotted and suddenly executed attempt to overthrow a government.
seditious Tending to incite resistance to or insurrection against lawful authority.
seriatim In a series.
sovereign One who exercises supreme political authority in a given realm.
stare decisis The doctrine that the rules or principles laid down in previous court cases should be followed in all subsequent court cases in which the basic facts are the same.
vagabond A person who wanders idly from place to place.
writ of mandamus An order issued by a higher court to a lower court or government official compelling the performance of a duty.

For Further Reading

Beeman, Richard. *Plain, Honest Men: The Making of an American Constitution*. New York, NY: Random House, 2009.

Carp, Robert A., Ronald Stidham, and Kenneth L. Manning. *Judicial Process in America*. Washington, DC: CQ Press, 2007.

Federman, Cary. *The Body and the State: Habeas Corpus and American Jurisprudence*. Albany, NY: State University of New York Press, 2007.

Fehrenbacher, Don E. *The Dred Scott Case: Its Significance in American Law and Politics*. New York, NY: Oxford University Press, 2001.

Forsyth, Christopher. *Judicial Review and the Constitution*. Portland, OR: Hart Publishing, 2000.

Hall, Kermit L., and Kevin T. McGuire. *Institutions of American Democracy: The Judicial Branch* (Institutions of American Democracy Series). New York, NY: Oxford University Press, 2006.

Hall, Kermit L. *The Oxford Companion to the Supreme Court of the United States*. New York, NY: Oxford University Press, 1992.

Hamilton, Alexander, and Thomas Jefferson. *Foundations of Freedom:* Common Sense, *The Declaration of Independence, The Articles of Confederation, The U.S. Constitution*. Radford, VA: Wilder Publications, 2007.

Hargrove, Julia. *History Speaks: Judicial Branch of the Government*. Carthage, IL: Teaching & Learning Co, 2000.

Hoffer, Charles, and N.E.H. Hull. *Roe V. Wade: The Abortion Rights Controversy in American History*. Lawrence, KS: University Press of Kansas, 2001.

Irons, Peter. *A People's History of the Supreme Court: The Men and Women Whose Cases and Decisions Have Shaped Our Constitution*. New York, NY: Penguin, 2006.

Lawson, Steven F., Charles Payne, and James T. Patterson, *Debating the Civil Rights Movement, 1945–1968* (Debating 20th Century America). Lanham, MD: Rowman & Littlefield Publishers, Inc., 2006.

McCloskey, Robert G., rev. by Sanford Levinson. *The American Supreme Court*. Chicago, IL: The University of Chicago Press, 2004.

Nelson, William Edward. *Marbury v. Madison: The Origins and Legacy of Judicial Review*. Lawrence, KS: University Press of Kansas, 2000.

Neubauer, David W. *Judicial Process: Law, Courts, and Politics in the United States*. Boston, MA: Wadsworth Publishing, 2009.

O'Connor, Sandra Day. *The Majesty of the Law: Reflections of a Supreme Court Justice*. New York, NY: Random House Trade Paperbacks, 2004.

Orth, John V. *Due Process of Law: A Brief History*. Lawrence, KS: University Press of Kansas, 2003.

Patrick, John J. *The Pursuit of Justice: Supreme Court Decisions that Shaped America*. New York, NY: Oxford University Press, 2006.

Rosen, Jeffrey. *The Supreme Court: The Personalities and Rivalries that Defined America*. New York, NY: Henry Holt and Company, 2007.

Stahr, Walter. *John Jay: Founding Father*. London, England: Hambledon & London, 2005.

Tarr, Alan G. *Judicial Process and Judicial Policymaking*. Boston, MA: Wadsworth Publishing, 2009.
Toobin, Jeffrey. *The Nine: Inside the Secret World of the Supreme Court*. New York, NY: Anchor Books, 2008.
Trachtman, Michael G. *The Supremes' Greatest Hits: The 34 Supreme Court Cases That Most Directly Affect Your Life*. New York, NY: Sterling Press, 2006.
Tushnet, Mark V. *Making Civil Rights Law: Thurgood Marshall and the Supreme Court, 1956–1961*. New York, NY: Oxford University Press, 1996.
Woodward, Bob, and Scott Armstrong. *The Brethren: Inside the Supreme Court*. New York, NY: Simon & Schuster, 1979.

Index

D

E

I

J

K

L

M

N

O

P

R